Literature of Luther

Literature of Luther
Receptions of the Reformer

EDITED BY
A. EDWARD WESLEY
&
J. CHRISTOPHER EDWARDS

☙PICKWICK *Publications* · Eugene, Oregon

LITERATURE OF LUTHER
Receptions of the Reformer

Copyright © 2014 Wipf and Stock Publishers. All rights reserved. Except for brief quotations in critical publications or reviews, no part of this book may be reproduced in any manner without prior written permission from the publisher. Write: Permissions. Wipf and Stock Publishers, 199 W. 8th Ave., Suite 3, Eugene, OR 97401.

Pickwick Publications
An Imprint of Wipf and Stock Publishers
199 W. 8th Ave., Suite 3
Eugene, OR 97401

www.wipfandstock.com

ISBN 13: 978-1-62564-529-6

Cataloguing-in-Publication Data

Literature of Luther : receptions of the reformer / edited by A. Edward Wesley and J. Christopher Edwards.

viii + 182 p. ; 23 cm. Includes bibliographical references.

ISBN 13: 978-1-62564-529-6

1. Luther, Martin, 1483–1546. 2. Literature and society. 3. German literature—Early modern, 1500–1700—History and criticism. I. Wesley, A. Edward. II. Edwards, J. Christopher, 1982–. III. Title.

BS1191.5 B75 2014

Manufactured in the U.S.A.   10/22/2014

Contents

Preface | vii
Contributors | viii

1   "A Most Stupid Scoundrel": Some Early English Responses to Luther | 1
    J. Patrick Hornbeck II

2   Reformation Never Ends: Jeremias Gotthelf Eavesdropping on Luther in 1828 | 26
    Peter C. Meilaender

3   A Conversation among the Reformers in Heaven (*Gespräch der Reformatoren im Himmel*, 1828) | 40
    Jeremias Gotthelf, translation by Peter C. Meilaender

4   Luther and Kleist: Breaking New Ground | 50
    Jean Wilson

5   Vocation, Holiness and Freewill in Luther and Grisez: An Interconfessional Exchange | 60
    R. J. Matava

6   Luther's Linguistic Innovation | 106
    Virgil Thompson

7   Luther, Libertines, and Literature | 120
    Jeffrey K. Mann

8   Release from Torment: Finding Grace in Arthur Miller's *After the Fall*, John Osborne's *Luther*, and C. S. Lewis's *Till We Have Faces* | 131
    Elaine Lux

9   Luther's Theology of the Cross: Redemptive Suffering and Vivian Bearing's Death in Margaret Edson's play, *Wit* | 144
    Anthony Grasso

10 Never Such Innocence Again: The Persistence of Hope in Cormac McCarthy's *The Road* | 163
    Stephen Sicari

11 Allusions to Wittenberg, the Four Last Things, and the Character of Hamlet, Prince of Denmark | 174
    Brigid Brady

Preface

THE SELECTED ESSAYS IN this volume began as papers given at the Northeast Regional Conference on Christianity and Literature, which was held at St. Francis College on 8–9 November 2013. In anticipation of increased interest in Luther and his impact due to the upcoming 500 year anniversary of Luther's *Ninety-Five Theses*, we decided that "Literature of Luther" should be the conference theme. As anyone who has ever held a small local conference knows, there is some uncertainty about what to expect after posting the initial Call for Papers. However, we are very pleased to have received excellent papers from talented faculty members, most of whom come from regional colleges and universities, as well as an outstanding Keynote paper from J. Patrick Hornbeck II. Almost all of the papers are interdisciplinary, crossing the boundaries between literature, history, and theology. Both Catholic and Protestant voices are well represented. While the papers themselves are wide ranging in terms of the topics covered, most will strike a chord with the growing interest in reception studies; in this case, the reception of Luther.

We would like to thank the St. Francis College administration and staff for allowing the use of SFC facilities for the conference. The Faculty Research Committee generously provided a grant that made this publication possible. We also received support of various kinds from our colleagues in the Department of English and the Department of Philosophy and Religious Studies. Finally, we would like to thank K. C. Hanson for agreeing to publish the volume, and to everyone at Wipf and Stock who provided timely advice and assistance as we navigated the manuscript toward publication.

A. Edward Wesley

J. Christopher Edwards

Contributors

Brigid Brady, OP, Professor of English at
Caldwell College

Anthony Grasso, C.S.C., Professor of English at
King's College, PA

J. Patrick Hornbeck II, Chair and Associate Professor of Theology at
Fordham University

Elaine Lux, Professor of English at
Nyack College

Jeffrey K. Mann, Associate Professor of Religion at
Susquehanna University

R. J. Matava, Assistant Professor of Theology at
Christendom College, Graduate School

Peter C. Meilaender, Professor of Political Science at
Houghton College

Stephen Sicari, Chair and Professor of English at
Saint John's University

Virgil Thompson, Senior Lecturer of Religious Studies at
Gonzaga University

Jean Wilson, Director of the Arts & Science Program at
McMaster University

1

"A Most Stupid Scoundrel"
Some Early English Responses to Luther

J. Patrick Hornbeck II

LET US BEGIN IN the year 1521. It is four years after Martin Luther published his ninety-five theses on indulgences, theses that today appear to many scholars to constitute less the laying down of an ecclesiopolitical gauntlet than a relatively ordinary academic act.[1] It is the year after Pope Leo X threatened Luther with excommunication and the year that, after Luther responded by burning the papal bull *Exsurge Domine*, the pope formally declared him to be outside the community of Christian faithful. Though what most contemporary scholars know as the Protestant reformations had therefore begun, in 1521 the English language does not yet contain the word "Protestant," which appeared for the first time in writing in 1539.[2] The word "Lutheran" had just begun to be used, for instance in the correspondence of Archbishop of Canterbury William Warham, and the word "Anglican," at least in its modern sense, is at least half a

---

1. On scholarly assessments of the posting of the theses, see Dixon, *Contesting the Reformation*, 205–7.

2. *OED Online*, "Protestant, n. and adj."

century off.[3] In 1521, Henry VIII of England, in the twelfth year of his reign, is stably married to Katherine of Aragon, and their one surviving child, Mary, is a girl of five.

Recalling these details about the early years of the Reformation period serves as a reminder of the uncertainty about its eventual outcome that the women and men alive at the time would likely have possessed. Lacking the historiographical and interpretative tools—not to mention the raw facts—that modern scholarship takes for granted, these women and men did not know, in 1521, that they were living at the beginning of what later generations would call the Reformation. Even if they had an inkling that with the writings of Luther and his successors the religious world they largely took for granted was about to change, it is unlikely that any of them could have predicted the series of upheavals—cultural, social, and especially religious—that would roil the kingdom of England through the rest of the sixteenth century. Instead of the retrospective and oftentimes confessionally self-aware perspectives that scholars today bring to the events of the 1520s, the women and men living then brought to bear on the defining events of their lives perspectives that reflect the categories they had available to them.[4] Their ways of thinking were profoundly influenced by medieval and early Christian ideas about the tasks of theology and of theologians, about orthodoxy and heresy, and about the boundaries of permissible change in the church. Their worldviews framed religious difference almost exclusively in the categories of heresy and schism. And as this essay will seek to demonstrate with regard to several highly visible English anti-Lutheran texts of the 1520s, the limitations of such perspectives led them often to misinterpret, or at least to be unwilling to take on their own terms, the emerging theologies and ecclesiologies of Luther and other reformers.

On May 12, 1521, Cardinal Thomas Wolsey, archbishop of York, Lord Chancellor, and universally acknowledged the second most powerful man in England, organized a public burning of Luther's books in front of London's St. Paul's Cathedral. While in some respects this conflagration

---

3. *OED Online,* "Lutheran, n. and adj;" "Anglican, n. and adj."

4. For a reassessment of confessionalism and so-called post-confessionalism in Reformation historiography, see Marshall, "(Re)defining the English Reformation," 564–86.

differed little from the many other burnings, both of books and of people, that marked much of the sixteenth century, in its own time it was for at least two reasons remarkable. First, there is little evidence for the reading of Luther's writings in England at the beginning of the 1520s, and even less evidence for the widespread dissemination of Luther's ideas. His German compositions had not yet widely been translated into English, and his Latin texts had not yet attracted the interest that English scholars were to pay them in subsequent years.[5] As Craig D'Alton has put it, Wolsey's burning of Luther's books therefore took place against the backdrop of only "a negligible Lutheran presence in England."[6] Second, even though Lutheran ideas were not a significant or even a significantly growing feature of English religious and intellectual life, Wolsey's book-burning and other elements of the government's official response to Luther far outstripped the measures that were taken by other European kingdoms. Thus in England, although there were few Lutherans, there were prominent anti-Lutheran sermons by churchmen such as John Fisher, Bishop of Rochester; there were other public book-burnings; and perhaps most extraordinary of all, King Henry himself entered into the fray by writing in Latin a book against Luther, the *Assertio septem sacramentorum* (*Assertion of the Seven Sacraments*).[7] It was of course this book that won Henry and his successors on the English throne the papal title Defender of the Faith.

Thus before we begin to explore the contents of the king's book, as well as of other anti-Lutheran tracts written by men close to the king, we must confront this paradox: why, with so few Lutherans, was there so much anti-Lutheran activity on the part of English royal and ecclesiastical officials? Perhaps the king and his advisors were far-sighted enough to predict that the Lutheran controversy would achieve the international and historical importance that it eventually did. However, it is more likely that when Henry, Wolsey, and their colleagues began to assess the significance of Luther's proposed reforms, they were looking not forward into the future, but backward into the past. For in 1521, England was still dealing with the remnants of another set of religious controversies, ones that in the immediately previous century had been thought to pose serious challenges to the stability of both church and crown.

5. On the reading of Luther in early Tudor England, see Lytle, "John Wyclif, Martin Luther and Edward Powell," 465–79.

6. D'Alton, "The Suppression of Heresy in Early Henrician England," 102.

7. Ibid., 99–112, 124.

I am referring, of course, to the Wycliffite or lollard heresy of what we know as the later middle ages, but what in 1521 would have been just a few decades prior. Much about lollardy—the meaning of the word itself, the coherence of the heresy as a "movement" or "sect," the extent of its dependence on the ideas of its putative founder John Wyclif—remains contested among contemporary scholars.[8] According to the narrative current in the early 1520s, however, lollardy owed its existence to primarily the heretical ideas of Wyclif, a once distinguished Oxford scholar who, perhaps out of spite at being denied promotion to the episcopacy, began toward the end of his career to articulate progressively more controversial views. Wyclif was exiled from the university in 1381 for denying the doctrine of transubstantiation, but even after he left Oxford, he continued to exert influence through his followers. These equally or perhaps even more sacrilegious clerics and laypeople illicitly translated the Bible and composed religious texts in the vernacular, rejected orthodox understandings of the sacraments, shunned traditional devotional practices like the adoration of images of the saints, and proposed the disendowment of ecclesiastical institutions.[9] Recent scholarship has demonstrated that accounts of lollardy like this one, which focus primarily or exclusively on the doctrines and practices that lollards rejected rather than on the alternative forms of Christianity that they embraced, are incomplete.[10] However, it was on account of what they refused to accept that at least five hundred women and men were brought to trial on charges of heresy in the late fourteenth through early sixteenth centuries; of these, some seventy ultimately went to the stake.

Even if the particulars about lollardy remain subject to debate, what is certain is that for self-consciously orthodox citizens in early sixteenth-century England, Wyclif and lollardy represented blemishes on the history of their national church. Wyclif was one of only two heresiarchs cited by name at the ecumenical councils of the western middle ages, and he was viewed as a prime source of inspiration for the other heresiarch to be so condemned, the Bohemian preacher and scholar Jan Hus, who with his

---

8. On lollardy generally, see Hudson, *The Premature Reformation*; Hornbeck, *What Is a Lollard?*; and a variety of collections of essays, including most recently Ghosh and Gillespie, *After Arundel*, and Bose and Hornbeck, *Wycliffite Controversies*.

9. This narrative draws implicitly on a variety of medieval sources, especially the chronicle of the Augustinian canon. See Knighton, *Knighton's Chronicle 1337–1396*, 243–325.

10. See especially Somerset, *Feeling Like Saints*.

own cohort of followers challenged ecclesiastical authorities in Prague in the first quarter of the fifteenth century.[11] Lollardy remained something of a specter in the eyes of English royal and ecclesiastical officials through the first decades of the sixteenth century: a series of heresy prosecutions coincided with the period between the accession of Henry VIII in 1509 and the dispatch of England's delegation to the Fifth Lateran Council in 1512.[12] In the 1510s and early 1520s, the bishops of London, Winchester, and Salisbury, as well as the archbishop of Canterbury, arrested and in a few cases burned those who were suspected of lollard beliefs. And neither these bishops nor the king would easily have forgotten that, at least insofar as earlier chroniclers had told the story, the theological errors of lollardy had given rise to political instability and sedition, both in the infamous so-called "Peasants' Revolt" of 1381 and in the unsuccessful rebellion of Sir John Oldcastle in 1414.[13] These circumstances created incentives for both the English crown and the English church to respond fiercely—and perhaps more importantly, *to be seen* to be responding fiercely—to the new heresy of Martin Luther. If England had spent much of the fifteenth century enduring its reputation as the kingdom that had nurtured Wyclif, English officials in the sixteenth century took steps to appear proactive in the fight against heresy, including by continuing heresy trials, attempting to seize Lutheran books arriving at English ports, and publishing anti-Lutheran tracts in both Latin and the vernacular.

Out of the many English writings against Luther published in the 1520s, three in particular reflect directly the engagement of the crown and the highest officials of state: King Henry's *Assertio septem sacramentorum* (1521) and Thomas More's two great anti-Lutheran books, the *Responsio ad Lutherum* (1523) and the *Dialogue concerning Heresies* (1528). This essay will refer to the *Assertio* as the king's book, although its authorship remains a matter of some uncertainty.[14] While it may be the

11. For the most recent account of the relationships between Wycliffite and Hussite thinkers, see Van Dussen, *From England to Bohemia*.

12. No fewer than 220 defendants were charged with heresy between the years 1501 and 1521, of which the largest groups were some sixty-seven tried in 1511 and 1512 in Coventry and Lichfield diocese, some forty-three brought to trial in those same years in Canterbury diocese, and a group of eleven charged in 1512 in Winchester diocese. The records of the Winchester cases are now printed in modern English translation in Hornbeck, et al., *Wycliffite Spirituality*, 319–66.

13. On the relationships between lollardy and the first of these rebellions, see Justice, *Writing and Rebellion*.

14. On the authorship of the text, see the introduction to *Assertio Septem*

case that the compilation of the book was the work of a cohort of authors, including Fisher, More, Wolsey, and others, the content was acceptable to the king, who conveyed the book to Pope Leo X the week after Wolsey's public burning of Luther's books. In the letter that he enclosed with the text, Henry wrote of what he called his duty to defend Catholic doctrine against Lutheran ideas, as well as of what he saw as his established record in doing so:

> Whereas we believe no duty to be more incumbent on a Catholic sovereign than to preserve and increase the Christian faith and religion and its lessons ... so when we learned that the heresy and pestilence of Martin Luther's had appeared in Germany and was raging everywhere ..., we were so deeply grieved at this atrocious crime of the German nation (toward which we are moved in no small way), and for the sake of the Holy Apostolic See, that we bent all our thoughts, energies, and zeal on uprooting in every possible way, this cockle, this heresy from the Lord's flock.[15]

The *Assertio* is primarily a response to Luther's 1520 treatise on the sacraments, *De captivitate babylonica ecclesiae* (*On the Babylonian Captivity of the Church*). In it, Henry touches briefly on Luther's views on indulgences and the papacy, but the bulk of the work seeks to rebut Luther's teachings on the sacraments in general and on each of the seven Catholic sacraments in particular. The longest single section deals with the eucharist, but Henry's replies about penance, marriage, and holy orders run for at least a dozen pages each.

Henry's book earned him the gratitude of Pope Leo and the papal title *Fidei defensor*, but within a year it also provoked the ire of Luther himself. In his *Martinus Lutherus contra Henricum Regem Angliae*, Luther vigorously, and with no small amount of invective, dismissed the king's arguments. Even though the primary focus of the present essay is on English arguments against Luther, rather than on the reformer's own

---

Sacramentorum, Or Defence of the Seven Sacraments, 53–94.

15. *Assertio*, 153: "Quoniam nihil magis ex Catholici principis officio esse arbitramur, quam ut christianam fidem et religionem atque documenta ita servet et augeat ... ubi primum Martini Lutheri pestem atque heresim in Germania exortam, ubique locorum ... atrox istud schelus tum germanicae nationis (cui non mediocriter afficimur), tum vero sacrosanctae apostolicae sedis gratia sic indoluimus ut cogitations omnes nostras, studium et animum eo diverteremus, hanc zizaniam, hanc haeresim e dominico grege." This and subsequent translations from the *Assertio* are my own, owing to the poor quality of the published translation.

writings, it may be worth quoting a characteristic passage from Luther's book against the king to illustrate its tenor and style:

> Is it not enough to have seen the wickedness of this supposed champion? Now see whether in such a body there can be even a drop of royal blood, or in his soul even the spark of a good man. What, I ask, does not burn more than this sophistical malice and impudence, which from the soul and by industriousness rages so madly against the known truth, which he wishes be extinguished and buried not only for himself but also for the whole world? Obviously, this is the chosen instrument of Satan and the most worthy defender of the papistical church.[16]

The tone of correspondence between England and Germany was not destined to improve much in the coming years. In 1523, a year after Luther published his response and two years after Henry had written the *Assertio*, the king commissioned his secretary, Thomas More, to produce a rebuttal to Luther's response. More's *Responsio ad Lutherum*, written under the pen-name William Ross, ratcheted the polemical stakes still higher.[17] The *Responsio* contains virulent and often scatological language; in it, More describes Luther as "a most stupid scoundrel" (*stolidissimus nebulo*), and he went on to write:

> [F]or as long as your reverend paternity will be determined to tell these shameless lies, others will be permitted, on behalf of his English majesty, to throw back into your paternity's shitty mouth, truly the shit-pool of all shit, all the muck and shit which your damnable rottenness has vomited up, and to empty out all the sewers and privies onto your crown divested of the dignity of the priestly crown, against which no less than against the kingly crown you have determined to play the buffoon.[18]

In addition to the *Responsio*, which he composed in Latin, More continued his polemic against Luther and Lutheranism in a variety of

16. Luther, *Contra Henricum*, 198–99: "Satis ne vidisti nequitiam huius assertoris? Tu nunc vide, an in tali corpore ulla sit gutta regii sanguinis, aut in animo eius scintilla boni viri. Quem, rogo, non urat haec plusquam sophistica malitia et impudentia, quae ex animo et de industria adversus agnitam veritatem sic insanit, ut non modo sibi sed et orbi toto velit extinctam et sepultam? Plane vas electionis iste est Sathanae et dignissimus defensor."

17. In this regard neither Luther nor More was unusual for their times: on invective in sixteenth-century religious writings, see Furey, "Invective and Discernment," 469–88.

18. More, *Responsio*, 311; *stolidissimus nebulo* is at 317.

vernacular publications, including in his 1528 work *A Dialogue concerning Heresies*; in *The Supplication of Souls*, his 1529 response to Simon Fish's *A Supplication for the Beggars*; and in *The Confutation of Tyndale's Answer*, his lengthy 1532 reply to William Tyndale's response to the *Dialogue*.[19] The remainder of this essay will concentrate on three major early English anti-Lutheran works, primarily King Henry's *Assertio*, but also More's *Responsio* and *Dialogue*, and will seek to uncover the ways in which these writings maneuver rhetorically as well as theologically through their arguments against Luther. These texts reveal how well the king and More understood Luther's ideas, what assumptions they brought to the task of refuting them, and how extensively they borrowed in doing so from the standard tropes of patristic and medieval heresiology.

Henry's *Assertio* is a mélange of theological argumentation, heresiological rhetoric, and straightforward polemical assault. For the most part, but not without exceptions, when the king seeks to summarize Luther's ideas, he recounts with no small degree of accuracy the Wittenberg reformer's objections to orthodox beliefs about the church and the sacraments. In at least one place Henry even appears to agree with the substance of Luther's opinion about the desirability of giving communion in both kinds, although he readily defers to the church's discretion in making only one kind available: "And though I cannot see any reasons why the church should not ordain that each species be ministered to the laity, yet it is not possible for me to doubt that it is very suitable, what was done in times past, that it be omitted, and what is done now, that it not be reinstated."[20] The *Assertio* follows the general structure of Luther's *De captivitate babylonica*, and only occasionally does the king's book neglect to respond to any of Luther's arguments about the sacraments. For instance, in treating the sacrament of the eucharist, Henry responds sequentially to Luther's claims that the doctrine of transubstantiation is a novelty, that the Latin grammar of the phrases of institution precludes transubstantiation, that the relationship between a heated iron and the fire that heats it is an appropriate analogy for Christ's presence in the eucharist, and that analogies

---

19. The works are STC 18085, 18093, 18079, respectively.

20. *Assertio*, 217: "etiam si causas non viderem, cur non decernat Ecclesia ut utraque species ministretur laicis, tamen dubitare non possem quin sint idoneae quae et olim fecerunt ut id omitteretur, et nunc quoque faciunt ne redintegretur."

between the eucharist and the incarnation are more appropriate still.[21] Yet the king does not engage with Luther's charge that transubstantiation is philosophically an overly complex, and worse yet an Aristotelian, explanation of the metaphysics of the eucharist.[22]

Among the rhetorical moves that the *Assertio* makes, three are particularly noteworthy. First, there are the king's heresiological claims, in which Henry attributes to Luther the types of errors, sins, and tendencies that he was taught characterized all Christian heretics. Second, the king discerns in Luther's writing what we might call theologically slippery slopes, arguments that at first appear to concede only superficial reforms but that in fact open the door for the wholesale revision of beliefs and practices. Finally, as was the case in so many of the debates of the sixteenth-century reformations, Henry disputes with Luther over scriptural hermeneutics, that is, how one is properly to read the Bible.

Heresiology is the term that customarily has been given to the ways in which Christians and others have thought about heresy and heretics. To simplify a far more complicated story, the Greek term *haeresis*, which originally denoted a choice and in philosophical usage connoted a particular school of thought, evolved over the course of the first two centuries of Christian history to mean specifically a theologically incorrect choice or, more precisely, a theological view or set of views at odds with the consensus of those whom the church regarded as authoritative.[23] Early Christians produced a number of heresiological classics: the second-century bishop Irenaeus of Lyons, for instance, declared in his *Adversus haereses* (*Against the Heresies*) that the heretics of his day could be traced back through earlier heretics to the biblical figure Simon Magus, just as orthodox bishops could trace their succession back to the apostles originally called by Christ.[24] Later writers, such as Epiphanius of Salamis, in his *Panarion* (*Medicine Chest*), and Augustine of Hippo, in his *De heresibus* (*On Heresies*), sought to catalogue what they took to be the many dozens of heresies that either had threatened or continued to threaten the faith of the orthodox.[25] Other writers engaged directly with

21. *Assertio*, 239–53.

22. For Luther's claims, see *The Babylonian Captivity of the Church*, 144–51.

23. Alain Le Boulluec, *La notion d'hérésie dans la literature grecque*.

24. References to "orthodoxy" prior to the Council of Nicaea must carefully be qualified, as Rowan Williams has argued in "Does It Make Sense to Speak of Pre-Nicene Orthodoxy?," 1–23.

25. *The Panarion of Epiphanius of Salamis, Book I (Sects 1–46)* and *Book II and III*

specific heresies or heretics: in fourth-century Alexandria, Athanasius produced four lengthy orations, among other writings, against the followers of the presbyter Arius, and in the following century, Augustine wrote extensively against Manicheans, Donatists, and Pelagians. While scholars no longer use heresiological literature as a guide to what those who were designated heretics might have believed, texts such as these do reveal much about how church authorities thought about the individuals and groups they sought to anathematize.[26]

The *Assertio* confirms that King Henry, or at least his advisors, were familiar with many of the characteristic tropes of earlier heresiological texts. Not only does the text explicitly compare Luther to the heretics of prior centuries, but it does so implicitly as well, charging Luther with the same kinds of deviations from orthodoxy. Perhaps nowhere is the king's book so overt in its invocation of heresiological rhetoric than in its preface: "How rotten is his soul, how execrable a way of living, that he resuscitates buried schisms and adds new ones to the old, and that he brings into the light heresies which ought to be put away in eternal darkness, as if Cerberus from hell, and that he judges himself worthy, by his own word, to direct all things, all ancient opinions notwithstanding—indeed, so that the church be subverted."[27] Again toward the conclusion of the text, Henry conjures up the specter of earlier heresies:

> For there have been few heretics who did not accept the Scriptures; but all of them established their dogmas on it, which they contended either were firmly in the Scriptures, or seemed to be consonant with reason, the contrary not having been defined in the Scriptures: for they contended that those things which were put forward against their sect should be understood otherwise than the orthodox church understood them. And lest it be able to be seen clearly, they either invented another sense or preferred other passages of scripture, which seemed to be contrary to the former, throwing all things into confusion such that they would appear ambiguous. Therefore, unless the public faith of the church had stood firm against Arius, I know not

---

(*Sects 47–80, De Fide*); Augustine of Hippo, *Heresies*. On Epiphanius, see Pourkier, *L'hérésiologie chez Épiphane de Salamine*.

26. See, for instance, Lyman, "A Topography of Heresy," 45–62.

27. *Assertio*, 189: "Quam putris hujus animus, quam execrabile propositum, qui et sepulta ressuscitat schismata, et vetustis adjicit nova, et haereses aeternis abdendis tenebris velut Cerberum ex inferis producit in lucem, dignumque ducit se, cujus unius verbo, posthabitis antiquis omnibus, universa regatur, imo subvertatur Ecclesia!"

whether he would ever have lacked material for disputing about the Scriptures.[28]

As we will see, the charge that Luther reproduced the exegetical errors of earlier heretics by twisting scripture for his own purposes is one that appears constantly in the anti-Lutheran texts of Henry and More. In this passage, however, the king is doing more than simply accusing Luther of hermeneutical improprieties: he is specifically linking Luther's arguments about the number of sacraments, which he goes on to refute in the following paragraph, with the trinitarian and christological debates of the early centuries, debates in which the reviled Alexandrian presbyter Arius was the most notorious participant.[29]

Both of these passages point to what Henry believed to be the temperamental and methodological errors that Luther shared with his predecessors in heresy. For the king, as for most patristic and medieval heresiologists, what all heretics have in common is that, rather than remaining in continuity with the church and its received traditions, they instead seek to introduce new theological ideas of their own making. We have already alluded to the early heresiologist Irenaeus, who in the second century definitively introduced into the anti-heretical rhetoric of the church the notion of apostolic succession: for him, the truth of theological claims is guaranteed by the unbroken line of bishops stretching from his time back to that of Jesus. The fifth-century monk Vincent of Lérins, likewise, associated theological innovation with theological error when he famously stated that those doctrines should to be held to be true which are believed "everywhere, at all times, and by everyone."[30] Therefore, when Henry accused Luther of holding new opinions, or of having "invented" alternative interpretations of scripture, he was in the

---

28. *Assertio*, 405: "Nam paucissimi fuerunt haeretici, qui non receperint Scripturas; sed omnes fere ex eo sua statuebant dogmata, quod aut ea contenderent esse firmata Scripturis, aut, quum illis viderentur rationi consentanea, contrarium non definiri Scripturis: quoniam ea, quae proponebantur adversus suam sectam, aliter contendebant intelligi, quam orthodoxa intelligebat Ecclesia, et, ne clara dici possent, aut alio excogitato sensu, aut prolatis aliunde ex eadem Scriptura loci, in speciem valde contrariis, omnia sic turbarunt, ut viderentur ambigua. Itaque adversus Arium, nisi publica stetisset fides Ecclesiae, haud scio an defuisset unquam de Scripturis disputandi materia."

29. Depictions of Arius in the Middle Ages and early modern period were uniformly negative, and the charge of Arianism was one of the most serious that one could make. For details, see Wiles, *Archetypal Heresy*.

30. On Vincent, see Guarino, "Tradition and Doctrinal Development," 34–72.

same breath accusing him of holding unorthodox opinions and incorrectly interpreting the Bible. Henry's reliance on the theological rule that novelty denotes heterodoxy sometimes took the form of sarcasm, as when he critiqued Luther's idea that the mass is neither a good work nor a sacrifice: "It is a wonder, therefore, that out of so many holy fathers, out of so many eyes which over many centuries read the gospel in the church, none of them was ever so quick-sighted to recognize a thing so obvious, and even that all are even now so blind as to not be able to discern that thing that Luther boasts to see himself."[31]

If for Henry innovation is chief among the features that Luther shares with the generations of heretics who came before him, another is the way in which Luther's heresy resurrects the nexus between theological error and social and political unrest. For instance, in asking rhetorically how Luther dares to challenge the witness of the scriptures, the church fathers, and "the custom of the whole universal church, confirmed by the usage of so many ages and the consensus of so many peoples," Henry characterizes Luther's strategy as one of spreading both ecclesiological and political sedition.[32] "His accustomed method runs riot, he seeks to plant discord and to spread seditions, to excite the common people against the nobles, and so that he might provoke the common people by his most stupid cleverness . . . he pretends that he has Christ as the leader of the whole army in his camps, and that the trumpet of the gospel sounds only

---

31. *Assertio*, 275: "Mirum est igitur ex tot sanctis Patribus, ex tot oculis, quot in Ecclesia tam multis saeculis idem legerunt evangelium, nullum fuisse unquam tam perspicacem, ut rem tam apertam deprehenderet, imo omnes etiamnum tam caecos esse, ut ne adhuc quidem queant id quod cerene se Lutherus jactat." It should be noted, however, that what we might call the orthodox hermeneutic of continuity—the underlying, often tacit principle that established ways of thinking and speaking theologically are for that reason authoritative—was not without its complications for sixteenth-century traditionalists. For instance, in the *De captivitate babylonica* Luther had accused the Roman church itself of having innovated by developing the doctrine of transubstantiation, a concept that does not appear in scripture. In response, in the *Assertio* Henry engaged in somewhat fancy theological footwork, distinguishing between the newer word *transubstantiatio* and the older belief about the presence of Christ in the eucharist that it sought to articulate. The latter, Henry wrote, had been present from the beginning of the church, even if the word had not been. Yet even at the same time the king quibbled with Luther about when precisely the word *transubstantiatio* came into use, claiming that the word was at least a century older than Luther had allowed. See *Assertio*, 243–45.

32. *Assertio*, 255: "totam denique totius Ecclesiae consuetudinem, tot saeculorum usu, tot populorum consensus corroboratam."

for him."³³ These references to social unrest cannot be allusions to the German rebellions from which Luther was eventually required to distance himself; Henry's book appeared three years before the beginning of the insurrections in Luther's native land, so in writing his words the king was not drawing primarily on contemporary experience. Rather, he was taking his place in a long line of anti-heretical writers who associated religious error with sedition and revolt. The emperor Constantine, in many of his public proclamations during the Donatist and Arian controversies, had declared that so long as his empire was at war with itself religiously, it was equally putting itself at risk from upheaval from within and invasion from without.³⁴ More recently, as we have seen, chroniclers and polemicists had ascribed the "Peasants' Revolt" of 1381 and the later rebellion of Sir John Oldcastle to the heretical ideas of John Wyclif and his lollard associates.³⁵

Other elements of Henry's arguments against Luther reflect existing heresiological tropes. First, like his predecessors who ascribed the actions of earlier heretics to their hatred of and malice toward Christ and the church, the king declares that Luther is "moved by hatred," is "blinded by malice," and wishes to spread his "word of malice."³⁶ When authorities attempted to correct him, he "immediately vomited his malediction against those who wished his good, doing so crazily with reproaches and insults."³⁷ Second, repeatedly the king charges Luther with inconsistency, both from one of his works to the next and even within the same work: the charge of internal contradiction was one that was also used by patristic anti-heretical writers, not least among them Athanasius of Alexandria in his orations against the Arians.³⁸ Third, repeatedly also Henry follows the

---

33. *Assertio*, 255: "Usitata via grassatur, laborat seminare discordiam, et serere seditiones, plebem in patres excitare, et quo vulgus ad defectionem provocet stultissima solertia, et facillime coarguenda, mentitur totius exercitus ducem Christum in suis sese castris habere, et evangelii tubam pro se simulate canere."

34. See, for instance, many of the documents collected in Coleman-Norton, *Roman State and Christian Church*, as well as the analyses of Barnard, "Church-State Relations," 337–55; Shepherd, "Before and After Constantine," 17–38; Armstrong, "Church and State Relations," 265–72; Hall, "Constantine and the Church," 1–9.

35. See n. 13 above.

36. *Assertio*, 208, 334, 188.

37. *Assertio*, 193: "quod simul atque a quoquam salubriter est admonitus, ilicet pro benefactor regessit maledictum, conviciis et contumeliis insaniens."

38. See, among many others, *Assertio*, 199, 201, 205, 217, 219, 223, and 351. On Athanasius's rhetorical strategies, see Stead, "Rhetorical Method in Athanasius," 121–37.

time-honored method of arranging against Luther's arguments lengthy quotations from celebrated theologians.[39] Finally, as Athanasius also did against Arius, the king accuses Luther of flattering simple persons in order to achieve his theological objectives.[40] Luther flatters the laity, Henry writes, in order to stir up their hatred against the clergy; he also flatters the Bohemians, but for a different set of reasons:

> he sees that the Germans, upon whom he previously imposed in the guise of a simple sheep, would reject him shortly upon recognizing him as a wolf. And for this reason he insinuates himself among the Bohemians and makes friends with the mammon of iniquity, as much as he is able, so that when he is exiled from his own place, he will be permitted to come into the place of the people into whose errors he has already entered.[41]

As historically far-fetched as this may appear, in making accusations of this sort Henry does not go nearly so far as his retainer Thomas More, as we will shortly see.

Thus one primary rhetorical strategy of the *Assertio* is to employ traditional Christian heresiological discourse against Luther. A second strategy is for the king to point the reader to what he believes to be the slippery slopes in Luther's arguments. In a manner reminiscent of some of the arguments made in twenty-first-century Christian churches about the perverse long-term consequences of ordaining women or blessing the marriages of same-sex couples, Henry's method is to argue that Luther will not be satisfied with only those reforms that he has explicitly advocated. Rather, the king alleges, Luther will not stop until whole swaths of the traditional ecclesiastical system have been overthrown.

There are at least three instances of slippery-slope rhetoric in the *Assertio*. First, the king charges that Luther's reduction of the seven sacraments initially to three, and then to two, is only a prelude to the wholesale destruction of all the sacraments:

> I would be strongly surprised if he were to put forth anything so serious, so stuffed with venom, as this whole swollen prelude

---

39. See, for instance, *Assertio*, 215, 285–87, 339.

40. See Athanasius, *Four Discourses against the Arians*, I.4–7.

41. *Assertio*, 225: "videt enim brevi fore ut Germani, quibus pridem per speciem ovinae simplictatis imposuit, agnitum tandem lupum sint ejecturi; atque ideo Boemis ante se insinuat, ac sibi, quoad potest, amicos facit de mammona iniquitatis, ut in quorum immigravit errores, extorris aliquando sua, illorum immigrare sinatur in patriam."

[i.e., the *De captivitate babylonica*]. In which immediately, from the seven sacraments, he leaves only three, nor them either, but only for a time, evidently indicating that before long he himself will take these away as well. For of the three he snatches one immediately after in the same book, by which he plainly indicates what he proposes to do with the rest.[42]

Likewise, in one of his more tendentious passages, Henry alleges that Luther's views on communion in both kinds secretly mask the Wittenberg reformer's true desire, which is to eliminate communion altogether. "Just as the old serpent, having been cast out of heaven, envied man for having paradise, so Luther, after he fell by his own sin into excommunication . . . seeks to trap all the remaining people in the same snare, so that being freed from the bond of receiving in both kinds, they might little by little become accustomed to receiving under neither kind."[43] It is of course ironic that Luther's own position, in the *De captivitate babylonica* and elsewhere, was to encourage communion in both the bread and the wine, and that it was Henry's own nascent Church of England that did not provide communion in both kinds through the 1530s. Finally, a third instance of the king's slippery-slope rhetoric occurs in his treatment of the sacrament of orders. Henry interprets Luther's critique of the sacrament of orders to be part of his hidden project to bring about the end of all the sacraments by minimizing the difference between the clergy and the laity. By making the claim that all are priests, Henry writes, Luther seeks to render the ministers of the church "contemptible" and the sacraments "despised and undervalued."[44] Not just here does Henry hold up the clergy and the sacraments as irreplaceable avenues for bringing laypeople closer to God; it is for the same reason that elsewhere in the *Assertio* the king argues that Luther's simpler communion service and less exalted theology of ordination are in fact obstacles to the faith of laypeople, since they leave nothing "that might move the simple souls of

42. *Assertio*, 211: "Quanquam vehementer admiror, si quicquam edet unquam tam serium, ut plus tumere veneno queat, quam totum hoc turget praeludium. In quo protinus, ex sacramentis septem, tantum relinquit tria, nec ea tamen, nisi pro tempore, nimirum significans illa etiam ipsa propediem sese sublaturum: nam e tribus unum aufert paulo post eodem libro, quo plane declaret quid proponet in reliquis."

43. *Assertio*, 227: "Nam quemadmodum serpens antiquus, ejectus e caelo, invidit homini Paradisum, ita Lutherus quoque, postquam sua culpa sic in excommunicationis incidit laqueum . . . reliquos omnes eodem laqueo cupit implicare, ut utriusque recipiendae vinculo soluti, neutram paulatim assuescant recipere."

44. *Assertio*, 399.

the common folk and might direct them toward the veneration of this invisible deity by the majesty of visible honor."[45] All three of these arguments—about the number of the sacraments, communion in both kinds, and ordination—share an almost identical purpose: namely, to stress that the dangers posed by Luther's reforms are even more serious than they might appear at first glance. Rather than restricting the number of sacraments, Luther intends to eliminate the sacramental system altogether; rather than encouraging more frequent communion, he means to take it away; rather than making priesthood the shared right of all, he means to undermine its sacred character. In one respect, Henry's arguments anticipate the emergence of more radical reformers, including those whom Luther was eventually to expel from Wittenberg. But subsequent events would demonstrate just how exaggerated Henry's fears would turn out to be: it was Luther, for instance, who famously and forcefully argued for Christ's presence in the eucharist in his 1529 Marburg meeting with Huldrych Zwingli. Yet the king's words have a clear rhetorical intent: they provoke the reader of the *Assertio* to a heightened state of fear about the possible consequences of failing to combat Luther.

In addition to the ways in which he criticizes Luther for reviving earlier heresies and fashioning theological slippery slopes, the king articulates in the *Assertio* a series of broader concerns about Luther's scriptural hermeneutics. Of course, debates about the interpretation of the Bible were not unique to the sixteenth century: almost all of the earlier heresiological writings we have encountered thus far also engaged in hermeneutical debates. But as Ian Christopher Levy has masterfully demonstrated in his recent book, *Holy Scripture and the Quest for Authority at the End of the Middle Ages*, the late fourteenth and fifteenth centuries were a time when arguments over the proper interpretation of scripture proliferated. Levy has shown that the conflicts that shaped much of fifteenth-century western Christianity, such as the debates over how to resolve the schism in the papacy and over the relative authority of the pope and ecumenical councils, were at their heart conflicts about who has the authority to determine if a particular reading of scripture is orthodox. On Levy's account, no universally acceptable solution to this problem was ever found, despite the efforts of theologians including Wyclif, William Woodford, Jean Gerson, and others; the ambiguity about the relationship between scripture and ecclesiastical authority that resulted from these prolonged

---

45. *Assertio*, 293: "simplices animos plebeculae commoveant, et in venerationem numinis invisibilis visibilis honoris majestate convertant."

but unresolved debates created part of the intellectual context for the reformations of the sixteenth century.[46]

King Henry's *Assertio* seeks repeatedly to intervene in the ongoing debate about the proper interpretation of scripture. Combining his arguments about the novelties and inconsistencies in Luther's teachings, the king charges Luther with selecting from scripture only those passages which suit his purposes:

> Nor in such a matter does he prove anything, nor does he bring forth anything by which he might confirm his doctrine, contenting himself to deny anything that the church has accepted. Whatever is believed by everyone, he himself mocks by his futile reasoning, and he accepts for himself that nothing is admitted except clear and evident scriptures. However, if anyone produces these, then he rebuffs them by some fabricated understanding or denies that they belong to their authors.[47]

Luther's way of proceeding, then, is in times of controversy to deny traditional interpretations of scripture when idiosyncratically he believes them to have no basis. The king gleefully points out a number of the contradictions that he believes follow from Luther's approach, and in the *Assertio* he seeks to hoist Luther on his own rhetorical petard. If every action of the church must be directly warranted by scripture, then many things that Luther seeks to retain cannot be found in the Bible. Yet if extrascriptural traditions are to be admitted, who is to determine which of them are and are not legitimate? The rhetorical force of Henry's argument appears perhaps most clearly in his discussion of Luther's treatment of the eucharist, where for instance the king argues:

> If Luther so rigidly summons us to the example of the Lord's Supper, in order not to permit the priests to do anything which Christ is not read to have done there, then they must never receive the sacrament that they consecrate. For it is not read in the gospel that Christ received his own body, where the Supper is written of. And though some doctors hold that he did receive it, and though the church celebrates the same, this does nothing

---

46. Levy, *Holy Scripture and the Quest for Authority at the End of the Middle Ages*.

47. *Assertio*, 453: "nec in tanta re probat quicquam, nec affert aliquid, quo confirmet sua, sat habens negare tantum quicquid recepit Ecclesia. Quicquid creditur ab omnibus, ratione futili solus eludit, ac se denuntiat nihil admissurum praeter claras et evidentes Scripturas. Quas ipsas tamen, si quis afferat, vel aliquo repellit commento, vel auctoris esse, cujus feruntur, negat."

for Luther... From this it follows, as I have said, that the priests should not receive the sacrament that they themselves consecrate, if Luther so rigidly binds us to the example of the Lord's Supper. But if for this reason he concedes that the priests are to receive, because the apostles received... then by this reason the priests should never consecrate, because Christ and not the apostles consecrated.[48]

The king's preferred hermeneutic, in contrast to what he takes to be Luther's ambiguities and evasions, is to follow the counsel of Augustine, whom he quotes: "you cannot know what the gospels are except by the church having handed them down."[49] For Henry, Christ's prayer for Peter that his faith should not fail, and Christ's sending of the Holy Spirit to give testimony to the church, both guarantee that the church can be confident in its ability to distinguish the truth from falsehoods. The king also relies upon John 22:25, in which the writer of the gospel states that "many things were done, which are not written in this book," clear proof, according to Henry, that the traditions of the church validly extend beyond those things explicitly recorded in scripture.[50]

As we have said, these debates about the interpretation of scripture and about the relationship of scripture to extrascriptural traditions represent a running theme through the history of Christianity. In the twentieth century, the great Reformation historian Heiko Oberman described two positions that he called "Tradition I" and "Tradition II"; subsequent scholars have proposed additional models for the relationship between scripture and tradition.[51] Of Oberman's paradigms, the former takes the history of biblical exegesis to constitute an essential part of the church's tradition, whereas the latter assumes that there is a separate source of tradition outside and alongside the Bible and its interpretation. One

---

48. *Assertio*, 277–79: "Si Lutherus tam rigide nos revocet ad exemplum Coenae dominicae, ut nihil sacerdotes permittat facere, quod ibi Christus fecisse non legitur, sacramentum, quod consecrant, nunquam ipsi recipiunt. Suum enim corpus Christus in evangelio non legitur, ubi Coena scribitur, ipse recepisse. Nam quod Doctores aliquot eum recepisse tradunt, et quod idem canit Ecclesia, nihil potest pro Luthero facere.... ex quo sequitur, ut dixi, nec sacerdotes debere, quod consecrant ipsi, recipere, si tam rigide nos obstringat Lutherus ad exemplus Coenae dominicae. Quod si ideo concedat recipiendum sacerdotibus, quia receperunt apostoli... hac ratione nunquam consecrabunt sacerdotes: consecrabat enim Christus, non apostoli."

49. *Assertio*, 357: "nisi tradente Ecclesia scire non posses quae sint evangelia."

50. See, for instance, *Assertio*, 356, 406.

51. Oberman, "*Quo Vadis?*," 225–55; see also McGrath, *Reformation Thought*.

might be tempted to think that Luther is a representative of Tradition I, while Henry represents Tradition II. Yet in reality Luther continued extrabiblical practices, such as infant baptism, in his own church, and he expelled from his community those who took a stricter line on such matters. As Catholic-Lutheran dialogues in our own time have continued to demonstrate, the differences between Lutheran and Catholic positions on a range of theological questions are far subtler than sixteenth-century polemics make them appear.[52]

Subtlety is not one of the virtues of Thomas More's anti-Lutheran writings, whether the 1523 *Responsio ad Lutherum*, the 1528 *Dialogue concerning Heresies*, or other occasional pieces. These works do demonstrate, however, the substantial theological and intellectual continuities between the king's *Assertio* and other near-contemporaneous English polemics against Luther and Lutheranism. Indeed, More's two books utilize almost all of the argumentative strategies we have observed in the king's writings. More labels Luther inconsistent. He maintains that the growth of the Lutheran heresy will lead to political unrest and sedition. He positions Luther on a slippery slope by seeking to demonstrate that his heresies change "from day to day, from worse to worse."[53] He attacks Luther for focusing only on those parts of scripture that support his positions, ridiculing him in particular for speaking ill of the Epistle of James. Like Henry, he rejects Luther's scriptural hermeneutics by quoting in the *Responsio* the Johannine text, "Many things were done which are not written in this book."[54]

All of these strategies echo those of the king's *Assertio*, but More's books go a step further in regard to the extent of the *ad hominem* assault that they launch on Luther's motives and character. Perhaps the most striking example of More's polemic comes in the fourth book of his *Dialogue*, where he offers an extended account of how Luther came to his heresies.

---

52. See, for instance, the "Joint Declaration on the Doctrine of Justification" by the Lutheran World Federation and the Roman Catholic Church.

53. More, *Dialogue*, 365; see also 368. In this and subsequent quotations I have silently modernized the early modern English of the *Dialogue*.

54. *Responsio*, 99.

> It is somewhat worthwhile to consider how this lewd friar began to fall into his mischievousness. You should understand that there was an indulgence announced in Saxony, and for this indulgence, as the custom was there, Luther was made the preacher, and he preached to the people, exhorting them and announcing the authority of the indulgence as much as he might possibly do . . . But it happened soon after that the distribution of the indulgence, with the advantages that came with it, was taken away from him and given to another. Out of his anger at this he fell into such a rage that immediately he began to write against all pardons. Because this was a new matter, he began first simply by raising doubts and questions, submitting himself and his writings to the judgment of the pope and desiring to be informed of the truth. He was thus answered in writing by the master of the papal palace. Then he became more angry and fell to railing against him, and he wrote another book against the power of the pope, alleging that the pope's earthly power was never instituted by God, but ordained only by the common consent of the Christian people so that schisms could be avoided. Still, though, he said that all Christian men were required to obey the pope and that the Bohemians were damnable heretics for doing the contrary. But soon after, when he was answered by good and knowledgeable men so that he perceived himself unable to defend what he had affirmed, then he slipped from reasoning into railing and utterly denied what he had affirmed. Then he began to write that the pope had no power at all, neither from God nor from people, and that the Bohemians whom he had previously called damnable heretics were good Christian men and their opinions good and catholic.[55]

It is breathtaking to consider the scope of More's counter-narrative about the genesis of Luther's reforms. In this passage, and in allusions to it elsewhere in the work, he depicts Luther as a failed indulgence-seller, as a man who quickly fell into anger when his job was taken from him, as a leader who is inconsistent, and as a false reformer who in his rage is looking only to cause the greatest possible damage to the church and the Christian people. Another passage finds More describing Luther as "a foolish friar . . . an apostate . . . an open, incestuous lecher, a plain limb of the devil, and a manifest messenger of hell."[56] In the *Dialogue*, written

---

55. *Dialogue*, 361.
56. *Dialogue*, 346.

in 1528, More repeatedly, indeed to the point of redundancy, condemns Luther's marriage in 1525 to the former nun Katharina von Bora.[57]

What are we to make of More's attempts at character assassination? First, in light of More's twentieth-century canonization by the Roman Catholic Church and in light of the hagiographic praise lavished on him in works like Robert Bolt's play *A Man for All Seasons*, it is important to recognize that More the polemicist, like many of his contemporaries, felt himself to be constrained by few limitations of decorum.[58] More importantly from an historical point of view, we must also note that many of More's calumnies echo those generated by the opponents of earlier heretics. Early church writers complained that heretics fell into heresy when denied church positions. Medieval chroniclers alleged the same about John Wyclif, claiming that he only began to speak against the church and the sacraments when he was passed over for promotion to the bishopric of Worcester.[59] Likewise, More's repeated emphasis on Luther's marriage calls to mind the charges of sexual misconduct lodged by churchmen against a variety of early and medieval heretics, and even in this brief study we have already encountered ample precedents for More's depiction of Luther as inconsistent, angry, and self-serving.[60]

Yet while in general More's arguments proceed along the same polemical trajectories as Henry's, there is at least one difference. Because he was writing more than a decade after Luther came to prominence, More was able to bring to his *Dialogue*, in particular, a longer historical perspective. He therefore was able to comment on the relationships between Luther and other reformers, including the Swiss theologians Zwingli and Johannes Oecolampadius. More takes men like these to be signs of both the proliferation of heresy and of the internal contradictions that he believes all heresies to possess:

---

57. See, among many other references, *Dialogue*, 304, 346, 366, 375.

58. The editor of More's *Dialogue* observes that the "slander" about Luther's past in the lengthy passage just quoted "is not repeated in his later polemical works. He probably discovered that it was untrue." (Part II, 707) It is difficult to believe, however, that someone as well-connected as More, who had been in royal service for ten years at the time he wrote the *Dialogue*, was so unaware of Luther's personal history.

59. For these allegations against Wyclif, see the historiographical survey in Crompton, "John Wyclif," 6–34.

60. On charges of sexual misconduct, see Brundage, *Law, Sex, and Christian Society*, 357, 493; and Bullough, "Postscript: Heresy, Witchcraft, and Sexuality," 206–10.

And also Zwingli and Oecolampadius, scholars of Luther, have built further upon the ungracious ground of their master, and they teach that the sacrament of the altar is not the true body or blood of our Lord at all. And Luther himself, although he now writes against them on this point, yet (as by many things it appears) intended to set forth at his leisure the same heresy himself, until he changed his mind on account of the envy that he bore toward them, when he saw that they wished to be the heads of a sect themselves, for he could permit no one to be that but himself.[61]

Thus for More, as for Henry before him, the heresies that Luther has set forth are by no means the only ones that lurk within his mind and heart. In this passage, More also specifically portrays Luther as a heresiarch: it is clear from his designation of Zwingli and Oecolampadius as "scholars of Luther" that More believes them to depend upon Luther for the content of their theologies, although of course historically their reforming ideas bear the stamp of multiple theological influences. It is also clear that More believes that Luther, motivated by pride like all heretics, will brook no rival for the title of heresiarch.

Were it not for the limitations of space, much more could be said about King Henry VIII's *Assertio septem sacramentorum* and about Thomas More's major anti-Lutheran works, the *Responsio ad Lutherum* and the *Dialogue concerning Heresies*. In addition, beyond the three works that this essay has been exploring, there are dozens more pamphlets, treatises, and other texts that shed light on how sixteenth-century traditionalists perceived their Lutheran opponents, as well as how they viewed Luther himself.

The kinds of arguments that Henry and More employed against Luther provide a window into the ways in which they believed that heresy came about, spread, and was to be combated by the orthodox. As we have seen, their arguments rely strongly on the heresiological discourses of earlier centuries. Consciously or otherwise, Henry and More drew upon a litany of existing tropes and accusations that by the time of Luther's birth Christians had employed against heretics for more than a thousand years. On the one hand, these anti-Lutheran texts testify to the endurance of patristic and medieval discourses at the start of the early modern period. On the other hand, they also testify to the extent to which Henry, More, and

---

61. *Dialogue*, 354.

many other traditionalist opponents of the new reformers saw Lutheranism as yet another heresy, indeed the most recent in a long line stretching back through those of Hus, Wyclif, Arius, and Simon Magus.

That so much anti-Lutheran rhetoric drew heavily on existing discourses suggests that church authorities and their defenders in positions of secular power were confident that they knew what kind of man and what kind of movement Luther and Lutheranism were. If I am right, then, it would not be surprising that these authorities were also confident that Lutheranism would eventually give way to orthodoxy, just as they believed Arianism, Pelagianism, and Wycliffism had all done. That Lutheranism would become one of the most established Christian denominations, that Lutherans in the twentieth century would enter into productive theological dialogue with Roman Catholics, and that in 2011 Pope Benedict XVI would declare that it was "deeply moving" for him to meet with Lutheran leaders at the Augustinian convent where Luther himself had studied—all these things would no doubt surprise and horrify sixteenth-century Catholic controversialists.[62] For them, to conceive of Luther as anything other than the "most stupid scoundrel" of this essay's title would have been to break faith with the many generations before them who had dedicated their lives to the defense of orthodoxy.

Bibliography

Armstrong, Gregory T. "Church and State Relations: The Changes Wrought by Constantine." In *Church and State in the Early Church*, edited by Everett Ferguson, 265–72. Studies in Early Christianity 7. Reprinted, New York: Garland, 1993.

Athanasius. *Four Discourses against the Arians*. In *Athanasius: Select Writings and Letters*. Edited by Philip Schaff and Henry Wace. Edinburgh: T. & T. Clark, 1903.

Augustine of Hippo. *Heresies*, in *Arianism and Other Heresies*. Translated by R. Teske. New York: New City Press, 1995.

Barnard, Leslie W. "Church-State Relations, a.d. 313–337." *Journal of Church and State* 24 (1982) 337–55.

Benedict XVI, Pope. "Meeting with the Council of the Evangelical Church in Germany: Address of His Holiness Benedict XVI." September 23, 2011. Online: http://www.vatican.va/holy_father/benedict_xvi/speeches/2011/september/documents/hf_ben-xvi_spe_20110923_evangelical-church-erfurt_en.html.

Bose, Mishtooni, and J. Patrick Hornbeck II. *Wycliffite Controversies*. Turnhout: Brepols, 2011.

---

62. Benedict XVI, "Meeting with the Council of the Evangelical Church in Germany."

Brundage, James A. *Law, Sex, and Christian Society*. Chicago: University of Chicago Press, 1987.

Bullough, Vern. "Postscript: Heresy, Witchcraft, and Sexuality." In *Sexual Practices and the Medieval Church*, edited by Vern L. Bullough and James Brundage. Buffalo: Prometheus, 1982.

Coleman-Norton, P. R. *Roman State and Christian Church: A Collection of Legal Documents to A.D. 535*. London: SPCK, 1966.

Crompton, James. "John Wyclif: A Study in Mythology." *Transactions of the Leicestershire Archaeological and Historical Society* 42 (1966–67) 6–34.

Dixon, C. Scott. *Contesting the Reformation*. Malden, MA: Wiley-Blackwell, 2012.

D'Alton, Craig William. "The Suppression of Heresy in Early Henrician England." Ph.D. thesis, University of Melbourne, 1999.

Epiphanius. *The Panarion of Epiphanius of Salamis*. 2 vols. Translated by Frank Williams. Nag Hammadi and Manichaean Studies 35. Leiden: Brill, 1987–1994.

Furey, Constance M. "Invective and Discernment in Martin Luther, D. Erasmus, and Thomas More." *Harvard Theological Review* 98 (2005) 469–88.

Ghosh, Kantik and Vincent Gillespie. *After Arundel: Religious Writing in Fifteenth-Century England*. Turnhout: Brepols, 2012.

Guarino, Thomas G. "Tradition and Doctrinal Development: Can Vincent of Lérins Still Teach the Church?" *Theological Studies* 67 (2006) 34–72.

Hall, Stuart G. "Constantine and the Church." In *Faith and Identity: Christian Political Experience*, edited by David Loades and Katherine Walsh, 1–9. Oxford: Basil Blackwell, 1990.

Henry VIII, et al. *Assertio Septem Sacramentorum, Or Defence of the Seven Sacraments*. Edited by Louis O'Donovan. New York: Benziger, 1908.

Hornbeck, J. Patrick II. *What Is a Lollard? Dissent and Belief in Late Medieval England*. Oxford: Oxford University Press, 2010.

Hornbeck, J. Patrick II, et al. *Wycliffite Spirituality*. Mahwah, NJ: Paulist, 2013.

Hudson, Anne. *The Premature Reformation: Wycliffite Texts and Lollard History*. Oxford: Clarendon, 1988.

Justice, Steven. *Writing and Rebellion: England in 1381*. Berkeley: University of California Press, 1994.

Knighton, Henry. *Knighton's Chronicle 1337–1396*. Edited and Translated by Geoffrey Martin. Oxford: Clarendon, 1995.

Le Boulluec, Alain. *La notion d'hérésie dans la literature grecque*. 2 vols. Paris: Etudes Augustiniennes, 1985.

Levy, Ian Christopher. *Holy Scripture and the Quest for Authority at the End of the Middle Ages*. Notre Dame, IN: University of Notre Dame Press, 2012.

Luther, Martin. *The Babylonian Captivity of the Church*. In *Three Treatises*. Translated by Charles M. Jacobs, et al. 2nd rev. ed. Philadelphia: Fortress Press, 1970.

———. *Contra Henricum Regem Angliae*, in *D. Martin Luthers Werke*, vol. 10. Weimar: Böhlaus, 1907.

Lyman, Rebecca. "A Topography of Heresy: Mapping the Rhetorical Creation of Arianism." In *Arianism after Arius*, edited by M. R. Barnes and D. H. Williams, 45–62. Edinburgh: T. & T. Clark, 1993.

Lytle, Guy Fitch. "John Wyclif, Martin Luther, and Edward Powell: Heresy and the Oxford Theology Faculty and the Beginning of the Reformation." In *From Ockham to Wyclif*, edited by Anne Hudson and Michael Wilks, 465–79. Woodbridge: Boydell & Brewer, 1987.

Marshall, Peter. "(Re)defining the English Reformation." *Journal of British Studies* 48 (2009) 564–86.

McGrath, Alister. *Reformation Thought: An Introduction*. Oxford: Blackwell, 1988.

More, Thomas. *A Dialogue concerning Heresies*. In *The Complete Works of St. Thomas More*. Volume 6. Edited by Thomas M. C. Lawler, Germain Marchadour, and Richard Marius. New Haven: Yale University Press, 1981.

———. *Responsio ad Lutherum*. In *The Complete Works of St. Thomas More*. Edited by John M. Headly. Volume 5. Translated by Scholastica Mandeville. New Haven: Yale University Press, 1969.

Oberman, Heiko. "*Quo Vadis*? Tradition from Irenaeus to *Humani Generis*." *Scottish Journal of Theology* 16 (1963) 225–55.

OED Online. "Anglican, n. and adj." Oxford: Oxford University Press, December 2013. Online: http://www.oed.com/view/Entry/153194?redirectedFrom=Anglican.

———. "Lutheran, n. and adj." Oxford: Oxford University Press, December 2013. Online: http://www.oed.com/view/Entry/153194?redirectedFrom=Lutheran.

———. "Protestant, n. and adj." Oxford: Oxford University Press, December 2013. Online: http://www.oed.com/view/Entry/153194?redirectedFrom=Protestant.

Pourkier, A. *L'hérésiologie chez Épiphane de Salamine*. Paris: Beauchesne, 1992.

Shepherd, Massey H. "Before and After Constantine." In *The Impact of the Church Upon Its Culture*, edited by Jerald C. Brauer, 17–38. Chicago: University of Chicago Press, 1968.

Somerset, Fiona. *Feeling Like Saints: Lollard Writings after Wyclif*. Ithaca, NY: Cornell University Press, 2014.

Stead, G. Christopher. "Rhetorical Method in Athanasius." *Vigiliae Christianae* 30 (1976) 121–37.

The Lutheran World Federation and the Roman Catholic Church. "Joint Declaration on the Doctrine of Justification." October 31, 1999. Online: http://www.vatican.va/roman_curia/pontifical_councils/chrstuni/documents/rc_pc_chrstuni_doc_31101999_cath-luth-joint-declaration_en.html.

Van Dussen, Michael. *From England to Bohemia: Heresy and Communication in the Later Middle Ages*. Cambridge Studies in Medieval Literature 86. Cambridge: Cambridge University Press, 2012.

Wiles, Maurice. *Archetypal Heresy: Arianism through the Centuries*. Oxford: Oxford University Press, 1996.

Williams, Rowan. "Does it Make Sense to Speak of Pre-Nicene Orthodoxy?" In *The Making of Orthodoxy: Essays in Honour of Henry Chadwick*, edited by Rowan Williams. Cambridge: Cambridge University Press, 1989.

2

Reformation Never Ends
Jeremias Gotthelf Eavesdropping on Luther in 1828

Peter C. Meilaender

My focus in this essay is on a short work that, I am confident, few of my readers—perhaps not a one—has ever encountered.[1] Though it was written by an author of considerable significance, few English readers are likely to be familiar with him, or perhaps even to recognize his name. The author is Albert Bitzius, better known by his pen name, Jeremias Gotthelf. Gotthelf was a Swiss pastor who lived from 1797 until 1854, spending his entire life, except for one trip to Germany as a student, in or near the capital city of Bern, mostly in the neighboring Emmental region. Though he did not begin writing until relatively late in life, his output was prodigious. His collected works comprise forty-two volumes, about two thirds of which is fiction—a dozen novels, plus numerous short stories and novellas, as well as the contents of an almanac he edited for several

---

1. The author wishes to thank the Katherine Lindley Project Fund of Houghton College for financial support in the preparation of this essay and the accompanying translation.

years—with the rest being letters, sermons, and the like.² Along with Gottfried Keller and Conrad Ferdinand Meyer, Gotthelf is considered one of the three great Swiss German authors of the nineteenth century. Though immensely popular in his own time, not only in Switzerland but also in Germany, Gotthelf's work is less widely read today. German readers know him mainly for what is usually considered his best novella, *Die schwarze Spinne* (*The Black Spider*); English readers hardly know him at all. Although a new translation of *The Black Spider* appeared in late 2013, very little of Gotthelf's work has ever been translated into English.³ His neglect may be due in part, at least, to his liberal use of the Swiss German dialect in his writing—an obstacle even to native German speakers, both because of its difference from high German and also because it is not ordinarily a written language at all.

In 1828, however, Albert Bitzius was not yet Jeremias Gotthelf. Not until 1837, when he was already forty years old, would he publish his first novel, *Der Bauernspiegel* (*Reflections on a Peasant's Life*), which purported to be the memoirs of one Jeremias Gotthelf, whom many readers took to be a real person and whose name Bitzius adopted for his later writings. But in 1828 he was still only Albert Bitzius. Already somewhat advanced in years never to have been appointed pastor of his own congregation, he was serving at the time as vicar to the church in Herzogenbuchsee, a town about thirty minutes by train (today) northeast of Bern, in the region known as Oberaargau. For Reformed clergy in the canton of Bern,

---

2. The standard edition of Gotthelf's *Sämtliche Werke* (SW) is that published by the Eugen Rentsch Verlag (Erlenbach-Zürich) between 1911 and 1977. (In late 2012 the Georg Olms verlag [Hildesheim, Zürich, New York] published the first volumes of what will eventually become a new historical-critical edition of Gotthelf's complete works.) The forty-two volumes of the SW include twenty-four initially planned main volumes, along with eighteen subsequent supplemental volumes. The initial volumes have Roman numerals, the supplemental volumes Arabic numerals. The usual way of citing from the SW, which I will follow here, is to give the volume number (either Roman or Arabic) followed by the page number. Thus the short "Conversation Among the Reformers in Heaven" that is the subject of this essay, which begins on p. 181 of the twelfth supplemental volume, is at 12.181–92.

3. Gotthelf, *The Black Spider*, tr. Bernofsky. See also Godwin-Jones, *Tales of Courtship by Jeremias Gotthelf*, which contains translations of five short stories and one novella; and Godwin-Jones and Peischl, *Three Swiss Realists*, which contains a brief introductory chapter on Gotthelf and a translation of a short novella. H. M. Waidson, who himself published a translation of *The Black Spider* as well as the only general introduction to Gotthelf in English (Waidson, *Jeremias Gotthelf*), supplies information on the few earlier English translations of Gotthelf, some of them based upon French translations rather than the German originals, in "Jeremias Gotthelf's Reception."

the year 1828 was of some importance. It was the 300th anniversary of Bern's adoption of the Reformation, an occasion marked by various festivities and remembrances.[4] It was in this context that Bitzius wrote a short dialogue entitled *Gespräch der Reformatoren im Himmel*, or "A Conversation among the Reformers in Heaven."

The short, early "Conversation" does not display the literary greatness of Gotthelf's mature work, though it does reveal his lively imagination and vigorous prose. Nor is it theologically profound. Some of the figures to whom it refers also leave it a bit timebound, so that it is, in essence, a contemporary satire. It is, however, an entertaining piece that has never before been translated into English. It nicely illustrates a certain late Enlightenment religious perspective that no longer expects human life to present a simple, straightforward narrative of continuous progress, but that has not given up hope for a more rational and humane social order shaped by Christian morality.[5] It also shows how the historic Reformers remained a source of inspiration for a later Christian writer seeking to awaken his readers to the need for a living faith. This is true of Luther in particular, who comes off especially well in the dialogue, not only speaking more lines than any other character, but also making a long, central speech that encapsulates the dialogue's message. Finally, by providing a glimpse into Bitzius's early understanding of the faith, the dialogue foreshadows in important respects later developments in Jeremias Gotthelf's complex and changing relationship to the political currents of his age.

The "Conversation among the Reformers in Heaven" rests upon a clever conceit. Bitzius imagines four of the great Reformers—Luther,

---

4. For the adoption of the Reformation in Bern in 1528, see Gordon, *The Swiss Reformation*, 101–8; Schaff, *The Swiss Reformation*, 102–6; and also Guggisberg, *Bernische Kirchengeschichte*, 608–12. Bitzius himself took a critical attitude toward at least some of the anniversary celebrations. He criticized the minting of a golden memorial coin, suggesting that the funds spent on this purpose might better have been used to create a foundation dedicated to supporting the education of schoolteachers or assisting poor communities in maintaining and improving their schools. See the brief account, in connection also with the *Gespräch*, in Fehr, *Jeremias Gotthelf*, 93–98; and, even more briefly, Fehr, *Jeremias Gotthelf (Albert Bitzius)*, 26. Gotthelf's own reaction can be found in his short essay "Zum Reformationsjubiläum von 1828" ("On the 1828 Anniversary Celebration of the Reformation"), in SW 11.196–204; here he also appeals to Luther and, especially, Zwingli.

5. For Gotthelf as exhibiting this kind of late Enlightenment mentality—chastened but still hopeful about the possibilities for improving the lot of the common people—see Braungart, "Aufklärungskritische Volksaufklärung"; and Jarchow, *Bauern und Bürger*.

Zwingli, Calvin, and Melanchthon—in heaven, where they are discussing the fate of the Reformation on earth since their time and the current state of the faith. Moreover, we learn that St. Peter, unable to come to grips with modern theologians, has created a sort of examining committee of the four Reformers, with the duty of questioning any theologians seeking admission to Heaven in order to determine their suitability. The dialogue falls roughly into three parts. As it begins, the Reformers are reminiscing about their earlier defiance of the authorities of their day. They express remorse at some of their own errors or shortcomings and lament that the Reformation has become bogged down, so that contemporary Christians are more interested in repeating ossified doctrines or having a reputation for holiness than in the continued living out of a vital faith that transforms lives. Then, not quite halfway through the dialogue, the angel Gabriel brings two theologians—Karl Friedrich Stäudlin and Johannes Schultheß—before them for examination.[6] They come off very poorly indeed, revealing themselves as far more interested in their reputations for scholarly learning than in either discerning doctrinal truth or leading lives of genuine holiness. Luther, having previously made clear his low opinion of the current tribe of theologians, remains in the background for the examination, but he brings it to its close by sending the two away again with Gabriel, who is to take them to Uriel, who will in turn give them their reward: "he should feed them with paper, give them ink to drink, and give them quills for dessert! When they've been thoroughly purged in this manner for some years, then perhaps one could employ them among those whose job it is to sweep out heaven and keep it clean" (12.190). The dialogue then concludes with a two-page coda in which, at Luther's urging, the others look out the window to observe the situation in countries other than Switzerland, only to discover that things are equally bad wherever they look. It ends with Melanchthon weeping at the state of things in his dear Germany. In what follows, I will first indicate a few of the dialogue's main themes and then attempt to suggest how they relate to the broader trajectory of Bitzius's later literary career as Jeremias Gotthelf.

One of the dialogue's chief themes—the importance of boldly proclaiming the truth of God—is introduced in its very first sentence, when the four Reformers are sitting around a table and together singing a line

---

6. The young Bitzius would have heard Stäudlin's lectures on church history during a semester spent as a student in Göttingen in 1821. See editor Guggisberg's note to line 188 at 12.306. Schultheß was from Zürich; Guggisberg suggests that he does not receive entirely fair treatment at Bitzius's hands.

from a popular student song: "Raise your glasses, let live the freely spoken word! Hurrah!" (12.183).⁷ Luther immediately states the idea of the song in terms of a religious principle: "Truly, the ability to speak freely is a precious gift of heaven; being permitted to speak freely is humanity's loveliest adornment; and a free word spoken in and for God is more powerful than the might of armies" (12.183). This idea forms the main theme of the dialogue's opening scene. Zwingli, reminiscing about his own and Luther's experience, agrees that "preaching, or speaking freely, has preserved the gospel for the world. Wherever tyranny, spiritual or bodily, has hoped to grow, first it shut people's mouths" (12.183). Luther reiterates the importance of speaking truth: "[T]hat which has once been recognized as truth must be proclaimed, even if Hell should burst on account of it" (12.184). And Melanchthon, remembering Luther's own preaching, says, "I would never have believed that words could have such incredible power" (12.184). A bit later, Luther, criticizing the failure of current generations to live up to the Reformation example, exclaims,

> [N]ame for me men who speak freely according to the Word of God wherever they are, and who, trusting in Him, regardless of consequences, without hesitation take up the task at hand, in small matters as well as great ones, each according to his circle of influence, men who never tire, never shrink back in fear, never let themselves be bought off, who dare to step before emperors and kings and steadfastly preach to them a hated doctrine! . . . By the devil, if God hadn't given me not only a heavenly home but also heavenly patience to go along with it, I'd plunge down upon the earth even today—how those little fellows would shake before my words of thunder! (12.187)

There can be no doubt that in putting these words into Luther's mouth, Bitzius has him enunciate an idea dear to his own heart.⁸ Later, as Jeremias Gotthelf, he would often give important fictional roles to pastors whose honest and wise words are critical to a story's development; the novels *Anne Bäbi Jowäger* (named after its main character) or *Geld und Geist* (*Money and Spirit*) are prime examples. But whether as Bitzius

---

7. In German, "Stoßt an und freies Wort lebe hurra hoch!" Though one can turn up varying versions of the song, the web address for an online text, with an additional link to hear the melody, can be found in the bibliography.

8. For a short comparison of Gotthelf to Luther, emphasizing in part their shared commitment to speaking the truth boldly, see Guggisberg, "Jeremias Gotthelf und die Reformation," 88–90. Guggisberg goes on to suggest, however, that Gotthelf may have had even more in common with Zwingli.

or Gotthelf, he was for his entire life a forceful, outspoken defender of whatever he regarded as true, just, or required by the gospel, whether he was demanding reforms of the educational system or denouncing the irreligiosity of political radicalism. Indeed, his friends, family, and publishers often pleaded with him to temper his views, sometimes fearing that his outspokenness might even cost him his parish. But Bitzius, whose combative nature never shied away from a fight, seems to have been constitutionally incapable of mincing words—or, as he has Luther say in German, "*Das versteht sich, daß ich auch im Himmel kein Blatt vor den Mund nehme*" ("It goes without saying that I don't mince words even here in heaven," 12.183). In the "Foreword" to his late political novel *Zeitgeist und Bernergeist* (*The Spirit of the Age and the Spirit of Bern*), Gotthelf reports that friends had begged him to leave politics out of his books. But, he continues—with, I think, a touch of pride—"Instead of following this advice, this book bristles like no other with so-called 'politics'" (XIII.8). In fact, Gotthelf's own gravestone, which can be found beside the church in Lützelflüh where he served as pastor for over twenty years, carries an inscription from *Proverbs* 12:17 and 19: "*Wer wahrhaftig ist, der saget frei, was recht ist, und ein wahrhaftiger Mund bestehet ewiglich.*" In English: "The truthful man speaks freely that which is right, and a truthful mouth shall be established forever."[9]

A second major theme of the dialogue emphasizes that the heart of Christianity lies not in explicating complicated doctrines or building up impressive theological systems but rather in a faithful life. The gospel calls for fidelity to the truth and service to others; moral purity is more essential than doctrinal purity.[10] This theme appears especially in the satirical examination of Stäudlin and Schultheß, but it emerges even before that. Calvin expresses regret at having encouraged the execution of the heretic Michael Servetus; Luther at his stubbornness in having allowed doctrinal disputes over the Eucharist to divide the Protestant churches at the Marburg Colloquy; and Zwingli at the "sins of my youth" (12.184), presumably a reference to an early affair with a barber's daughter. All three, in other words, focus on moral failings, and in the cases of Calvin and Luther, failings caused by a too strict concern for doctrinal correctness. Later, when Zwingli attempts to praise the advances in theological knowledge that have been made since their own time, Luther will have

9. As seen by the author; see also Fehr, *Jeremias Gotthelf*, 416.

10. The most thorough treatment of Gotthelf's theology remains Guggisberg, *Jeremias Gotthelf: Christentum und Leben*.

none of it. Lamenting the sorry state of the contemporary churchmen who show up to be examined, he complains that when asked to speak on their own behalf, they can point only to a dozen forgotten books they had written. But occasionally a more humble servant of the Lord appears:

> Only now and then a humble little pastor came creeping along, who had refreshed his flock in the wilderness and raised up a congregation for the Lord in peace and quiet. Shyly he remained standing at the door, and those other fellows looked down their noses at him with pity. But when placed upon the scales, he weighed more than all the others put together; for he had been a laborer not in his own, but in the Lord's vineyard. (12.185)

We are then treated to an example of just such theological snobs in the examination of Stäudlin and Schultheß. Both men believe they deserve a place among the four Reformers on account of their scholarship and learning. They introduce themselves with boasts about their importance in Germany and Switzerland, respectively, listing off their scholarly achievements and confident that their wide reputations, which they assume precede them even in Heaven, will win them a place at the Reformers' sides. (Schultheß, from Zürich, is especially confident that Zwingli will have been eagerly anticipating his arrival.) Luther quickly points out that this is the first time he and his colleagues have ever heard of the newcomers, and then he invites the others to begin the examination. In reply to Melanchthon's opening question—"What do you believe about Jesus Christ?" (12.188)—both of the new arrivals display considerable indifference. Stäudlin admits that in his writings he confirmed that the New Testament presents Jesus as the literal Son of God, while also discreetly hinting that one might interpret the text differently; to a more pointed follow-up question about what he himself actually believes, he replies, "Yes, my good man, I can't really tell you that, I didn't have time to think about my own belief. I was busy building up a system for my works, on which I spent the greater part of the day laboring, for I was paid well by the page" (12.189). Schultheß, for his part, is even more blunt. "Already as a lad," he boasts, "I noticed there was nothing to that business about the Son of God" (12.189). Jesus was simply a "clever man" who understood that every religion requires a "mythological cloak" (12.189). This prompts Zwingli to intervene with an expression of shock that this fellow could have been a professor in Zürich. Luther wraps up the interview by asking them about their deeds on earth (a counterpart to

Melanchthon's initial query about their beliefs). Again, they have little to say for themselves, pointing only to their numerous writings, the lectures they've given, classes they've taught, and the theological disputes from which they emerged triumphant. At this, Luther has heard enough and summons Gabriel to drag the protesting and incredulous professors off for their punishment.

Bitzius thus appears to suggest that the true heritage of the Reformation lies not in theological controversy or doctrinal niceties, but rather in the hearts of those who lead lives of genuine Christian charity—lives, we might say, that give evidence of having been reformed by the gospel message. This goes hand in hand with his concomitant criticism of much of what Bitzius saw around him in contemporary "official" Christianity, as represented (fairly or not) by Stäudlin and Schultheß—a portrayal that presumably reflects impressions the vicar Bitzius had received during his recent studies at Bern and a year abroad in Göttingen. Combining this emphasis on a life of faithful service with the previous theme of boldly speaking the truth, we can see that this dialogue functions itself as a call to spiritual renewal. In other words, it is an appeal to continue the work of the Reformation. This is the third and last theme I wish to highlight in this short work: the way in which it draws inspiration from the historical Reformation in order to summon us, the readers, to continued reformation in our own lives.

In the dialogue's longest and most important speech, Bitzius puts this idea explicitly into the mouth of Luther—fittingly, given Luther's central role in framing the scene's action. After Luther's praise of the "humble little pastor" worth more than all those learned churchmen with their forgotten books, Melanchthon suggests that he is being too harsh in his judgment. "The people are now reformed; what else is there for those men of God to do but write? We did all the deeds for them in advance" (12.186). Zwingli points out how much these learned churchmen have advanced the science of theology and the many new discoveries they have made. And Calvin praises their increased humanity: "No more are pyres of fresh wood erected for another Servetus!" (12.186) But Luther replies to them all with indignation: "You all talk according to your own limited understanding of things. What!? We left them nothing more to do? Don't you know what Reformation is? It never comes to an end" (12.186). He continues, describing the sorry state in which humanity still finds itself:

> Just look at the peoples of earth, how infinitely much work still needs to be done on them, how they're still stuck in papism, not just with one foot but with almost their whole heart, or how they make up scattered flocks in need of a shepherd! In what way is the church not still oppressed in most places? And how utterly have all religious establishments decayed! Is there really nothing more to do for this race of men? Yes, they've built up the sciences, just like those who worked on the Tower of Babylon, until they no longer understand each other; they want to erect palaces of stone on foundations of straw. They made a lot of noise, all right, like a quack doctor pulling a tooth, but never at the right place or in the right tone. Science was for them simply a cow that they milked; and they racked their brains, not in order to discover the truth, but in order to cover a certain number of papers from top to bottom with their scribbling, or perhaps they felt the prick of ambition to find their own name listed in the catalog at the book fair. They didn't burn people any more, but just like fighting cocks flying at each other's feathers, scolding each other, slandering, mocking, beating each other to death with charges of immorality—you can see examples of these things every day. They argued over who had correctly discerned the destination of man, but they didn't strive to arrive at it themselves. While each of them was looking out for his own concerns, the poor people remained neglected; and when from time to time a bread crumb fell into their mouths from the revelers' table, they got an upset stomach as a result. (12.186–7)

In Luther's words, we hear the voice of the Bernese vicar who criticized the minting of special golden coins to commemorate the anniversary year of 1828, arguing instead that the money could be put to better use by funding educational establishments for the poor, or who cared less for the learned tomes of a leading theologian than for the work of an obscure pastor shepherding his little flock. Here is the battle cry of the dialogue: "Don't you know what Reformation is? It never comes to an end."

This bold assertion also provides a small window from this admittedly rather obscure dialogue onto Albert Bitzius's broader thinking about the role of the Reformation heritage, and of Christianity more generally, in the modern world. For the ideal of the Reformation with which he presents us here—with its call to speak the truth boldly, its summons to deeds rather than words, and its insistence that a life of true Christian faith is one lived in service to others—appears as the voice of progress. True Christianity improves the lives of men and women. Think again of those two ideal figures that Luther describes: the "humble little pastor . . . who had refreshed his flock in the wilderness and raised up a congregation for the Lord in peace and quiet," a "laborer . . . in the Lord's vineyard"; and the man "who speak[s] freely according to the Word of God . . . and who, trusting in Him, regardless of consequences, without hesitation take[s] up the task at hand, in small matters as well as great ones, . . . who never tire[s], never shrink[s] back in fear" (12.185, 186). These are people who defend their neighbors' freedom, attend to the common good, and work to ensure a decent life for every person, however poor or ordinary. Christianity here is a spiritual ideal, to be sure; but it is also a positive force in the world for good, improving the social order by infusing it with its spirit.

This outlook is fairly characterized as a typical late Enlightenment understanding of Christianity—with the important reminder, of course, that Bitzius is not the outsider appreciating the functional usefulness of Christianity as a tool of social order, but rather an insider fervently persuaded that his faith plays an essential role in transforming the world for the better. Unlike those strands of Enlightenment modernity that viewed religion as a reactionary power from whose yoke modern men and women needed to be freed, Bitzius, inspired by the example of Luther and the other Reformers, is confident that Christianity is, or can be when rightly understood, a progressive force. A fuller discussion of Bitzius—and also, we should now add, of Jeremias Gotthelf—would only clarify that this was indeed his perspective. We see this vision at work in his passionate engagement on behalf of social and political causes, in particular his tireless efforts at educational reform, or his lively interest and participation in the activities of Bern's liberal political party that ultimately led to a revolution overthrowing the city's old patriciate in 1831.[11] And we see it clearly in his early writings: a first novel devoted to exposing the abuses of the common practice by which towns provided for poor, orphaned or abandoned children by effectively auctioning them off to whoever would accept them for the least compensation (and who could therefore be expected to spend as little as possible on their care and upbringing); a second novel focused on the flaws of the educational system, especially the extremely low pay that was common for teachers; and a pair of early

11. For Bitzius's political sympathies and activity, see Fehr, *Jeremias Gotthelf*, 111–21; Hans Ulrich Dürrenmatt, *Die Kritik Jeremias Gotthelfs*, 31–53; and Holl, *Jeremias Gotthelf*, 52–77. For an English introduction to Gotthelf as a political thinker, see my "The Conservative Liberalism of Jeremias Gotthelf."

stories exposing the horrors of alcoholism, which had become a widespread rural problem in the wake of reforms liberalizing the granting of permits to operate an inn.[12]

In both words and deeds, then, Bitzius-cum-Gotthelf clearly demonstrated that for him religious Reformation and political reform were not only compatible, they were mutually reinforcing. Interestingly for our purposes here, in 1833, several years after writing the "Conversation among the Reformers in Heaven," Bitzius—by now no longer a vicar, but not yet embarked upon his literary career as Jeremias Gotthelf—made this very argument in an essay that he read before a group of his fellow pastors on the topic of "Christian Freedom and Equality in the Past and Present."[13] In this essay, Bitzius argues that the ideals of freedom and equality are specifically Christian ideals, and he describes the Reformation as the beginning of a historical process by which they have become more fully realized over time. Christianity is distinct from other religions, he argues, in recognizing the ultimate perfection of our natures as the truest form of service to God. At the individual level, the best sign of this perfection is our growth in loving our neighbors.

> But the surest evidence of this perfection of human or social institutions is when they tear down the barriers separating brother from brother, when they take from those of high rank their pride and give self-confidence to the lowly by assuring that even in these institutions we value not only people's external appearance but also, just as before God, their inner substance, when those institutions offer every person the means to cultivate that inner substance, and when everyone can make the same claim upon their protection and aid. Where, therefore, institutions repeal all privilege and treat all people equally as brothers, there we find progress, and indeed, mark you, Christian progress. (12.198)

Bitzius argues that the Reformation began to establish this Christian equality and freedom with respect to religious belief. But its full promise

---

12. Gotthelf's first novel is *Der Bauernspiegel, oder Lebensgeschichte des Jeremias Gotthelf, von ihm selbst beschrieben*, SW I; his second novel is *Leiden und Freuden eines Schulmeisters*, SW II and III. The two early novellas are *Wie fünf Mädchen im Branntwein jämmerlich umkommen*, SW XVI.5–90, and *Dursli der Brannteweinsäufer, oder Der heilige Weihnachtsabend*, SW XVI.91–212. On the legislative reforms governing inn licenses and Gotthelf's reaction to them, see Dürrenmatt, *Die Kritik Jeremias Gotthelfs*, 120–25.

13. "Christliche Freiheit und Gleichheit in Vergangenheit und Gegenwart," SW 12.193–212.

was not yet realized, because in the social and political sphere people remained trapped in relations of privilege and subordination. Only recently, at the end of the eighteenth and beginning of the nineteenth centuries, have people come to understand that the ideals of freedom and equality must also be extended into our political relationships. As an example of this process, Bitzius points to the progress of liberalism in Switzerland and in particular in Bern, where in 1831 the liberal movement, of which he was an active member, succeeded in ending the dominance of the city over its surrounding rural areas. Although the revolutionary movements sweeping Europe at this time took a range of forms and were not always friendly toward religion, Bitzius argues that it is a mistake for the church to look upon them as alien and hostile, or as irreligious for refusing to submit to the governing authorities. To the contrary, they are rooted in ideals which, properly understood, are profoundly Christian. Three hundred years earlier these ideals had prompted reforms emerging within the church. "Now that reform proceeds from the state, that is, from political society; it has thoroughly political formulae and affects at first only our civil relationships. But who could well deny that the idea lying at its foundation is the Christian one of freedom and equality, or fraternity!" (12.206) Bitzius insists, in other words, that the Christian vision of humans free and equal before God, and united in love of neighbor, is an ideal with social as well as spiritual consequences. "Christianity is not only a manner of worshipping God; Christianity is also the spiritual constitution that God has given us for this life, not only in relation to the church but also to the state, not only in relation to our domestic but also to our public affairs, not only for our inner but also for our outer life" (12.206).

This vision of a Reformation that "never comes to an end," which we find in both the "Conversation among the Reformers" and the essay on Christian freedom and equality—a vision of God at work in human history and of Christian ideals transforming the world—also provides some insight into the subsequent literary career of Jeremias Gotthelf. For the same Gotthelf who would begin by writing novels of social reform would end his career as an equally vehement critic of radical political ideologies such as socialism and communism. (English readers looking for a more familiar parallel might consider the very similar trajectory of Edmund Burke.) Many of Gotthelf's contemporaries thought that he had inexplicably, and inexcusably, become a reactionary late in life. Subsequent critics have also often felt that Gotthelf's apparent political about-face represented a puzzling change in need of special explanation. But as

Albert Tanner has persuasively argued, Gotthelf's broader consistency of outlook comes into focus precisely when we understand that his political views always rested upon his underlying religious convictions.[14] In the early decades of his life, it was easy to believe that political reform in the name of freedom and equality went hand-in-hand with, even arose out of, a Christian vision of those same ideals. But as liberalism became increasingly radicalized, often becoming openly hostile to Christianity in the process, Gotthelf grew ever more certain that the ideological trends of his age—the *Zeitgeist*, as he routinely labeled them—were after all in tension with the Christian understanding of freedom and equality, of whose success and spread he had initially hoped political reform might be a harbinger. Ironically, the Bitzius whose early dialogue among the Reformers ends on a note of sorrow at the Reformation's aborted spiritual progress would later, as Jeremias Gotthelf, grow disillusioned at political reformation's similar failure to realize its own ideals in a Christian spirit.

In conclusion, although the "Conversation among the Reformers in Heaven" is not a work of great literary or theological merit—not one that would have caused a reader to foresee its author's future literary greatness—it nevertheless remains of interest. It shows the continuing potential and availability of Luther and the other Reformers as a source of spiritual inspiration and a touchstone for discerning the essence of Christian faith. It provides an illustration of the complex interaction between Christianity and late Enlightenment ideals such as liberty, reason, and progress. And, not least, it provides one of our few windows upon the early ideas of a thinker who would go on to become one of the greatest Christian authors of the modern West: a "truthful man speaking freely that which is right," and one who as pastor, reformer, and writer spent his life in service of a reformation that never comes to an end.

Bibliography

Braungart, Wolfgang. "Aufklärungskritische Volksaufklärung. Zu Jeremias Gotthelf." *Fabula* 28 (1987) 185–226.

Dürrenmatt, Hans Ulrich. *Die Kritik Jeremias Gotthelfs am zeitgenössischen bernischen Recht*. Zürich: Buchdruckerei Berichthaus, 1947.

Fehr, Karl. *Jeremias Gotthelf*. Zürich: Büchergilde Gutenberg, 1954.

---

14. Tanner, "Vom 'ächten Liberalen' zum 'militanten' Konservativen?," 11–59.

———. *Jeremias Gotthelf (Albert Bitzius)*. 2nd ed. Stuttgart: J. B. Metzlersche Verlagsbuchhandlung, 1985.
Godwin-Jones, Robert. *Tales of Courtship by Jeremias Gotthelf*. New York: Peter Lang, 1984.
Godwin-Jones, Robert, and Margaret T. Peischl. *Three Swiss Realists: Gotthelf, Keller, and Meyer*. Lanham, MD: University Press of America, 1988.
Gordon, Bruce. *The Swiss Reformation*. Manchester: Manchester University Press, 2002.
Gotthelf, Jeremias. *Sämtliche Werke*. Edited by Rudolf Hunziker et al. XXIV and 18 vols. Erlenbach-Zürich: Eugen Rentsch, 1911–77.
———. *The Black Spider*. Translated by Susan Bernofsky. New York: New York Review of Books, 2013.
Guggisberg, Kurt. *Bernische Kirchengeschichte*. Bern: Paul Haupt, 1958.
———. *Jeremias Gotthelf: Christentum und Leben*. Zürich and Leipzig: Max Niehans, 1939.
———. "Jeremias Gotthelf und die Reformation." *Zwingliana* XII.2 (1964) 81–92.
Holl, Hanns Peter. *Jeremias Gotthelf: Leben, Werk, Zeit*. Zürich: Artemis, 1988.
Jarchow, Klaus. *Bauern und Bürger. Die traditionale Inszenierung einer bäuerlichen Moderne im literarischen Werk Jeremias Gotthelfs*. Frankfurt: Peter Lang, 1989.
Meilaender, Peter C. "The Conservative Liberalism of Jeremias Gotthelf." *Anamnesis* 2.1 (2012) 75–103.
Schaff, Philip. *The History of the Reformation: The Swiss Reformation*. History of the Christian Church VIII. Grand Rapids: Eerdmans, 1910.
"Stosst an! Jena soll leben!" Song. No pages. Online: http://www.markomannenwiki.de/index.php?title=Stosst_an!_Jena_soll_leben!.
Tanner, Albert. "Vom 'ächten Liberalen' zum 'militanten' Konservativen?: Jeremias Gotthelf im politischen Umfeld seiner Zeit." In "*. . . zu schreien in die Zeit hinein . . .": Beiträge zu Jeremias Gotthelf/Albert Bitzius (1797–1854)*, edited by Hanns Peter Holl and J. Harald Wäber, 11–59. Bern: Burgerbibliothek Bern, 1997.
Waidson, H. M. *Jeremias Gotthelf: An Introduction to the Swiss Novelist*. Oxford: Blackwell, 1953.
———. "Jeremias Gotthelf's Reception in Britain and America." *The Modern Language Review* 43.2 (1948) 223–38.

3

A Conversation among the Reformers in Heaven

(Gespräch der Reformatoren im Himmel, 1828)

Albert Bitzius (Later to Be Better Known as Jeremias Gotthelf)

Translation by Peter C. Meilaender

Text taken from Volume 12, *Frühschriften*, ed. Kurt Guggisberg, of Jeremias Gotthelf, *Sämtliche Werke*, eds. R. Hunziker, H. Bloesch, K. Guggisberg, and W. Juker (Erlenbach-Zürich: Eugen Rentsch Verlag, 1954), pp. 181–92. The editor's comments and notes on this text can be found on pp. 301–307 of the same volume. All references to this volume take the form "SW 12.[page number]."

∽ ∽ ∽

Luther, Zwingli, Calvin, and Melanchthon are sitting around a table in heaven and singing, "Raise your glasses, let live the freely spoken word! Hurrah!"[1]

They toast. Luther lays his pipe aside and, with his hands folded over his stomach, says, "Truly, the ability to speak freely is a precious gift of heaven; being permitted to speak freely is humanity's loveliest adornment; and a free word spoken in and for God is more powerful than the might of armies."

Melanchthon: "You, brother, certainly don't need to reproach yourself with not having spoken freely. My ears are still ringing from your sermons, and I think you'd read our dear Lord Himself the riot act, if He didn't step right along to your liking."

Luther: "You tame fellow, I'm amazed that you, in your shyness, dare to say such a thing to me. It goes without saying that I don't mince words even here in heaven. Tell me, Zwingli, what would have become of the world if we hadn't spoken freely and snapped the neck of darkness with unconcealed light!"

Zwingli: "Yes, brother, preaching, or speaking freely, has preserved the gospel for the world. Wherever tyranny, spiritual or bodily, has hoped to grow, first it shut people's mouths, only then did it make splendid progress. If you had feared for yourself in Wittenberg and Worms, and I had not been permitted to speak in Zürich, Baden, and Bern, the whore of Babylon in Rome would still be all-powerful."

Melanchthon: "Easy, good sirs, no need to grow so fierce, I was only jesting; I only meant that one's candor should always be finely tempered, taking consideration of the existing circumstances."

Luther: "You're always the same, a little better than that sneaking fellow Erasmus. That blasted 'taking consideration of circumstances' would have never allowed you to become a Reformer, however; but in reality, while I was breaking through, you did a great deal to secure my flanks and cover my back. But that which has once been recognized as truth must be proclaimed, even if Hell should burst on account of it."

Melanchthon: "Yes, true enough; I would never have believed that words could have such incredible power. To be sure, I have seen from the example of Christ and the Apostles what the speech of one possessing true

---

1. Gotthelf is quoting a line from a popular student song. The verse beginning with this line reads, "Raise your glasses! Let live the freely spoken word! Hurrah! Whoever knows the truth and speaks it not will verily remain a miserable wretch. Free is the man, free is the man!" See the editor's note by Guggisberg at SW 12.304.

power is capable of. But I still would never have believed that this miracle would renew itself, and that a poor little monk and a common preacher would win the hearts of so many thousands and shatter the might of lofty princes with mere words. But with the Lord all things are possible."

Calvin sighs: "Yes, we accomplished much, with fiery zeal we proclaimed that which we believed true. But was all of it good, all true? Ah, now indeed I am in heaven and grace has taken from me the burden of my sins, has pardoned my errors; but when I think back on poor Servetus, whose death I caused in my fervor, then I still seem to feel the pain of the flames in my own heart."[2]

Luther: "Yes, yes, I admit we were only human and made plenty of mistakes, we wanted to know that our own pronouncements were treated as equal to the Word of God and even started to curse others just like the pure and spotless lords at their pure and spotless Council of Trent. My dear Ulrich, I'm ashamed every time I think back on the events at Marburg, on your willingness to make concessions and my rough obstinacy, where I was to blame that out of one church there became two. But dear God be praised, that He gave me grace rather than justice."

Zwingli: "Nor has God let me forget the sins of my youth and many an error, so that I might praise His Grace all the more fully."[3]

Calvin: "It's a good thing that our Lord God has left us our memories, so that we can test our prior acts and omissions with a more perfected understanding. Now we know that our work was vain and fragmentary, and in heaven we've grown more humble than we were on earth. For how little we knew, how little we did!"

Melanchthon: "Yes, Paul is right; all our knowledge is partial. We forgot that, our successors forgot it still more. Hence so much controversy, so much error."

Zwingli: "We had hardly struggled ourselves free from the muck of the papacy; some of it still stuck to us, though we weren't aware of it. And how could we have known better? Gesenius had not yet published his abbreviated grammar; Rosenmüller, Kuinöl, and Paulus hadn't yet brought rational understanding to the New Testament; and Father Planck was still to illuminate the cathedral of the Christian church with the torch of history.[4] People of quite another sort are alive today; one has climbed

---

2. Michael Servetus (1511?–53) was a Spanish theologian who was burned as a heretic in Geneva in 1553.

3. Probably a reference to a youthful affair.

4. Wilhelm Gesenius (1786–1842), a theologian and professor at the University of

up upon the shoulders of another, and soon it will come to pass that an impudent human face will suddenly peer right into heaven at us."

Luther: "Pah, listen to you talk! For three hundred years now, as you well know, we've been examining all the servants of the church, since St. Peter just couldn't seem to figure out these new theologians. Many have come pompously mouthing their own names and knowing how to talk about everything. But when one questioned them about their works, they just named a dozen titles of forgotten books, along with (to determine their value even more precisely) a half dozen societies of which they were members, and they looked damned askance at God's not setting them above even the Redeemer himself. Only now and then a humble little pastor came creeping along, who had refreshed his flock in the wilderness and raised up a congregation for the Lord in peace and quiet. Shyly he remained standing at the door, and those other fellows looked down their noses at him with pity. But when placed upon the scales, he weighed more than all the others put together; for he had been a laborer not in his own, but in the Lord's vineyard."

Melanchthon: "Easy, Brother Martin, you're awfully hard in your judgment. People are reformed nowadays; what else should those men of God do except write? The deeds we already did for them in advance!"

Zwingli: "And just think how far they've nurtured the sciences! Oh, if we'd known all their new discoveries, we'd have been fellows of a different stripe! We wouldn't have allowed ourselves to be divided on account of the Eucharist."

Calvin: "And just look at the Christian humanity with which they treat each other. No more are pyres of fresh wood erected for another Servetus!"

Luther: "You all talk according to your own limited understanding of things. What!? We left them nothing more to do? Don't you know what Reformation is? It never comes to an end. Just look at the peoples of earth, how infinitely much work still needs to be done on them, how they're still stuck in papism, not just with one foot but with almost their whole heart, or how they make up scattered flocks in need of a shepherd! In what way

---

Halle; Johann Georg Rosenmüller (1736–1815), cleric, theologian, and professor in Leipzig; Christian Gottlieb Kuinöl (1768–1841), theologian and professor in Leipzig and Gießen; Heinrich Eberhard Gottlob Paulus (1761–1851), professor and theologian in Jena and Heidelberg; Gottlieb Jakob Planck (1751–1833), professor of church history in Göttingen, whose lectures on this subject Bitzius attended with interest in 1821. For additional details on these figures and their noteworthy writings, see Guggisberg's notes to the text at SW 12.304–5.

is the church not still oppressed in most places? And how utterly have all religious establishments decayed! Is there really nothing more to do for this race of men? Yes, they've built up the sciences, just like those who worked on the Tower of Babylon, until they no longer understand each other; they want to erect palaces of stone on foundations of straw. They made a lot of noise, all right, like a quack doctor pulling a tooth, but never at the right place or in the right tone. Science was for them simply a cow that they milked; and they racked their brains, not in order to discover the truth, but in order to cover a certain number of papers from top to bottom with their scribbling, or perhaps they felt the prick of ambition to find their own name listed in the catalog at the book fair. They didn't burn people any more, but ruffling each other's feathers like fighting cocks, scolding each other, slandering, mocking, beating each other to death with charges of immorality—you can see examples of these things every day. They argued over who had correctly discerned the destination of man, but they didn't strive to arrive at it themselves. While each of them was looking out for his own concerns, the poor people remained neglected; and when from time to time a bread crumb fell into their mouths from the revelers' table, they got an upset stomach as a result."

"Or name for me men who speak freely according to the Word of God wherever they are, and who, trusting in Him, regardless of consequences, without hesitation take up the task at hand, in small matters as well as great ones, each according to his circle of influence, men who never tire, never shrink back in fear, never let themselves be bought off, who dare to step before emperors and kings and steadfastly preach to them a hated doctrine! A pox upon this feeble race that screams like children but doesn't speak like men, that quarrels like women but doesn't fight like men, that like a young girl seeks appearances instead of desiring the truth, that complains like an old dotard instead of coming to the rescue in time of need like men, that makes eyes at the devil while it prays to God, that blusters godless ideas like a windbag and secretly trembles at the fear of ghosts! By the devil, if God hadn't given me not only a heavenly home but also heavenly patience to go along with it, I'd plunge down upon the earth even today—how those little fellows would shake before my words of thunder! Then you'd see, Calvin, that people will still commit murder nowadays. For it wouldn't take long before they dispatched me right back up here again."

Zwingli: "How you do go railing against them again! Just think about so many brave men in all countries!"

Someone knocks loudly on the door of the heavenly chamber. Zwingli calls out, "Come in!"

The angel Gabriel appears. "Your servant, most worthy lords! St. Peter sends me to inquire whether it would be convenient for you to examine two men who give themselves out to be pillars of the church and demand to be placed at your sides."

Luther: "They come at just the right time. Just lead them in, Gabriel, and you others, pay attention."

A small, powdered little man with a dark red face and somewhat crooked legs appears, along with a haggard, pale, carelessly dressed fellow. They bow deeply.

The first clears his throat and speaks as follows: "I am the well-known Stäudlin, doctor, professor, consistorial councilor, and knight, the pride of Göttingen, a light in Germany. Because I have shed light not only in Germany but throughout the entire learned world, and have unearthed so much that is new and remarkable in scientific theology, ethical doctrine, and church history, therefore I believe that I deserve a place among you, most learned, most worthy lords."

The other stretches himself and says: "You all know me already, and especially you, Zwingli, will have been eagerly awaiting me for a long time; for not only do I come from Zürich, the diamond of Switzerland, but I am the famous Schultheß, one of the leading exegetes ever; and since exegesis is the foundation for everything, I hope, your worthy Highnesses, that you will not fail to prefer me to that boaster, who is neither an exegete nor—especially—stems from Zürich."[5]

Stäudlin: "What! You boor, you, of whom I've never even heard at all, you who come from that dark nest Switzerland, you want to compare yourself to me?!"

Schultheß: "Silence, you—"

Luther: "Gently, gently, my lords, you can't go about things like that in heaven, just wait decently now until you're questioned; we'll assign you to your proper pastures in accord with your answers. Besides, now is the first time that we here in heaven have the honor of hearing your names. Ask them something once about their faith, Philipp!"

Melanchthon: "Stäudlin, what do you believe about Jesus Christ?"

---

5. For more on Karl Friedrich Stäudlin (1761–1826), whose lectures Gotthelf probably also heard in Göttingen, and Johannes Schultheß (1763–1836), see Guggisberg's notes at SW 12.306.

Stäudlin: "In my dogmatics I have demonstrated with the purest objectivity that he is truly presented in the New Testament as the Son of God, and I have only obliquely hinted that one could also take it differently."

Melanchthon: "I'm not asking what you wrote, but rather what you believe."

Stäudlin: "Yes, my good man, I can't really tell you that, I didn't have time to think about my own belief. I was busy building up a system for my works, on which I spent the greater part of the day laboring, for I was paid well by the page; then I read two to three lectures per day; and finally I had to trouble myself a good deal with my Marianne. How could I have even thought about my own belief!"

Schultheß: "Just look at that pitiful wretch! Already as a lad I noticed there was nothing to that business about the Son of God. Jesus was a clever man, who understood that no religion can be successful unless it is wrapped in a mythological cloak. He wove one with considerable skill, accommodated it extremely suitably to human beings, and in this fashion achieved his purpose quite successfully."

Zwingli: "Did you also write thus?"

Schultheß: "God forbid! That would have gotten me into a pretty kettle of fish with the antistes! I wrote in the way I thought would lead to the greatest success. *Mundus vult decipi, ergo decipiatur*;[6] if it was permitted to Christ, then I was allowed to venture it myself."

Zwingli: "What, you were a professor in Zürich?"

Schultheß: "But of course, well-reputed and held in great esteem."

Zwingli is about to explode, but Luther interrupts him: "Enough of belief, then; both of you, recount your deeds!"

Schultheß: "Now what kind of a question is that to ask me, when you've already heard who I was! I've given lectures, written, reviewed books, destroyed Pastor Gyger in a mighty battle,[7] had it out with my wife also from time to time, and grappled with my children."

Stäudlin: "You, as it appears to me from your heavy head, are Luther; I think your hearing must have also suffered in heaven, since I've already said that I wrote almost innumerable volumes, gave many lectures, certainly also reviewed books thoroughly, and on the side amused myself with my Marianne when she was in a good mood, and, when she was in a

---

6. "The world wants to be deceived; therefore, let it be deceived."

7. He refers to an insignificant polemical writing directed against one Franz Geiger, a professor and ecclesiastic in Luzern. See Guggsiberg's note at SW 12.307.

bad mood, drank cherry brandy—apart from cheese, the only good thing that comes from Switzerland."

Luther's face turns red and he pounds the table with his fist so that the bottles and glasses crash together. Gabriel appears.

Luther: "Take these two fellows and throw them to Uriel; he should feed them with paper, give them ink to drink, and give them quills for dessert! When they've been thoroughly purged in this manner for some years, then perhaps one could employ them among those whose job it is to sweep out heaven and keep it clean. But tell Peter he should do a better job of keeping his eyes open in the future, so that he doesn't admit any more such rabble!"

Stäudlin whines: "Ah, if only no one reports this in Göttingen, if only Marianne doesn't get word of it!"

Schultheß blusters: "This is the thanks I get for having done battle for you all! Just wait, I'll turn Catholic and will make things so hot for you that you'll be sorry!"

Gabriel seizes them. Stäudlin seeks to plead for mercy. Schultheß lays about with his hands and feet, but Gabriel departs with them like a whirlwind.

Melanchthon: "Heaven help us, what kinds of fellows are those!"

Zwingli: "A fellow like that boasts that he stood in high esteem in Zürich? No, it isn't possible. I'll go and ask the Father to let me back down to earth again in order to purge out the old leaven."

Calvin: "God have mercy on these poor humans!"

Luther: "Now you see for yourselves whether my zeal was well-founded! Just take a look out of the window at our little old star down below; it will be clear to you soon enough how the peoples of earth are doing at this moment! Calvin, you're letting your head hang especially today. Snap out of it, look through the telescope at France, England, and America, and give me a report on how the salvific doctrine is doing in these places!"

Calvin opens the window and looks out for a while. Then, sighing, he again takes his seat.

Melanchthon: "Dear brother, what sorrows have you seen? We want to help you bear your sorrow."

Calvin: "The longer I looked, the dimmer my eyes grew. In England I saw much stiff formality, a great hustle and bustle in religious societies; but of true Christianity there was little. Their piety was mere appearance, the societies a fashionable trend, their great expenses for religious purposes a mere financial show of splendor. I saw stout vicars living even better than bishops and their flocks given over to miserably paid hirelings, saw dissenters under inhuman pressure; at the universities the old, expired corpse of the strictest orthodoxy is industriously dissected; with the living religion of Christ they are unacquainted.

In North America there prevails great indifference; everyone cuts his cloak according to his own taste, can even go naked if he likes. The entire state is still in the process of coming into being; how it will take shape, God only knows.

In France I looked, lamenting, and saw the little church shamefully oppressed and sinister Jesuitism opening its wings ever wider; but there in France, precisely on account of the oppression, a countervailing power is showing itself, giving witness to a religious life that I did not discern in other lands.

But all in all, how little have our hopes been fulfilled, how slowly the race of men plods forward! It's a good thing for them that God is eternal and that a thousand years for him are like a day, otherwise they would never reach their goal."

Luther: "That is our consolation, and here in Heaven we don't need merely to hope, rather we see the slow but certain course of providence clear and undisguised. But the zealous friend of Christ on earth must feel his heart sink when things don't seem to make any progress, when the efforts of the most strenuous seem to be in vain and when one race seems to destroy what the previous one built up."

Melanchthon: "To be sure, what Calvin saw is no cause for rejoicing; but just think, he only saw moneygrubbing England, where it surprises me that no one's yet thought to speculate in selling places in heaven, payable in advance; frivolous France, where proper gravity hardly finds a place; and America, populated with the riff-raff of all countries. In our dear, earnest, decorous Germany—the hearth of the Reformation and nursery of the sciences, of princely virtue, of pious civic life—surely there things look different and happier."

Luther: "Oh, my dear Philipp, I'm afraid you've been sleeping, or going around pregnant with some new work; or, if in heaven one still took a wife in marriage, you would court one of our beauties and never reach the goal because of your shyness. Otherwise you wouldn't speak like that; with your words, you betray that you haven't taken a good look at your lauded Germany in many a year. Open the window yourself and make up for lost time!"

Melanchthon obeys and sticks his head out.

Meanwhile the other three converse, making many apt observations about the vanity of human understanding, how no race of men is able to behold the truth clearly, only approximating it instead, but how every race surrenders to the delusion of having grasped the pure truth and wants to force others to see it through the same lens, which is the source of so much calamity.

While they are thus talking, Melanchthon creeps away from the window and tries to reach the nearest door without being noticed. Calvin spots him and cries out: "Hey, brother, where are you trying to get off to? Don't like admitting you were wrong, even now in heaven?"

Melanchthon turns around, wipes his red eyes, and says: "Ah, no, a mere error I would confess gladly; but what I saw pains my heart, and I would fain have wept out my woe in private."

4

Luther and Kleist

Breaking New Ground

Jean Wilson

INSPIRED IN PART BY Northrop Frye's theoretical inquiry into the value of literary studies,[1] the following discussion explores an early nineteenth-century literary text in which Martin Luther appears as a central character: the novella *Michael Kohlhaas* (1810) by German author Heinrich von Kleist (1777–1811).[2] Borrowing from a sixteenth-century chronicle that documents the response of a man by the name of Hans Kohlhase to an injustice he had experienced (it records the feud that began with the theft of his horses and ended with his execution in 1540), Kleist's imaginative rendering tells of a principled citizen who becomes a terrorist, "one of the most honorable as well as one of the most terrible men of his age."[3] His fictional recasting of the factual account, the "old chronicle" (*MK*, 114) acknowledged to be the source text, has had a remarkable reception. Its influence can be traced in a number of subsequent creative recastings:

---

1. Frye, *The Educated Imagination*, 437.

2. Partly excerpted from a previous publication and published with the permission of Cambridge Scholars Press.

3. Kleist, *Michael Kohlhaas*, 114. Hereafter, *Michael Kohlhaas* is abbreviated as *MK*.

E. L. Doctorow's 1975 novel *Ragtime*, for example, which was followed by the 1981 Miloš Forman film and ultimately the Broadway musical of the same name, and the 1999 film *The Jack Bull*, a western starring popular American actors John Cusack and John Goodman, written by Cusack's father. In what I argue is a groundbreaking work in its provocations to our thinking about issues of peace and conflict—about what Ursula Franklin calls a culture of "militarism"[4] and the possibility of its transformation—Kleist imaginatively explores the relationship between his protagonist and Martin Luther, to whom the unjustly treated citizen appeals, as the historical Hans Kohlhase had done in his protest against the abuses of authority he had suffered. In its description of Kohlhaas' attempts to justify his behavior, especially to the character of Luther, on whose actions he apparently models his own, the text draws upon a range of theological and philosophical discourses. As a literary text, however, *Michael Kohlhaas* refuses an argument that endorses or condemns the protagonist's claim to be waging a "just" war. Instead it engages in what we might, following the suggestion of another German author, Christa Wolf (1929–2011), conceive of as a kind of literary "peace research."[5]

In her Büchner Prize acceptance speech of 1980, faced with the global threat of nuclear annihilation and working on the assumption that "maps already exist which record the phases of our extinction," Wolf contends that literature should be "taken at its word," its alternative mappings attended to, as they "counteract those maps of death."[6] Literary peace research, as I see it, is carried out in works from antiquity to the present day. Poems as ancient as Homer's *Iliad* confront human experience marked by fear and by "structures of threat and violence," as Franklin defines militarism,[7] but also map other realities and possibilities; they expose what Wolf elsewhere refers to as a desperate "lack of alternatives,"[8] but at the same time chart openings into new life beyond the limits of what is normally conceived of as possible. Far from being a fully theorized concept, Wolf's vision of literature as peace research emerges only briefly at the end of her acceptance speech, but the idea is exemplified in the Homeric war poem and in works by Kleist and by other authors read

---

4. Franklin, *Pacifism as a Map*, 100.
5. Wolf, "Speaking of Büchner," 185.
6. Ibid., 186.
7. Franklin, *Pacifism as a Map*, 100.
8. "Alternativlosigkeit" is the term in the original German. See Wolf, *Die Dimension des Autors*, 670.

alongside it in a course I teach—works that counteract dominant cultural narratives by drawing their "own map," as Wolf puts it, both in the exploration of overwhelming conflict and in the suggestion of alternatives to personal and cultural devastation.[9]

Kleist's writing, like the *Iliad*, engages profoundly with the question of what it means "to reconcile," one definition of which is simply "to render no longer opposed."[10] The *Iliad* ends with the astonishing coming together in peace of the Greek hero Achilles, feared as "the most violent man alive,"[11] and Priam, the Trojan king, who has suffered the atrocity of Achilles' slaying of his son Hector. Such a spectacularly positive resolution is by no means duplicated in the conclusion to Kleist's tale; indeed, what fascinates is the ironic spectacle of compromise with which the novella ends. As Kleist scholar Elystan Griffiths suggests, a text such as *Michael Kohlhaas* represents "an opportunity for [the author] to think his way into problems (and to set related problems for his readers)."[12] In reading *Kohlhaas*, we may initially find completely understandable the failure of the protagonist to follow his wife's deathbed directive—to forgive his enemies—but the nature and consequences of his refusal lead us to consider anew the challenge that she actually presents, which would entail asking who his enemies are, discovering what it might mean to forgive them, and moving beyond the false alternatives of giving in to intimidation and violence or giving up on peace and justice altogether. Literary peace research thus invites the active participation of readers; the interpretive challenges posed both in and by Kleist's works enable his readers to go, as he once expressed it, "where no one ever goes,"[13] to follow new maps of human problems and possibilities.

Here is a brief summary of the situation: Kohlhaas, a law-abiding horse-dealer, who is arbitrarily detained by the keeper of a new toll-gate and asked to furnish a non-existent permit with his horses left as surety until he does so, becomes the latest victim of "shameful" (*MK*, 119) ill-treatment at the hands of the Junker Wenzel von Tronka. Vowing that he will see justice done, Kohlhaas institutes legal proceedings, and then settles back into his peaceful and well-ordered life. In time, however,

---

9. Wolf, "Speaking of Büchner," 186.
10. "Reconcile," *Random House Dictionary*, Def. 1.
11. Homer, *Iliad*, 82.
12. Griffiths, *Political Change and Human Emancipation*, 43.
13. In a letter to his sister, 5 Oct. 1803. See Kleist, *Sämtliche Werke*, 4:736.

his world is turned upside down with his discovery of what has somehow become the official view: that he, rather than the Junker who has wronged him, is the problem, that he is a "vexatious litigant" (*MK*, 130), with absurdly trivial concerns. Thus, when he is sent a message advising him to refrain from bothering the courts with such "contentions and complaints" (*MK*, 130), not only has justice been denied, but the tables have been turned in an infuriating narrative of blame, which puts the horse-dealer in an enraged state, unable to function. The text literalizes Kohlhaas' inability to live in such a state: he cannot live in a place where he is not protected, where his "rights are not defended" (*MK*, 134), and so he prepares to sell his property and move away if one final appeal, as suggested by his wife, Lisbeth, fails. She travels to Berlin to approach the Elector of Brandenburg in her husband's stead, but encounters such extreme resistance from an "overzealous" (*MK*, 136) bodyguard that she is brought back in a state of unconsciousness, from which she rallies only briefly before expiring. Upon her death, Kohlhaas undergoes a dramatic change; the upright citizen relinquishes his lawful attempts to seek justice. What happens here is reminiscent of a decisive turn in Homer's *Iliad*. When Kohlhaas sets out to avenge his wife's death, he is filled with a rage reminiscent of that of Achilles after the death of Patroclus, one of a number of significant parallels that can be traced between the two texts.

Like Kohlhaas, the Iliadic hero is an exemplary figure in his society. He too has been treated arbitrarily and shamefully; he too has lost control of a prized possession, a determinant of cultural identity—in his case a woman, whom the Greek commander Agamemnon seizes as his own war "prize" (*Iliad*, 81). She is an economic object of exchange, as are Kohlhaas' prized horses, taken from him by the Junker, and Kohlhaas' demand that they be returned in their original condition recalls Agamemnon's assurance, when later trying to make amends, that the woman recognized as Achilles' property will be restored to him unchanged: "I never mounted her bed, never once made love with her" (*Iliad*, 256). Furthermore, Achilles, like Kohlhaas, has attempted to argue his case publicly; he too has been unsuccessful and branded a troublemaker, too proud for his own good, overly concerned with a trivial matter. "All for a girl" (*Iliad*, 273), mutters Ajax, whose disdain for Achilles' behavior corresponds to that of Martin Luther for the horse-dealer's dispute "about some trivial possessions" (*MK*, 149). In the end, Achilles and Kohlhaas, respectively, feel "like some outcast stripped of all [his] rights" (*Iliad*, 273), placed "outside society and its laws" (*MK*, 156), and each of them, from this position as outlaw, witnesses the loss of a loved one acting in his place. Patroclus, the man Achilles loves "as [his] own life" (*Iliad*, 470), goes into battle in the hero's stead, wearing Achilles' armor, and is killed by the Trojan warrior Hector. His death mirrors, in a remarkably literal way, Achilles' own vulnerable state with respect to his community, and when Patroclus dies, something inside Achilles dies as well: his contentiousness, his readiness to expose and oppose Agamemnon's abuse of power, to challenge the structures of authority that are making an ordered life impossible. Kohlhaas' assertion—*before* Lisbeth's death—that justice must be achieved if he is "to go on practicing his trade" (*MK*, 135) echoes Achilles' acknowledgment *before* the death of Patroclus that he has lost the "desire to battle glorious Hector" (*Iliad*, 263), for the Greek warrior's quarrel is not with the Trojans, but with Agamemnon. Whereas Kohlhaas is said "peacefully" to earn a living "by his trade" (*MK*, 114), Achilles is accustomed to belligerence—his job, after all, is to plunder "wealthy Trojan stronghold[s]" (*Iliad*, 83)—but the experience is comparable: neither man can continue to participate in social life when his rights are not protected, and each of them, prior to the death of Patroclus and Lisbeth, respectively, is willing to stand up for such rights.

Once their loved ones die, however, both characters undergo a significant development: the kind of anger that enriches their humanity also dies, and what takes over, as they are "driven mad by . . . grief,"[14] is a monstrous desire for revenge. Having "lost the will to live" (*Iliad*, 470), Achilles arms for battle, intent on nothing but avenging Patroclus' death by taking the life of Hector. His "barbaric" (*Iliad*, 551) actions are what psychiatrist Jonathan Shay has described as typical of soldiers in our own time when they are betrayed by their commanders, as Achilles is by Agamemnon. Shay analyzes the move, experienced by many of the Vietnam veterans he interviewed, from "indignant rage" at the "violation of 'what's right'" to "berserk rage."[15] The former, indignant rage, is what Kohlhaas feels in regard to the wrong done by the Junker, what Achilles feels in regard to that done by Agamemnon; the latter, berserk rage, characterizes the state entered by those who once felt a healthy anger at injustice, when they, as Shay says, "los[e] it."[16] Achilles indeed in more ways than one "loses it" after the death of Patroclus, and dramatically

---

14. As Seán Allan describes Kohlhaas. See Allan, *The Stories of Heinrich von Kleist*, 57.

15. Shay, *Achilles in Vietnam*, 21.

16. Ibid., 82.

acts out his giving up on the real fight—that is, with Agamemnon—by becoming a killing machine for the Greek forces in their war against the Trojans. Kohlhaas, for his part, begins "the work of his vengeance" (*MK*, 137), setting fire first to Tronka Castle, and then to entire towns, killing those who come between him and the Junker. The paragon of civility becomes fanatically embroiled in a self-proclaimed "just war" (*MK*, 140), lost in an absurd parody of Martin Luther; Kohlhaas issues numerous edicts, even posts a declaration on a Wittenberg church door (*MK*, 143), but, unlike Luther, finds no ground on which to stand.[17]

In the *Iliad*, new ground is eventually broken in Priam's disarming appeal to Achilles for the return of Hector's body; the Trojan king "endures," as he describes it, "what no one on earth has ever done before— / I put to my lips the hands of the man who killed my son" (*Iliad*, 605). In the final book of the epic poem, Hector's corpse is ransomed, but it is Achilles who is brought back to life, rendered no longer opposed to it, as he had been after the death of Patroclus, when he gave in to his berserk fury. The moving reconciliation of Achilles and Priam exposes the common enemy of militarism, and while it does not end the war, it models the possibility of social transformation through the regaining of individual agency and the workings of creative human power. In Kleist, a promising development comes in the form of Martin Luther's "disarming" (*MK*, 151) condemnation of his imitator's presumptions and the "insanity of [the latter's] blind passion" (*MK*, 149), followed by Kohlhaas's equally disarming gesture of paying Luther a personal visit instead of madly issuing another edict. Rather than leading to reconciliation, however, and to a recognition of a common cause against abuse, their exchange remains thoroughly discordant; it culminates in the failure to achieve communion, literalized in their inability to share in the sacrament, to serve and receive the Eucharist. When Luther's measured and dispassionate subsequent intervention on behalf of Kohlhaas leads to naught, swallowed up by political wrangling that includes a debate between the Electors of Brandenburg and Saxony about who is bound by what and by whom, the social chaos reflects the disorder of the meeting between Luther and Kohlhaas, in which, despite a measure of agreement, the two men remain fundamentally at odds. In its description of the protagonist's explanation of his violent actions, the literary text neither supports nor dismisses his claims; it privileges neither Luther's position

---

17. The echo is of Luther's famous defiance of the Diet of Worms in 1521: "Here I stand. I can do no other."

nor the Hobbesian justification anachronistically advanced by Kohlhaas that being denied the protection of the law has "put into [his] hands the club [he is] wielding to defend [himself]" (*MK*, 152).

Unlike the *Iliad*, which establishes a paradigm for tragedy, *Michael Kohlhaas* follows neither a tragic nor a comic trajectory, but instead calls forth the interpretive energies of readers to make sense of a singular and often bewilderingly ironic narrative. The power of this particular work of peace research arises, in part, from the text's parodic strategies, which ultimately lead readers to confront the social and psychological realities exposed in the spectacular failure to achieve a genuinely satisfying resolution. To an obviously wronged man who has reached an impasse in his quest for justice, Martin Luther offers the opportunity of getting beyond what has become an untenable situation. But Luther disappoints. As Seán Allan observes, "Kohlhaas has little difficulty in countering most of Luther's arguments," which "for the most part ... amount to little more than a blustering, ill-judged attempt to preserve the stability of public order at all costs."[18] Luther fails truly to hear the charge of injustice Kohlhaas has leveled, fails to reach the individual who has been wronged, fails to meet him on common ground. Griffiths notes that in contrast to the historical account, which "records that the men debated openly and at length," Kleist's tale depicts Luther "retreat[ing] from argument" and "cut[ting] short the discussion by turning his back on Kohlhaas."[19]

Indeed, in a complex parodic approach, the correspondences that emerge are surprising and revealing; the text disrupts expectations of precise fictional-historical equivalents. The fictional Luther, in his reluctance to become involved, bears more of a resemblance to Erasmus (1466–1536), positioned historically in the middle ground between the Church and those who would reform it, than to his real-life counterpart. And if Kohlhaas corresponds to the historical Luther (1483–1546) in, for instance, his indignant anger, the posting of his declaration on the church door in Wittenberg, and his being outlawed, he recalls more strongly, in his violent excesses, Thomas Müntzer (1490–1525), the radical Reformer who broke with Luther and whose pursuit of a so-called "just" war included taking up arms in the Peasants' Revolt of 1524. As observed above, unlike the historical Luther, Michael Kohlhaas cannot find a ground on which to stand. He imitates the leader of the Reformation poorly, acting

---

18. Allan, *The Stories of Heinrich von Kleist*, 62.
19. Griffiths, *Political Change and Human Emancipation*, 136.

on no basis other than the authority "inborn in him" (*MK*, 137) and ignoring that of Scripture. Obvious differences aside, the character in Kleist's novella who in important ways perhaps most recalls the position of the historical Luther is neither Kohlhaas, who becomes a parody of the great Reformer, nor Luther himself, but rather Lisbeth, Kohlhaas' spouse, who plays a literally short-lived, but highly significant role in the narrative.

Caught within the binary terms of an identity as law-abiding citizen or terrorist, and an equally confining conception of justice, Kohlhaas cannot seize opportunities for "life and freedom" (*MK*, 207) presented repeatedly: first, by his wife; second, by Luther, and third, by the mysterious gypsy-woman (who in a strange subplot has scribbled the Elector of Saxony's fortune on a scrap of paper and given it to Kohlhaas). While the gypsy offers an easy way out—simply surrender the coveted piece of paper to the Elector in exchange for a lifting of the horse-dealer's life sentence—it would allow Kohlhaas to save his own skin but leave matters unresolved. Both Luther and Lisbeth set forth a potentially more satisfying but also more difficult means of saving his life, of reconciling with God and man: they challenge him to forgive. In the end, however, the recipe that Luther gives Kohlhaas is perhaps not so difficult, but rather, in its prescriptiveness, a little too easy: "forgive the Junker who wronged you, go to Tronka Castle, mount your two [horses] and ride them back [home]" (*MK*, 155). Dictated by a figure of authority, it is a formula that leaves little room for individual initiative or complexity; it specifies the party to whom forgiveness is owed, and requires no further thought or independent action from Kohlhaas. His wife's simple directive, in contrast, is not spelled out. On her deathbed, unable to speak at all, she takes the Bible from the hands of the minister, searches through its pages, and then simply points to the verse, "Forgive your enemies: do good also unto them that hate you."[20] After pressing her husband's hand and gazing at him soulfully, she dies, at which point he, unable to see what she sees—unable to *follow*—sets out to avenge her death.

It is significant that Lisbeth does not issue explicit instructions, does not even identify the enemies to be forgiven. She does not preach, argue or declare. She is, of course, literally unable to speak, but her actions constitute a voice that is neither compromising nor uncompromising. She leaves it to Kohlhaas to discover what forgiveness might entail and to move beyond the options of giving in to violence—both direct and

---

20. *MK*, 137. This is not an exact biblical quotation, either in the original German text or in the English translation.

structural, and that of others as well as his own—or giving up on peace and justice altogether. As has consistently been her position, she neither supports the impulse toward vengeance nor advocates the abdication of his grievance, but rather points to the need to find a new way. Scripture becomes authoritative here, but interpretive responsibility rests with the reader; Kohlhaas must figure out where he should go with what he reads.

The historical Luther's translation of the Bible made the text directly available to a far greater public; Lisbeth has no need of the minister to read it to her, and neither does her husband. That Kohlhaas fails to accept the challenge of interpretation, however, corresponds to his subsequent failure to go beyond a poor imitation, a mere parody of Luther. The endless issuing of edicts throughout his campaign of vengeance only exposes a lack of direction and initiative, in contrast to the historical Luther's contributions to what became a groundbreaking movement. Justice, in Kleist's tale, is in the end neither denied nor established. Ironically, in the absurd public spectacle with which the novella concludes, the uncompromising Kohlhaas is satisfied with the compromise of regaining his lost property but relinquishing his life, the only apparent way of putting a stop to the proliferation of false alternatives, which entail either giving up or giving in. Unlike Achilles, whose reconciliation with Priam opens up a way beyond such dead ends—the either/or of killing or being killed—to what Wolf calls the "third alternative" of living,[21] the protagonist of Kleist's tale has reached an impasse. Moreover, the tongue-in-cheek rendering of the march to the scaffold, the horse-dealer apparently satisfied that he has recovered his losses (his two horses, his neckcloth, and his groom's bundle of washing), makes a spectacle of his blockage.

We are not told exactly how we should think about Kohlhaas, who ultimately reflects readers' own positions in the shifting terrain of social (dis)order. What emerges clearly, however, is the absence of a reconciliation that would mark not the end of the road, but rather a new path, new ground on which to stand and along which to move. And so Kleist's ironic resolution offers a new reading of an old story. By this I mean not only the Hans Kohlhase chronicle, but also the age-old story of injustice and the human desire to overcome it. Like the Biblical passage to which Lisbeth points, the text poses an interpretive challenge, which grants readers the responsibility—and the opportunity—to engage in the possibly groundbreaking work of peace research. Thus, to the underlying

---

21. Wolf, *Cassandra*, 118.

question acknowledged at the beginning of this paper, that concerning the value of literary studies, Kleist's fiction provides a compelling response, as it invites practices of reading that have the potential to be both socially and personally transformative, and opens up new, creative ways of thinking and interacting.

Bibliography

Allan, Seán. *The Stories of Heinrich von Kleist: Fictions of Security*. Rochester, NY: Camden House, 2001.

Franklin, Ursula M. *The Ursula Franklin Reader: Pacifism as a Map*. Toronto: Between the Lines, 2006.

Frye, Northrop. *"The Educated Imagination" and Other Writings on Critical Theory, 1933–1963*, edited by Germaine Warkentin. Vol. 21 of *The Collected Works of Northrop Frye*. Toronto: University of Toronto Press, 2006.

Griffiths, Elystan. *Political Change and Human Emancipation in the Works of Heinrich von Kleist*. Rochester, NY: Camden House, 2005.

Homer, *The Iliad*. Translated by Robert Fagles. New York: Penguin, 1990.

Kleist, Heinrich von. *Michael Kohlhaas*. In *The Marquise of O—and Other Stories*. Translated by David Luke and Nigel Reeves, 114–213. Harmondsworth: Penguin, 1978.

———. *Sämtliche Werke und Briefe in Vier Bänden*, edited by Helmut Sembdner. Munich: Hanser, 1982.

"Reconcile." Def. 1. *The Random House Dictionary of the English Language*. 1981.

Shay, Jonathan. *Achilles in Vietnam: Combat Trauma and the Undoing of Character*. New York: Simon & Schuster, 1994.

Wolf, Christa. *Cassandra: A Novel and Four Essays*. Translated by Jan van Heurck. New York: Farrar, Straus, and Giroux, 1984.

———. *Die Dimension des Autors: Essays und Aufsätze, Reden und Gespräche 1959–1985*. Frankfurt: Luchterhand, 1990.

———. "Speaking of Büchner." In *The Author's Dimension: Selected Essays*, edited by Alexander Stephan, 176–86. Translated by Jan van Heurck. New York: Farrar, Straus, and Giroux, 1993.

5

Vocation, Holiness and Freewill in Luther and Grisez
An Interconfessional Exchange

R. J. MATAVA

THE CONCEPT OF VOCATION is a repeated theme in Luther's writings on Christian life. He was, perhaps, the first Christian thinker to introduce a concept of personal vocation as an explicit and developed theme in theological reflection. Various factors help to explain this, including Luther's experience as an Augustinian monk and his consequent teaching on justification *sola fide*. Convinced that holiness was not to be attained through penance and the monastic life, Luther held that each of the baptized has a unique calling from God which encompasses all the duties and providentially ordained circumstances of his or her personal station in life.

One remarkable though likely unexpected characteristic of Luther's theology of vocation is its similarity in important respects to the Catholic understanding of vocation that emerges after Vatican II. Hinging upon the doctrine of the universal call to holiness in Chapter Five of *Lumen Gentium,* there emerges in both the teaching of the council fathers and subsequently, John Paul II, the idea that each of the baptized has a unique personal share in Christ's threefold *munus* of priest, prophet, and king. Thus not only those called to priesthood or religious life have a vocation. Moreover, one's personal vocation is here conceived not merely as one's state in life, but encompasses all life's aspects, similar to Luther's view.

While the idea of personal vocation is explicit in Vatican II, it is not systematically developed by the council fathers. It has been developed however, by the Catholic theologian, Germain Grisez (1928–). Grisez has pioneered the postconciliar renewal in Catholic moral theology, chiefly through the production of his monumental opus, *The Way of the Lord Jesus*.[1] Since the conciliar teaching on vocation is central to Grisez's theological project, he is a fitting, though perhaps initially surprising, dialog partner for a study of Luther on vocation.

Scholars such as Gustaf Wingren have established the centrality of vocation in Luther's writings on the Christian life.[2] However, the connections between Luther's theology of vocation and contemporary Catholic thought, as well as the underlying issues of grace and freedom remain relatively unexplored. This, in connection with the moral importance of vocation emphasized by both Luther and Grisez, makes this an investigation worth pursuing.

What follows is a Catholic theologian's attempt to understand Luther's teaching on vocation in dialog with that of his own native confession. I hope I have understood Luther and represented him here fairly, and I also hope I will be corrected if at any point I have not.

This essay will be divided into three sections. In the first section, I will present an overview of Luther's theology of vocation and in the second, of Grisez's. In the third section, I will highlight key points of similarity and difference, weighing the merits of each view.

---

1. Grisez, *Christian Moral Principles*, vol. 1 (hereafter *CMP*); *Living a Christian Life*, vol. 2 (hereafter *LCL*). The third volume, *Difficult Moral Questions*, is not cited in this essay. What exists of the unfinished fourth volume—which amounts to hundreds of pages of material—can be found Online (see Bibliography). Pages 185–221 of the first chapter of this fourth and final volume provide an excellent overview of Grisez's developed thinking on personal vocation.

2. Wingren, *Luther*. I am chiefly reliant on Wingren's seminal exposition for my presentation of Luther's theology of vocation. Prior to Wingren, Max Weber also pointed out Luther's important place in the historical development of the idea of vocation. See chapter 3 of his *The Protestant Ethic*.

Core Argument

Luther's theology of vocation develops out of his doctrine of justification by faith alone—the article on which all Christian doctrine and practice, in his view, stands or falls.³ Justification *sola fide* is the principle that gives life to Luther's distinctive idea of vocation. It is also what ultimately distinguishes Luther's view from the Catholic understanding of personal vocation, which depends respectively on Trent's doctrine of justification. I shall argue that one probable reason Catholics generally did not catch on to the idea of personal vocation before Vatican II is traceable to this difference over justification: Resistance to Luther's exclusion of contemplation and monastic life from the scope of vocation (out of concerns over works righteousness) may have obscured from Catholics the fact that believers other than contemplatives have vocations. Related to this, I also argue a pivotal point of divergence between Luther and Grisez is revealed in a consideration of the complex question of whether fidelity to one's personal vocation is sanctifying. For both thinkers, vocation is in some sense sanctifying, but the manner in which it is differs because of each thinker's respective soteriology. I will show that ultimately, the difference between Luther's theology of vocation and Grisez's is a function of their differing views on the relationship between divine causality and the human will—a matter of fierce debate not only between Catholics and Lutherans, but within each confession as well. The final adjudication of the two theologies of personal vocation under consideration here depends then on the strength of each thinker's account of the relation of divine and human agency.

I. Luther's Theology of Vocation

Luther's theology of vocation develops chiefly from an idea and an event. The underlying idea is his thesis that man is justified not by works, but by faith alone. The event is his repudiation of monastic life in 1521, which occurred in conjunction with his conception of the thesis on justification. Since vocation's purview is the range of human actions (or works) to which one is called by the Lord, these two factors—the idea and the event—decisively shape Luther's theology of vocation insofar as they bear upon his view of the place of works in the economy of salvation.

---

3. Luther, *Smalcald Articles*, II.1.4–5.

A. Luther's Experience of Monasticism

Luther joined the Augustinian order in 1505 at the age of twenty-one. His decision to enter monastic life was not entirely peaceful. As Luther himself later related, one day in July of 1505—the same month he entered the monastery—he found himself caught without shelter in the midst of a violent storm while on the way to Erfurt. Seized by fear after having been thrown to the ground by a bolt of thunder, Luther beseeched the intercession of St. Anne for safety, promising to become a monk if safely delivered. The Lord proved to be Luther's helper amidst the flood of mortal ills, but monastic life did not quell Luther's anxiety over his eternal welfare. Luther's experience of monastic life seems in fact only to have exacerbated his early fears about salvation. Life as an Augustinian was quite rigorous and austere. Luther sought Christian perfection through a punctilious observation of his order's rule. But Luther found himself unable to observe the rule perfectly, and so—it seemed—he was incapable also of pleasing the Lord and winning his favor. As Luther later related, "I wanted to live so devoutly and so strictly through my own works that I could appear before God and say: 'Here, you have holiness.'"[4] Luther's breakthrough came around 1512 while studying St. Paul's Letter to the Romans. It was then he fastened upon the idea that salvation is not a function of one's own efforts, but of one's faith—really, trust—in the divine promise of salvation. This faith or trust was a divine gift, wrought in us by God, at his own initiative, freely and irrespective of the believer's own merits. It was ultimately this insight that led to Luther's repudiation of monastic life in 1521.

From that point forward, Luther clearly saw the idea of a Christian's calling not as something that pertained only to the elite few, such as those with explicitly religious vocations. For Luther, a Christian vocation was now understood to be anything but that. In fact, it is not until Luther's break with monastic life that the word *Beruf*—calling or occupation, a key term Luther uses for vocation—appears with frequency in his writings.[5]

---

4. As quoted in Pfurtner, *Luther and Aquinas on Salvation*, 32.
5. Wingren, *Luther*, xviii.

B. Justification, Faith, and Works

While Luther is an occasional, not a systematic writer, it is impossible to overstate the thematic role his teaching on justification plays within his theology as a whole. For Luther, the doctrine of justification *sola fide* "is master and head, lord and governor and judge, over all the kinds of doctrine"; it is the article "on which the Church stands or falls."[6] For Luther, this, more than anything else, is the Gospel, for it contains what he perceives to be the essence of Christ's teaching, the core truth of the Christian faith.

Luther's juxtaposition of works and faith with respect to justification is characteristic of a series of related dichotomies that run throughout his thought, giving shape to it overall: Just as works and faith are juxtaposed, so too are law and Gospel, outer and inner man, earth and heaven, Satan and God. It is a mistake, however, to interpret Luther's juxtaposition of works and faith (or the members of any of the aforementioned couplets) as a strict opposition between them, for Luther does not see works and faith as mutually exclusive. It is rather for Luther that works and faith have sharply distinct but complimentary roles in the life of a Christian. As Wingren affirms, they are both "parts of a single reality" and "constitute an organic unity."[7] While one is justified by faith alone, works remain important and necessary. But given the radical distinction between the earthly and heavenly realms, how is the exact relationship between faith and works to be explained?

Luther turns to the Incarnation as a model for understanding the relationship between faith and works. Luther states in his Galatians commentary, "Faith is the divine nature of works and it is poured out in works even as in Christ the divine nature is poured out in the human."[8] Just as God breaks through the boundary of earth and heaven by his kenotic act of becoming man, so too faith becomes incarnated in kenotic love for neighbor, breaking through from the heavenly realm into the earthly.[9] But just as the Incarnation is a miracle, so too is the emergence of love from faith a miracle: There is no systematic, logical explanation. Faith

---

6. Luther, *WA* 39/1:205, as cited and translated in Placher, *The Domestication of Transcendence*, 45; Luther, *Smalcald Articles*, II.1.4–5.

7. Wingren, *Luther*, 73–74; see also 85.

8. Luther, *Large Commentary on Galatians*, WA 40-I, 417, 427, as quoted in Wingren, *Luther*, 41.

9. Wingren, *Luther*, 41.

does not demand any works, yet works—love—cannot but accompany faith.[10] As Luther states, "faith forever justifies and makes alive, but it does not remain alone, i.e., idle . . . but is incarnated and becomes man, that is, it does not remain idle or devoid of love."[11] The Incarnation was a most unexpected miracle, yet such is the character of the eternal and unchanging God—he *has* become man.

Strictly however, it seems a mischaracterization of Luther's view to say good works flow from faith. Luther's view seems not to be that *faith* is positively productive of good works, but rather that good works flow from the legitimate demands that press in upon one from the world. These works must be done *in faith*. The exigencies of the created order impose works on us and we must respond by working in *accordance with* faith. That means not by directing our works upward to God, but outward to creatures. Faith is not incompatible with works as such, but only with works that threaten to usurp faith's soteriological function, that is, with works thrust into the heavenly realm. When engaged in works, one can only maintain faith by giving one's works a horizontal trajectory rather than a vertical one. The purpose of works then is to serve the needs of one's neighbor and all other creatures to the extent they serve his or her good.

C. Vocations as "Masks of God"

Thus works, and by extension, vocation, find their significance entirely in the earthly needs of humankind. God works in and through the established offices or stations of human life to sustain and govern the whole created order, and principally for the sake of the human person.[12] By discharging the responsibilities of one's place in life, one becomes an instrument of God—"a medium which receives from above and gives forth downward—like a vessel or pipe."[13] Luther therefore calls the human person a "mask of God" or *larva Dei,* for in establishing the various offices or stations of human life, it is God who actually acts through these vocations. Here we see another point of connection to the incarnational dimension of human works: Like the way the humanity of Christ con-

---

10. Ibid.

11. Luther, *Large Commentary on Galatians,* WA 40–I, 417, 427, as quoted in Wingren, *Luther,* 41.

12. Wingren, *Luther,* 6, 9.

13. Luther, *Kirchenpostille,* WA 10–I 1.100, as cited in Wingren, *Luther,* 207.

ceals his divinity, so too the earthly, human aspect of vocation conceals that it is God working through the works of human persons. It is God who milks the cows through the one whose vocation it is to milk.[14] It is God who provides clothing through the ones whose office it is to tend the flock, sheer the sheep, spin the wool, and weave the cloth.[15] However, the principal idea of the metaphor is not so much that man disguises God, but to the contrary, that man is an instance of God's presence and operation whenever he discharges the works of his particular station. The human person serves as God's hands in the world and so in this way is a co-worker with God.[16]

Thus, while the human person does not cooperate with God in the heavenly realm, with respect to justification (since that is by faith alone and not works), Luther's doctrine of justification does entail a kind of divine-human cooperation *in the earthly realm* insofar as the human person cooperates with God in the preservation and governance of creation.[17] Moreover, this cooperation takes place whether or not man wills it. Similar to the way God confers sacramental grace through an unworthy minister, so too God provides for creation through the various offices or life stations he has ordained.[18] Just as God's operation through the unworthy minister is intended not for the minister's own benefit, but for the benefit of the people, so too a vocation is not ordained for the benefit of the person who fulfills that vocation, but rather his or her neighbor.[19]

Because works, and by extension, vocation, find their significance entirely in relation to the earthly needs of humankind (and not one's justification), vocation is the frame of reference for Luther's understanding of Christian love. As Wingren points out, "[s]ince vocation involves my relation with others, love for others is *eo ipso* the fulfillment of my vocation. It is the vocabulary of vocation itself, the terms 'station' and 'office,' which Luther uses when he speaks of spontaneous love toward others."[20] Rather than eliminating a motive for service to one's neighbor, the fact that man cannot merit by his good works frees him, in Luther's view, to

---

14. Wingren, *Luther*, 9, 19, 139, 140, 196.
15. Ibid., 8–9.
16. Ibid., 27.
17. Ibid., 16–17, 123–43.
18. Ibid., 131–33.
19. Ibid., 29.
20. Ibid., 120.

engage in disinterested service to his neighbor. Faith, then (in Luther's sense), is a necessary prerequisite for altruism. When one performs works in order to achieve one's own salvation, love is impure because it is mixed with self-interest.[21] In contrast, the tranquility of conscience one has through assurance of salvation by faith alone allows one to focus all one's efforts externally on meeting the needs of neighbor. With the inner man free of anxiety about salvation, the outer man can be fully engaged in meeting whatever needs one's neighbor has.

Thus a central aspect of vocation—and thus of Christian love—for Luther, is the idea that it entails a certain amount of freedom or spontaneity, a particular adaptability and flexibility in responding to specific and changing circumstances.[22] One must look to one's neighbor's situation to hear there the voice of God calling. God makes his will known in the concrete and particular situations of life. It is here that we see Luther's pivotal metaphor of the mask—the *larva Dei*—cut both ways: It is not only that man is a mask of God, an occasion for divine action in the world, when he fulfills the duties of his office. It is also that each of the particular circumstances of the Christian's life, each of his or her neighbor's needs, is a mask of God insofar as through these, God makes his will—and so the Christian's calling—manifest.[23]

D. Christian Freedom and the Unique, Concrete Character of Vocation

All of this entails that there is no model or blueprint of *the* Christian life. There is no pre-given template—let alone a single template—for Christian holiness.[24] For Luther, vocation is not a matter of the outworking of some law, some set of predetermined norms or rules, but of faith. Faith is incarnated in love, and love is spontaneous, adaptable, and unpredictable. It overcomes all circumstances and finds a way to meet the changing needs of neighbor whatever they are.[25] It is this idea that Luther captures by his stress on the believer's freedom "to do or not to do" in respect to temporal affairs. The Christian is not bound to perform any prescribed

---

21. Ibid., 109.
22. Ibid., 123–24.
23. Ibid., 137–140.
24. Ibid., 47–50, 153–54, 184.
25. Ibid., 178.

set of outward activities, but only to faith and love. He or she must "become all things to all people" as St. Paul did (1 Cor 9:19–23). Thus, the Christian acts or omits in accordance with the changing exigencies he or she discovers in the world.

This freedom to do or omit is, for Luther, the core feature of Christian freedom.[26] In his view, a Christian is free in at least two related senses. On the one hand, the earthly realm is a sphere of unrestricted autonomy for man, wherein he has the liberty to do or omit as the situation demands. He is bound by no prescribed rule of life, but only to love, which is no law, but the outworking of faith. On the other hand, the Christian is free in the heavenly realm in the sense that he is free from works and his conscience rests untroubled in the assurance of salvation by faith alone.[27]

Conversely, a Christian's freedom in the heavenly realm is at the same time bondage in the sense that he is powerless before God with respect to his salvation.[28] Not only is he or she free from works, he or she is obliged *not* to proffer works—*not* to exercise his or her free will—before God to earn salvation or holiness.[29] Conversely also, one's freedom in the earthly realm is at the same time bondage in the sense that man on earth is subject to the law—understood here as the obligations that pertain to his office or station in life. While faith and love transform the drudgery of one's earthly service into cheerful willingness, it is still the case one is obliged to perform it.[30] One *cannot* work in the heavenly realm; one *must* work in the earthly realm. Man is at once slave and free in different respects both on earth and in heaven.[31] Luther sums up the paradox of Christian liberty thus: "A Christian is a perfectly free lord of all, subject to none," and, "a Christian is a perfectly dutiful servant of all, subject to all."[32]

However, while man is free to act as he must *in* his vocation (and is free *from* obligation before God and *from* anxiety by faith), he is not free *to actually choose* his vocation. Luther says, "a Christian does not select

---

26. Ibid., 95, 147–50.
27. Ibid., 16, 94.
28. Ibid., 94, 123–24.
29. Wingren goes so far as to say that "before God . . . every work stands as sinful and worthless" and that freedom "exists before God only as evil" (Ibid., 13, 16). The thought seems to be not an outright denial of man's freewill before God, but assumes man has freewill before God—it is just wrong for man to exercise it there.
30. Ibid., 47.
31. Ibid., 102.
32. See Luther's *Treatise on Christian Liberty*, 53.

what he will do, nor does he start any divisions. He contents himself with his vocation."[33] Luther's idea seems to be that each individual finds him or herself in given circumstances, in a particular place in the world and state of life, and he or she should live out his or her Christian calling there, rather than flee from this providentially assigned context into a state of life that is of human design.

E. The Rejection of Monastic Life as a Legitimate Vocation

In light of vocation's givenness, reference to neighbor and the freedom in external behavior that its reference to neighbor requires, as well as Luther's consequent rejection of the idea there can be a set pattern of Christian life, it is no surprise that he vehemently rejects monastic life as a legitimate vocation. The problem Luther sees with monastic life is that it prescribes a specific course of external behavior as *the* path to Christian holiness.[34] In so doing, monastic life preoccupies the Christian with activity that does nothing to alleviate the burdens of his or her neighbor and which attempts in vain to win salvation before God. In Luther's view, since the works of the cloister are a substitute for the works one should be doing to serve one's neighbor, the monk has only an ersatz love of his fellow man and so an ersatz love of Christ.[35] Faith and love (and so righteousness) cannot be attained through monastic life insofar as "before God . . . every work stands as sinful and worthless" and freedom "exists before God only as evil."[36]

Moreover, Luther charges not only that monastic life is incompatible with faith and love, but also that it is incompatible with genuine prayer. Ironically, Luther's view is that the one state uniquely ill-suited to prayer is contemplative life. The reason is that, for Luther, the experience of desperation is a necessary requisite for genuine prayer.[37] So long as one sees how one's needs will be met, it is impossible to truly pray. As in Luther's experience, genuine prayer—and indeed, faith itself—emerges from the predisposing anguish of distress, of hopelessness, of the cross. Because the monk's temporal welfare is ensured through the works of laypeople,

---

33. *WA* 17/2:37, as quoted by Wingren, *Luther*, 179.
34. Wingren, *Luther*, 100–101, 201–4, 231.
35. Ibid., 33.
36. Ibid., 13, 16; see 31.
37. Ibid., 189.

he does not experience insecurity, and so cannot enter into real prayer.[38] Therefore, the monk, in Luther's view, is a thoroughly non-productive member of society: He does not work and to the extent he is provided for, he cannot even pray. For Luther, monastic life is not a state intended by God; it is an anti-vocation.[39]

F. Vocation and the Crucifixion of the Outer Man

Rather than seeking out the cross in a life of intentional asceticism and penance, Luther's view is that suffering is naturally inscribed in the various offices and states of life which the Creator in his providence has instituted for the good of creation. While the primary purpose of works and thus of vocation, is the care of one's fellow man and of all things to the extent they serve his or her good, for Luther, a second foundational purpose of works and vocation is to crucify the outer man. In order to understand this, it is necessary to grasp first, Luther's distinction of inner from outer man, and second, his perspective on the Christian meaning of human suffering.

Luther's distinction of inner from outer man originates in his reading of St. Paul. For St. Paul, the inner man is a reference to *nous*, the locus of faith and conscience. When man is justified, it is the inner man that is justified, while the outer man retains a propensity to sin and remains fallen. Thus the inner man is regenerate, while the outer man is the human person in his or her unredeemed, unregenerate state. The outer man denotes one's carnal aspect and passions, especially to the extent they resist the influence of right reason (conscience) and the Gospel.

The chief purpose of human suffering, in Luther's view, is to serve as a propaedeutic to the Gospel and faith.[40] As with prayer, Luther thinks it is impossible to come to faith without first experiencing despair.[41] One meets despair in and through the hardships that naturally arise from undertaking the works of one's station in life—not through some self-imposed cross. Through these hardships, one's conscience is terrorized, and

---

38. Ibid., 33.

39. Thus Luther maintains that monastic life is a "vow to do evil" and that ordained and religious life in his day was "sinful orders like robbery, usury, and prostitution" (ibid., 2).

40. Ibid., 60–63.

41. Ibid., 35–36.

with no further recourse to one's own efforts available, one seeks refuge in the Gospel's promise of salvation. However, the cross is instrumental not only for coming to faith, but it also remains instrumental for the maintenance and deepening of faith throughout Christian life. Because one has faith, one confines one's works to the earthly realm; there—where the devil holds sway—one experiences the hardships fidelity to one's vocation entails. The devil attacks one and in desperation, one turns to prayer. In turning to prayer, faith is renewed and invigorated, and with this revitalized faith, one continues on faithfully discharging one's earthly duties, confining them to the earthly realm.[42]

G. Vocation and Salvation

This dialectic of the cross—a dialectic between heaven and earth, faith and works, which is mediated by prayer—provides a window into the nature of sanctification and its connection to vocation in Luther's view. Salvation is a matter of justification, of being made righteous in God's sight, and Luther envisions justification as an ongoing process for wayfarers.[43] This ongoing process is sometimes called sanctification. During a believer's time on earth, he is *simul iustus et peccator*—at the same time, righteous and a sinner. Earthly life is a time of continual movement toward the kingdom of heaven during which the believer must be prepared to enter that kingdom through the crucifixion, the putting to death, of the outer man.[44] The believer is thus sanctified in and through the cross, but it is not that suffering positively causes the believer's sanctification or is a means of gaining heavenly reward. Rather, the sufferings that come with the fulfillment of one's vocation check—really, kill—the outer man and thereby keep justifying faith alive. Vocation occupies the believer during his earthly life with charitable endeavors, channeling his efforts in a neighborly direction, while faith accomplishes his salvation in parallel.

This explains how Wingren can assert, "vocation has nothing to do with salvation" while at the same time maintaining that "sanctification is hidden in offensively ordinary tasks" and that it "occurs in the vocations of men."[45] For Luther, works do not play any positive role in

---

42. Ibid., 119.
43. Geisler and MacKenzie, *Roman Catholics and Evangelicals*, 223–24.
44. Wingren, *Luther*, 234–51.
45. Ibid., 14, 19, 64, 73, 110, 182. Wingren notes that Luther explicitly rejects the

the economy of salvation, but they do play an important positive role in the order of creation and they also play an important negative role in the economy of salvation. Human works play a positive role in the order of creation because by God's plan, they are the means whereby human persons and all things that serve their good are sustained and cared for. Correspondingly, good works play an important negative role in the order of salvation because to the extent the exigencies of the created order horizontally channel one's willing and striving, human activity is confined to the earthly realm and kept out of the heavenly realm, which is the proper domain of justifying faith. The confinement of works to the order of creation ensures that justifying faith is not displaced from its place in the economy of salvation and so nullified. It is faith that positively justifies; works, by contrast, allow faith to justify when they do not try to usurp its soteriological function. In simple terms, when faith and works each mind their own business, man is sanctified and creation is sustained. Man is sanctified insofar as faith justifies the inner man while the outer man is crucified through the performance of works. The two operations—justification and crucifixion—occur in parallel. Conversely, when faith and works meddle in each other's business there is a double cost: Creation goes neglected while faith is nullified by works that are themselves futile before God. Disorder is introduced to both the earthly and heavenly realms.

II. Grisez's Theology of Vocation

Given the centrality of Luther's conviction that works are not instrumental in salvation, and especially his repudiation of monastic life as a pretender to the title of authentic vocation, it is perhaps surprising to discover significant resonances between his teaching on vocation and that which has been proposed in documents of the Catholic Magisterium over the last fifty years. This magisterial teaching has been developed most systematically by Germain Grisez, a Catholic lay theologian who has distinguished himself during this same period through his leading contributions to the field of Christian ethics. Besides the discovery of certain convergences between Grisez's theology of vocation and that of

---

idea that vocation is instrumental to man's salvation in his *Kirchenpostille*, which contains perhaps the single most important discussion of vocation in all Luther's writings (ibid., 10).

Luther, a further reason for examining this theme in Grisez is the architectonic role it has within his moral theory as a whole.[46] The idea of personal vocation is a golden thread that runs throughout the entirety of Grisez's theology. Nevertheless, the idea's decisive influence—whether in terms of its own theological merit or in terms of understanding Grisez's account of Christian life—has not yet been fully appreciated.

A. The Historical Context of Grisez's Theology of Personal Vocation

For Grisez, as for Luther, every believer has a unique vocation. There is no single blueprint of the Christian life, and God's call—indeed holiness—is not reserved for a select group of the spiritually elite. In order to appreciate the significance of this idea within the teaching of Vatican II and its subsequent development by Grisez, especially in relation to Luther's thought, it is necessary to trace the idea's origins and recognize the extent to which it has, for centuries, been obscured within Catholic thought and life.

1. The Scriptural Basis for Personal Vocation

Grisez maintains the general idea of vocation emerges within the OT, but the idea of personal vocation emerges with greater clarity in the NT.[47] In the OT, God's personal call is addressed to certain key individuals who are instrumental in relating God's word, carrying out religious rituals or forming covenants with God, and ruling over the people. For example, God's personal calling is addressed in different ways to figures such as Noah, Abraham, Moses, Samuel, David, and Jeremiah. These OT figures

---

46. In chapter 23 of *Christian Moral Principles*, Grisez remarks, "[h]ere we reach the heart of this entire work, for it is now possible to explain clearly what it means to follow the way of the Lord Jesus" (*CMP* 23–C.1). Further on, he also states, "[f]or us Christians, to follow Jesus means to accept and carry out our personal vocations faithfully" (*CMP* 23–C.11). The significance of these passages can be seen in light of the title of Grisez's multivolume opus, *The Way of the Lord Jesus*. It is not unreasonable to say—though at some risk of oversimplification—that Grisez's entire four-thousand page attempt to articulate a science of Christian life is a detailed, systematic exposition of the idea of personal vocation.

47. Grisez and Shaw, *Personal Vocation*, 37–40. See also Grisez, "Personal Vocation," 10–11.

tend to be prophets, priests, those who fill roles of headship over the people, or some combination of these. Otherwise, God's call is not addressed to individuals as such, but to the people collectively, and the principal form his calling takes is the Mosaic Law. The detailed prescriptions of the Mosaic Law and the social roles defined by one's place in the people of God provided the normative framework necessary to guide one's life under the old covenant. Under the new covenant however, the Law finds its fulfillment in the Gospel. The ceremonial and judicial precepts of the Law are abrogated, and the new law is written inwardly on the hearts of believers through the gift of the Holy Spirit. Now, not only certain individuals, but every member of the whole people is Spirit-endowed, priestly, prophetic, and kingly. Grisez believes personal vocation emerges within the context of the new covenant in part because the gift of the Holy Spirit "provides a law of freedom which renders a detailed code of precepts no longer necessary."[48] Moreover, through faith and the Holy Spirit, the people of God under the new covenant are members of Jesus, incorporated into him through baptism. This mystical (i.e. sacramental) union with Jesus entails believers drawn up into the life of the Trinity because the Jesus into whom they are incorporated by baptism is the Eternal Word. Thus Grisez asserts "[a]n even more profound" reason why personal vocation emerges with clarity only within the new covenant, "is the enhancement of the dignity of the individual person which comes with the Christian understanding of God's kingdom, in which created persons will enter into communion with the Trinity."[49]

2. *The Medieval Obfuscation of Personal Vocation*

Grisez argues that while the idea of personal vocation emerges from the NT and is evident in some patristic writings, such as the Epistle to Diognetus,[50] it became eclipsed during the medieval period, due largely to social, economic, and political factors inherent to feudalism.[51] In a

---

48. Grisez, "Personal Vocation," 11.
49. Ibid.
50. Grisez and Shaw, *Personal Vocation*, 45–46.
51. Ibid., 47–53. Grisez and Shaw note that despite centuries of obfuscation, the idea of personal vocation has been clearly attested (even if not systematically developed) by thinkers in every century from the sixteenth to the present day (Ibid., 52–60). In the sixteenth century, Ignatius of Loyola speaks in his *Spiritual Exercises* of Christ's call issued to "all" and "each one." In the seventeenth century, Francis de Sales' *Treatise*

feudalistic society, one's life is mainly settled by one's birth. A person's geographical place, class, employment, economic status, and even marriage partner are chiefly determined by factors outside of one's control. The lack of social mobility characteristic of medieval feudalism meant that there was far less need or opportunity for most people in this period to make the sort of large, life-organizing choices that became imperative especially in the modern period and which confront most young adults in the West today (for example, undergraduates).[52] While on the one hand, this makes identifying the content (and to that extent, the fulfillment) of one's personal vocation comparatively easy, on the other hand, it makes identifying this content *as vocation* comparatively hard. Since little discernment and often no real choice is required, the idea that one's place in the world with its assigned tasks is a unique personal calling from the Lord to which one must respond with a commitment is almost laughably obscure.[53] One's situation is *simply given*. The sense of the person *as an individual self* to whom the Lord addresses a unique call is eclipsed by the wider collective sense of one's identification with and within the society as a whole. Moreover, the practice of one given religion which involves sacramental mediation and contemplative intercession by members of society whose office is, by contrast, not simply given, but assumed by discernment and free choice, helps to solidify the sense that vocation is limited to priestly and religious life.

---

on the Love of God acknowledges that while all are called to perfection, not all are called to the evangelical councils. DeSales goes on to provide guidance for vocational discernment. In the eighteenth century, Jean-Pierre de Caussaude speaks of the "sacrament of the present moment" whereby God's will for the believer is manifest in his or her concrete circumstances. In the nineteenth century, John Henry Newman, in one of his Anglican sermons, speaks of God's specific call present at every juncture of one's life. Beyond this, the idea of personal vocation is also implicit in such pre-conciliar twentieth-century campaigns as Catholic Action and the Liturgical Movement. All of these currents prepared the ground for the teaching of Vatican II on personal vocation, not only in its core documents *Lumen genitum* and *Gaudium et spes*, but also *Apostolicam actuositatem* and *Presbyterum ordinis*. These documents are a point of departure for the subsequent teaching of the Magisterium, including Pope Paul VI's social encyclical *Populorum progressio* and the many writings of John Paul II which touch on personal vocation, such as his seminal post-synodal apostolic exhortation, *Christifideles laici*.

52. Grisez, *LCL*, xi–xiv.

53. On Grisez's understanding of choice as a specific kind of will act, see *CMP* 2–B–E. See also Boyle et al., *Free Choice*, 11–15.

3. *The Genesis of a Two-Track idea of Christian Life*

The rise of religious life as a manifestly intentional form of Christianity is revealing in this regard.[54] The medieval period was a mixed blessing for Christian life. While the social stability and cultural reinforcement of the faith typical of medieval Europe made it comparatively easy for ordinary, earnest Christians to live exceptionally holy lives, in other ways it also facilitated religious mediocrity, secular compromise, and a mindless, merely cultural Christianity for believers who were less earnest. The faith could be taken for granted.

Prior to the fourth century, when the predominant culture in which the Church was situated was not Christian, believers had to be quite intentional about their Christian lives.[55] The prevailing culture did not buttress faith the way it would in, for example, medieval Europe or even the immigrant Catholic subculture of preconciliar twentieth-century America. In the earliest centuries, one could not take being a Christian for granted: To become, or at any rate, to remain a Christian typically required an explicit decision. This decision meant a new way of life, one noticeably different from the lives of unbelievers. The juxtaposition of the Gospel with the cultural situation of the first three centuries brought the Gospel's hearers face-to-face with a literal *krisis*: What was to be chosen, the faith or the program of the world? Given the concrete possibility of persecution and probability of social marginalization, the stakes in this decision were high.

With the legalization of Christianity and the end of exogenous persecution, believers sought a new way to radically live the Gospel. The result was the dawn and development of eremitic and cenobitic life. While the development of this new way of intentionally living the Gospel was itself good (pace Luther), any increase of good in this world at least makes possible an increase of evil—a privation—as a side effect. More specifically, with the development of religious life it became possible for a mentality to take root among the faithful which bifurcated them into a specially consecrated spiritual elite, called to Christian perfection, and the rank-and-file laity concerned merely with meeting minimal obligations and avoiding hell.

---

54. In this connection, see Shaw, *To Hunt*, 45–49. More broadly, chapter 5 of Shaw's book also provides a helpful summary of the idea of personal vocation from Grisez's perspective.

55. Grisez, "Personal Vocation," 11.

It is not by accident, then, that Luther's idea of vocation as something pertaining to all the baptized develops in significant part from his rejection of monastic life. However, it is exactly Luther's rejection of monastic life, coupled with the resultant entrenchment of Catholic clericalism in the period that followed, that contributed in no small part to steeling many Catholics' sensibilities against the idea that ordinary layfolk have personal vocations.[56] The association of what Charles Taylor has called "the affirmation of ordinary life" with the repudiation of monastic life made it practically impossible for those who did not share Luther's profound criticism of monasticism to recognize and appreciate his positive insight that the actual purview of vocation is much broader and deeper.[57] Thus, while the idea of personal vocation was not completely absent within the Catholic theological tradition from the time of the Reformation, it was not until the time of the Second Vatican Council that the idea received any sustained or systematic attention.

4. Personal Vocation and Modern Secularism

It is noteworthy that the turning point for a Catholic recovery of the idea of personal vocation was the Second Vatican Council. One of the Council's principal aims was *aggiornomento*, or a renewal of the relationship between the Church and the modern world. Such a renewal was necessary because the Church's evangelical efforts had become trammeled by a defensive culture of opposition to modernity which had set in during the centuries following the Reformation and Enlightenment. This period, especially the long nineteenth century, saw the rise of what was called "laicism"—a somewhat unhappy title, though one that suggests the problem's partial origin in clericalism.[58] Laicism effectively denotes the uncoupling of the Gospel from the secular order and its receding influence

---

56. Grisez and Shaw, *Personal Vocation*, 51. One significant factor that fostered the growth of clericalism was the problem lay investiture. The Church's need to resist lay political influence had the side effect of widening the gap between the Church's pastoral hierarchy and the laity. See Shaw, *To Hunt*, 53–56 as well as the related discussion of lay trusteeism 68–73.

57. See part III of Taylor's, *Sources of the Self*. Cf. Weber, *The Protestant Ethic*, 80–81.

58. For a period sketch of the problem of laicism and its connection to Catholic Action, a movement that anticipated the postconciliar development of a theology of personal vocation, see, for example, Bandas, *Catholic Action*, 3–7.

on daily life and culture. It was this problem—what we today would call "secularism"—that the fathers of Vatican II identified as one of "the more serious errors of our age."[59] Their choice of words is arresting: "One of the gravest errors of our time is the dichotomy between the faith which many profess and the practice of their daily lives."[60]

Grisez's theology of personal vocation must be understood against this backdrop. The idea of personal vocation lies at the very heart of a response to the challenge of modernity identified by Vatican II because a life lived in response to one's personal vocation is precisely an implementation of faith as the fundamental commitment of one's life. An understanding of personal vocation is the key to an intentional Christianity for all of the baptized, not only those who assume a certain state in life, such as religious or ordained. Writing for a principally western audience, Grisez stresses while "[i]n simpler and less affluent societies than ours [perhaps like those of Christian Europe in the high Middle Ages], Christians who entered one or another state of life with the right intention embodied the principle of personal vocation in their lives without becoming explicitly aware of it," today, it is impossible for people to "live good Christian lives by passively accepting roles and responsibilities which are thrust upon them; they must reflect critically on culturally defined roles, examine their gifts and opportunities in the light of faith, discern what God asks of them, and commit themselves to doing it. Therefore, it has become necessary to stress personal vocation as the organizing principle of a good Christian life."[61] In other words, if ever they could, Christians can no longer rely upon socially defined roles and responsibilities to define and structure their lives. Rather, they must consciously reflect on what Jesus demands as that is manifest through the deposit of faith, the particular, concrete, providentially ordained circumstances of their lives, and make life-organizing commitments in response to the call those circumstances embody.

B. The Idea of Personal Vocation

For Grisez, a personal vocation is the calling of God addressed in a unique way to each of the baptized.[62] This calling is to a certain way of life—a

---

59. *Gaudium et Spes*, 43.
60. The translation is from the Flannery ed. of *Vatican Council II*.
61. Grisez, *LCL*, xiii.
62. Ibid., 114.

singular, unrepeatable way of following Jesus. Viewing the same reality from the angle of human response, a personal vocation is the life of good deeds that God prepared beforehand for each of those who have been justified by faith to walk in (Eph 2:8–10). This life of God-given good works must be discerned within the concrete, providentially ordained circumstances in which one finds oneself. And while one's personal role in God's universal plan is limited, the extent of that role relative to the whole of one's life is comprehensive—no aspect of one's life falls outside the purview of God's call.[63] Thus, personal vocation is universal in scope insofar as it encompasses every aspect of life and it is universal in extent insofar as all believers, and not only some, are called. Moreover, there is no one-size-fits-all template of *the* Christian life. Personal vocations are as singular as the persons themselves who receive God's call.[64]

More evidently than for Luther, personal vocation is, in Grisez's view, a deeply sacramentally and ecclesiologically embedded reality. Thus, to understand Grisez, it is important to consider vocation in relation to the sacramental life of the Church and especially the implications such sacramental encounters with the risen Lord have for Christian life. To this end, it may be useful to explicitly set forth the following three triplets of related themes in terms of which Grisez's theology of personal

63. Grisez, *CMP*, 25–F.2.

64. It is interesting in this connection to note the conspicuous lack of attention to virtue as a structuring motif in Grisez's moral theory (contrast the thematic layout of *The Way of the Lord Jesus* with the second part of Aquinas' *Summa theologiae*, for instance). Grisez's ethics is not a virtue theory (though neither is it a Kantian deontology as is sometimes inaccurately alleged). This aspect of Grisez's work has sometimes drawn attention from critics. See for example, Ashley, "The Scriptural Basis," 36–49. Often, this characteristic has been seen (not incorrectly) in light of the "is"/"ought" distinction Grisez's commitment to the irreducibly practical character of ethics drives his adoption of a normative, rather than virtue-based approach. However, I would suggest it is also important to understand the absence of virtue as a structuring motif in *The Way of the Lord Jesus* in relation to the dominance of personal vocation there. See Grisez and Boyle, "Response to our Critics," 214, 232–36. For Grisez, there is not one sufficiently specific template of the good life. Living a good life is not so much about striving to cultivate certain universal virtues as finding, accepting, and fulfilling God's specific plan for one's life. Of course, there is in reality no conflict between vocation and the cultivation of virtue and Grisez acknowledges this: The virtuous person discerns and discharges his or her vocation, and one becomes virtuous in striving to answer God's call. Nor is there a conflict between virtue and propositional norms. But Grisez's preoccupation in *The Way of the Lord Jesus* is not with articulating a theoretical description of *the* virtuous character. Rather it is with providing concrete, biblical and practical guidance for decision-making, insofar as it is principally through the choices one makes that one becomes good or bad.

vocation can be understood. These themes are, first, the sacraments of initiation—baptism, confirmation, and the Eucharist—which initiate one's life in Jesus and consummate one's incorporation into his body; second, the dispositions of faith, hope, and charity, which are infused at baptism and translate one from a state of sin to a state of righteousness; and third, the priestly, prophetic, and kingly dimensions of the mission of Jesus, into whom one is incorporated by living faith and the sacraments. Before proceeding however, it is necessary to make the following two caveats.

First, the identification of three converging triplets of architectonic themes is not, as such, explicit in Grisez, but is rather a heuristic I am imposing on this thought. The themes are explicit in Grisez and their relations to one another are explicit, but Grisez does not organize these into a sort of system for understanding personal vocation. Moreover, it would be a mistake to reduce Grisez's account of personal vocation strictly to the nine related themes I have just proposed. As will become evident, other ideas, such as human free choice and discernment, conscience and the limitations of specific positive moral norms also play a crucial role in Grisez's account of vocation.[65] So the reader should beware of my attempt to systematize the original sources and should not take my presentation as an exhaustive summary.

Secondly, while the above themes overlap in a variety of ways, it is not the case that there is an exact or mere one-to-one correspondence across the triplets between the first, second, and third members of each. The convergences between the themes are, in reality, more complex than that, as even the structure of the following discussion shows. So the reader is cautioned against over-systemizing my heuristic.

1. Baptism, Church Membership, and Participation in the Work of Christ

For Grisez, baptism is the basis for a personal vocation. Baptism unites the believer with Christ humanly by making him or her a member of Christ's mystical body, the Church.[66] Through this human communion with Jesus, the believer also receives a share in Jesus' divinity.[67] United

---

65. Grisez, *CMP*, 2; 27–B–D, H; 31–E; *LCL* xi–xii; 5–J.
66. Grisez, *CMP*, 30–H–I.
67. Ibid., 24–C, app. 2. Crucially, for Grisez, this participation in the divine nature,

with Jesus both bodily and in his divine nature, the baptized have the capacity to cooperate with Jesus in his human actions.[68] As members of Jesus' mystical body, the Church, every believer has a particular and irreplaceable function (Rom 12:4; 1 Cor 12:12–14). This specific function is a participation in the mission of the Church, but not necessarily for that reason a participation in the hierarchy of the Church, for the hierarchy is not the Church, but a part of it. Thus a personal vocation as such is not a participation in the clerical ministry, but a participation in the mission of Jesus.[69] This mission is continued through believers endowed with Jesus' Spirit. Every personal vocation, both those that include ordination (or, for that matter, religious vows) and those that do not, is, therefore, a concrete specification of Christ's extended mission to the world.[70] A personal vocation is the actual, individual form Christ's extended mission takes as it is carried out by each of his people.

Jesus' mission was to proclaim repentance and the Gospel of the kingdom of God and thereby establish a communion between human persons and God.[71] The kingdom Christ proclaimed was a kingdom whose coming his followers were to pray for, and yet at the same time, it was a kingdom already at hand. Indeed, the reign of God was already at hand in the very person of Jesus.[72] God's reign is established in principle, though in the Incarnation and earthly life of the Word—the kingdom God is creating starts with the humanity of Christ. By extension, the Church, endowed with the Holy Spirit, is the earthly, human prolongation of Jesus' person. So the Church too is the kingdom, though not

---

typically called habitual grace or more vividly, *theosis* or deification is "no mere metaphor" (Ibid., 24–F). In his view, the baptized are literally divinized through the waters of baptism so that they share in divine nature just as really as the Incarnate Word shares in human nature by the Incarnation. There is this pivotal difference, however: Just as the Word remains a divine person when he assumes human nature, so conversely believers remain created human persons when they sacramentally receive a share in the divine nature. This qualification is not intended to mitigate the reality of the believer's divinization; rather it is to affirm that it is the *created person as such* who is divinized. In other words, receiving a share in divine life at baptism does not amount to absorption into the divine whereby one loses one's creaturely identity and being.

68. Ibid., 19–C, F.

69. This marks a significant difference between personal vocation and the earlier idea of Catholic Action, which was defined as the laity's participation in the hierarchical apostolate. See Bandas, *Catholic Action*, 1.

70. Grisez, *LCL*, 2–C.

71. Ibid.

72. See *Catechism of the Catholic Church*, 2816.

its complete, definitive form, but its embryonic stage.[73] Thus, while the kingdom includes believers, believers also cooperate in Jesus' work of building the kingdom because they are mystically part of him. Because of this union, his mission is theirs, though not in the sense that the personal vocation that belonged to Jesus as man is each believer's own (or for that matter, that believers' vocations are identical with one another because of an identity with Christ's).[74] Just as union with Christ is relationship, not assimilation, so too there remains a corresponding distinction of roles within that relationship of communion.[75] Continuing Jesus' mission is not a matter of imitating his outward pattern of behavior. Rather it is a matter of cooperating with the Holy Spirit by seeking the will of God for one's life, accepting the unique, specific form that takes at any given moment and doing it. The idea is captured by St. Paul's teaching on the mystical body: There is one body with many members, each unique and indispensable, with Christ as the head (Eph 4:11–16). As an individual human, Jesus had a personal vocation that was circumscribed and when viewed relatively to his total mission, incomplete. Christ's work, and indeed his human body, is still being completed until he attains full stature through his members (Eph 4:13). This is what allows St. Paul to make the otherwise audacious claim that he makes up what is lacking in the sufferings of Christ (Col 1:24).

2. Faith, Hope and the Kingly Dimension of Jesus' Mission

Believers cooperate in Jesus' work of building the kingdom to the extent they allow faith to be the organizing principle of their lives. Faith can serve as a life-organizing principle because it is a commitment.[76] Grisez understands a commitment to be a large choice which must be carried out by means of smaller, subsequent choices.[77] It is a choice to accept the Gospel of the kingdom—really, Jesus himself and his offer of relationship.[78] Faith thus initiates a communion of the believer and Jesus that both enables and demands the believer's cooperation in Jesus' work. Just

73. Grisez, *CMP*, 23–C.7.
74. Ibid., 23–C.
75. Ibid., 19–B.6, C.5.
76. Ibid., 20–B, D; 23–D.
77. Ibid., 2–G, 9–E.
78. Ibid., 20–C.

as one cannot simply give marital consent and then live as one wishes (for the covenant forged in the exchange of vows entails a whole way of life structured around and executive of that initial commitment), so too the initial "yes" to Jesus, the acceptance of what he offers, as in any other real, living, interpersonal relationship, demands that one determine, accept and fulfill what Jesus asks.[79] This threefold task of finding, accepting and fulfilling God's will can only be done by making further choices that carry out the initial commitment of faith. Faith is thus the Christian's fundamental option which is executed in and through these subsequent smaller choices.[80]

For Grisez, the ultimate end one desires and so then intends in the act of faith and the subsequent choices which implement it is the kingdom Jesus promised.[81] By intending the kingdom as the ultimate end of what one does—that is, in responding to one's personal vocation—one fulfills one's responsibility to hope.[82] Whereas faith is a commitment—a kind of choice—hope is not a choice, but a willing of the kingdom as an end. Hope begins as a motivating interest in the kingdom (a volition), but it becomes an intention in the very act of choosing.[83] In desiring the kingdom and choosing for the sake of its realization, believers hope in God for the coming of his kingdom, for the kingdom cannot be realized by their own choices.[84] Thus, hope is in God for the coming of his

---

79. Ibid., 23-C.9.

80. Ibid., 20-C.7. As Grisez points out, the only alternative to integrating the whole of one's life with the faith is to have some aspects of one's life not integrated with faith. Thus, Grisez observes, ignorance of or inadvertence to the idea of personal vocation stunts spiritual growth and impedes the attainment of Christian holiness. See *CMP*, 28-D; *LCL* xii; "Personal Vocation," 16; and this essay, below. On the distinctive sense of "fundamental option" in Grisez and his critique of other applications of the notion, see *CMP*, 16-G, app. 1.

81. Grisez, *LCL*, 2-A.4.

82. Ibid., 2-B.2.

83. Ibid., 2-A.4. Grisez also discusses the way charity—which he understands as analogous to volition—motivates the act of faith (*CMP*, 24-D.9-13; 25-A.7-9). One thing this discussion reveals is Grisez's recognition of two senses of faith in justification: There is a preliminary, dispositive act of faith made for the sake of human goods (though not without grace), which is then transformed into saving faith (which is motivated by the infused gift of charity). For an elaboration of the distinctions between volition, intention, and choice, see Finnis, "Object and Intention," 1–27.

84. Grisez, *LCL*, A.1-2.

kingdom and, by extension, for all one needs here and now to follow and so remain in Jesus.[85]

3. Confirmation and the Prophetic Dimension of Personal Vocation

By intending the kingdom in what they do, believers help Jesus to extend the Father's reign. In this way, Christians participate in the kingly aspect of Christ's threefold *munus* through their personal vocations. Yet to the extent believers put their faith into practice by intending the kingdom in what they do, they also bear witness to Christ and the truth of the Gospel with their very lives. In this way, personal vocation is also a share in the prophetic dimension of Christ's threefold mission.[86] Grisez sees an important connection between this prophetic, or witness-bearing aspect of personal vocation and the sacrament of confirmation. Whereas baptism initiates the relationship by virtue of which believers have a personal vocation, confirmation is the sacrament that empowers the believer to discharge the responsibilities of his or her personal vocation.[87] Through the sacrament of confirmation, there is a second, abundant bestowal of the Holy Spirit whereby believers are strengthened for bearing witness as mature Christians. For this reason, while personal vocation is related in important ways to all three sacraments of initiation (baptism, confirmation, and Eucharist), Grisez sees confirmation especially as the sacrament of personal vocation.

4. The Priestly and Eucharistic Dimension of Personal Vocation

Insofar as a personal vocation is an individual believer's share in the total mission of Christ, it has not only kingly and prophetic aspects, but a priestly aspect also. For Grisez, all of the baptized, and not only the ordained, share in Christ's priestly office. According to Vatican II, believers exercise their share in Christ's priesthood especially by their full, conscious and active participation in the liturgy of the Eucharist, the source and summit of Christian life.[88] Participation in the Eucharist is

---

85. Ibid., 2-A-B.
86. Grisez, *CMP*, 31-C.
87. Ibid., 31-A-E; *LCL* 2-B.4.
88. See *Sacrosanctum Concilium*, 11, 14; *Lumen gentium*, 10–11. It is worth noting the important connections between the Liturgical Movement, which anticipated the

an exercise of priestly capacity because the proper function of a priest is to offer sacrifice and the Eucharist is sacrificial in character insofar as it re-presents the one atoning sacrifice of Christ.[89]

But the precise manner of the laity's participation in the liturgy of the Eucharist reveals the way in which believers, through their personal vocations, exercise their share in the priesthood of Christ. It is not only that each of the baptized is called to participate in the ritual performance of the Eucharistic liturgy; it is that fidelity to one's personal vocation throughout day-to-day life becomes the material, as it were, of spiritual sacrifice that is offered (1 Pet 2:5).[90] As members of Christ, the baptized are capacitated to unite their sufferings, joys, work, and rest—the whole of their lives—to the sacrifice of Christ, to the extent these are carried out for the sake of the kingdom as part of the believer's "yes" to Jesus (cf. 2 Cor 1:20). In this way, just as believers make up Jesus' mystical body, so too they also make up, as St. Paul did, what is lacking in the atoning work of Christ (Col 1:24).[91] The liturgy is the precise means whereby this conjunction of the work of the believer and the work of Christ takes place. By fidelity to their personal vocations, Christians live out the public worship of the Church through all the elements of ordinary, everyday life and their lives thus become permeated by the liturgy.[92] Christian life leads up to the liturgy as material prepared for the offering, and Christians go forth refreshed and strengthened by the Eucharist for living the life of good deeds God prepared beforehand for them to walk in.

---

teaching of *Sacrosanctum Concilium* and *Lumen gentium*, and growing awareness of personal vocation and the universal call to holiness (*Lumen gentium*, 5). By seeking to reform the liturgy from a narrow professionalization, the Liturgical Movement contributed toward breaking down the broader mentality that holiness was outside the purview of the majority faithful.

89. Grisez, *CMP*, 23–B.

90. *Sacrosanctum Concilium*, 48; *Lumen gentium*, 34.

91. It is worth noting that not only the sufferings of believers can be joined to Christ's sacrifice, but the whole of their Christian lives. In this way, the priesthood of believers is congruent with the priestly work of Christ the head, insofar as it is not only his sacrifice on the cross, but the whole of his life, lived in obedience to the Father's plan (culminating in the cross), which accomplishes our salvation. For a classic Lutheran perspective on the soteriological value of the Incarnation, not solely the paschal mystery, see Aulén, *Christus Victor*.

92. Grisez, *CMP*, 23–D.7; app. 1.

5. Free Choice, Charity and Sanctification

For Grisez, walking in the good deeds God prepared beforehand—fidelity to one's personal vocation—is sanctifying.[93] How this is so can be understood from considering the person and work of Jesus against the reality of human free choice.

On Grisez's view, acts of free choice are not discrete, transient realities that exist only in the moment they are made. Rather, choices are realities that last as dispositions of character.[94] Thus, choosing is not simply a matter of doing; more fundamentally, it is a matter of becoming. Free choices are soul-forming. They forge one's existential identity. The specific character and moral quality of the act of free choice is left as a determination of the agent's character. A free choice, once made, lasts until a further, contrary choice is made. For example, by lying, one becomes a liar and one remains a liar until one repents of lying and commits oneself to truth-telling. Conversely, the decision to accept the Gospel (that is, the person of Jesus and what he offers) and all the subsequent decisions by which one responds to his demands for the sake of this new relationship (the kingdom he is building), last as dispositions that integrate one's self around Jesus and the love he offers through his gift of the Holy Spirit. Through these decisions, one becomes increasingly informed by God's love.[95]

Grisez understands Christian charity or the love of God principally as God's love for us poured forth in our souls by the Holy Spirit (1 John 4:19; cf. 4:22).[96] This love establishes our communion with God and quite literally divinizes us. For Grisez, growth in holiness is precisely a matter of growth in charity. However, it is not that charity itself increases or undergoes some intrinsic change. Rather, by choosing in accordance with their fundamental commitment of faith, Christians allow more and more of their lives to be pervaded by charity. Believers become holier as God's love reaches into more aspects of their lives (and therefore, themselves). The change is not objectively one of charity, but subjectively one of the Christian.[97] Crucially, the love of God by which we become holy is not something we do, but something we abide in by what we do. To the extent we, by our good works, remain in and become increasingly

---

93. Ibid., 28–C–E.
94. Ibid., 2–A–B, E.
95. Ibid., 27–E.5.
96. Ibid., 25–A, app. 4.
97. Ibid., 28–C.3, 5.

integrated around the divine love which makes us holy, those works are really and intrinsically, but only secondarily effective of our sanctification and salvation. Hence the intrinsic connection between good works and Christian perfection: It is not that holiness is some sort of reward or divine payment to man for good works.[98] Holiness is rather the natural effect in one's character of the good free choices made for the sake of the kingdom that execute the commitment of faith and by which we continue in God's gratuitous love. Most importantly, both this gift of sanctifying love and the good actions whereby we remain in it are God's gifts to us.

III. Comparison and Evaluation

A. Similarities

As will already have become apparent, there are several points of significant agreement between Luther's theology of vocation and Grisez's, despite the historical and confessional distance between the two thinkers.

Most centrally, both Luther and Grisez see vocation as the central organizing feature of Christian life. It would be possible to say both thinkers conceive of the substance of Christian life in vocational terms. For both thinkers, the particular roles of service to which God calls one comprise the whole of one's Christian life after conversion. Thus, both Luther and Grisez acknowledge that each and every believer has a vocation, not only those called to some special form of religious life. Moreover, a vocation is not merely a general state in life (even a lay state) but is a unique and specific life of good deeds. For both thinkers, vocation is something that touches every aspect of the believer's life, not just a certain sphere, such as explicitly religious activity. Accordingly, both acknowledge one's vocation is discovered through attention to the providentially ordained, concrete circumstances in which one finds oneself. These central points of similarity are noteworthy because in Luther, they arise largely through a definitive break with monasticism—an institution the Catholic Church has upheld with great solicitude. These similarities are also noteworthy in Grisez because the Catholic faithful in general still have not been well catechized in the idea of personal vocation. Consequently, Grisez's view continues to be the exception rather than the norm, despite a half-century of clear Magisterial teaching that vocation can be (and perhaps

---

98. Ibid., 28–C.5.

principally is) something more particular than a general state in life, or more narrowly, a clerical or consecrated state. Beyond this, both Luther and Grisez conceive of vocation primarily as a form of loving service. The works of vocation are meant to address the concrete needs of creation (and principally of human persons) that surround one.[99] Additionally, for both Luther and Grisez, the believer encounters the cross in these works of service. Both theologians see suffering and vocation as inextricably linked, although this connection plays out in alternative ways due to differences in soteriology.

B. Three Points of Difference

While there are several important similarities between Luther and Grisez on vocation, several points of divergence will by now also have become apparent. I shall outline in the remainder of this essay those differences which I find most important for understanding and evaluating each perspective, though more or other points of difference than these could certainly be explored.

1. Different Controlling Ideas: Justification vs. Christocentric Ecclesiology

Perhaps most clearly, there are different controlling ideas behind Luther and Grisez's respective understandings of vocation. We have seen that for Luther, the principal controlling idea is a certain reading of Paul on justification. Man is justified by faith alone, not by his own works or striving. To the extent man's works play any role at all in his salvation, that role is a negative one: works directed toward one's neighbor occupy man's efforts, channeling them in the right direction so that faith is not displaced from or encumbered in its function of positively effecting justification. Indeed, for Luther, the whole significance of vocation arises from his doctrine of justification. Vocation is the corollary to justification by faith alone, for it answers the question of the place works—which are a necessary part of every human life—occupy in the life of a Christian. In contrast, while a different doctrine of justification is very much in play behind Grisez's theology of vocation, the controlling idea for him is not so much justification as a Christocentric ecclesiology.

99. Grisez, *LCL*, 2-E.3.a.

While the doctrine of justification bears in significant ways on Grisez's account of personal vocation, that account of personal vocation is not so much an implication of the doctrine of justification as rather an implication of sacramental incorporation into the Church, which is the mystical extension of Christ's own human body. One who is baptized enjoys a new existence. As reborn through water and the Spirit, he or she exists in and by the created humanity of the incarnate, eternal Word and therefore shares in doing what the incarnate Word does. His redemptive mission becomes in some delimited, individually specified way, the believer's own. In this regard, while Luther's theology of vocation is best thought of an aspect of this theology of creation (since it is by man's works channeled in a horizontal direction by which Creation is sustained and cared for), Grisez's theology of vocation is best thought of more in terms of Christ, the Church, and the eschatological renewal of all things Christ is effecting in and through her. Whereas for Luther, earth and heaven are sharply distinguished realms, vocation pertaining to the former; for Grisez, man's earthly work and progress is directly related to the furtherance of the incipient kingdom of God. For Grisez, vocation is one's cooperation here and now in Jesus' work of building the heavenly kingdom. This is not to say Grisez conflates earthly progress with the growth of the kingdom. It is only to say that there is continuity between man's earthly work and Jesus' eschatological kingdom, which is impossible on Luther's two-kingdoms doctrine.

Different ideas of the Gospel underlie this first divergence. For both thinkers, Christian life is one informed by the Gospel, but whereas for Luther, the Gospel is in essence the doctrine of justification by faith alone, Grisez conceives of the Gospel chiefly as the very person of Jesus and by extension, the message of the NT as a whole (principally the canonical gospels).[100] For Grisez, the Gospel is not something Christ merely preaches and salvation something he merely brings. Christ himself *is* our salvation. He is the Gospel in personal form.

Hence, whereas the doctrine of justification drives Luther's theology of vocation, it is more obviously the person of Jesus and one's sacramental-ecclesial communion with him that drives Grisez's. Overall, Grisez's theology of vocation is more Christological than Luther's.

---

100. Grisez, *CMP*, 20–A, C.8

2. The Relationship of Faith and Life

A second crucial difference between Luther and Grisez is their understanding of the relationship between faith and life, or human action. Really this amounts to a pair of related differences. One is the relationship of faith to life; the other is the relationship of life to what faith initially accomplishes, namely the making holy of the believer—what Trent identifies as the "increase of justification" or what is simply referred to across confessions as sanctification (even while the exact nature of sanctification and its relation to justification is differently conceived). Behind this pair of differences, what is really at stake is a difference in each thinker's understanding of justification.[101]

A. Vocation and Sanctification

We have seen that for Grisez, Christian life consists in the very implementation or execution of faith as the primary life-organizing commitment of a believer. In Grisez's view, there ought to be no separation of faith from life. Rather it is imperative that faith directly and positively inform every aspect of the believer's life. In turn, by living out one's faith—one's acceptance of Jesus and the relationship he offers—one becomes gradually more and more integrated around the love of God poured forth in one's heart at baptism, and so is sanctified. For Grisez, fidelity to one's personal vocation makes one holy. Conversely, one's failure to do what God wills stunts one's spiritual growth and can even imperil one's

---

101. It is possible less difference exists between Luther and Grisez on the gospel and the nature of justification than I suggest below if the new Finnish Interpretation of Luther is correct. See Braaten and Jenson, *Union with Christ*. See also chapter 4 of Malloy, *Engrafted into Christ*. According to the Finnish Interpretation, Luther conceives justification as something much more ontological, intrinsic, participatory, and Christological than it is on the forensic imputation with which Luther is typically associated. The Finnish Interpretation thus finds significant resonances between Luther's understanding of justification and the Orthodox and Catholic idea of deification. Some have questioned the objectivity of the Finnish Interpretation and suggested it does not sufficiently attend to the shifts that occurred between Luther's earlier, more Catholic years and his later thinking, while others consider it to have redefined the field of play in our understanding of Luther. It is impossible, however, to explore here all the complexities of the debate over the Finnish Interpretation. It suffices to say that if the Finnish Interpretation is correct, there is a further significant point of contact between Luther and Grisez that would require a reassessment of their differences on vocation. However it also remains that many of the differences outlined here would persist.

salvation. Someone who has been initially justified but who subsequently fails to live according to the Gospel, can—and indeed, if he or she dies unrepentant, will—be lost.

In contrast, there is a sharp distinction of faith and works in Luther's theology of vocation. We have seen that for Luther, faith alone justifies. By implication, since works do not positively justify, neither can they imperil one's justification, that is, so long as they are confined to the earthly realm and not presumptuously thrust into the heavenly so as to win God's favor. Two points are being made here. The first is that one is not positively made holy by what one does, but rather by faith. Thus, in contrast to Grisez, fidelity to one's vocation is not per se sanctifying for Luther. At the most what can be said is that fidelity to one's vocation allows for one's sanctification as a sine qua non condition, but not an actual cause of it. The second point is that justification cannot—with perhaps one exception—be lost through sin, if indeed one was justified in the first place (appearances to the contrary notwithstanding). For Luther, justification is not tantamount to immediate perfection. Sin is in some regard compatible with holiness in man's actual condition, for the Christian wayfarer is *simul iustus et peccator*. So long as one maintains faith in Christ—is confident in his forgiveness—bad works, or the failure to do good works, cannot jeopardize one's justification. At most, they are simply evidence that one was never truly justified. The only exception, perhaps, is if the sin amounts to a negation of the sine qua non condition for justification: An action that displaces faith—that is, a work proffered to God for merit, rather than directed toward the service of one's neighbor—must imperil one's justification because it undercuts the possibility of that by which one is saved. It would seem this is the only sin incompatible with salvation on Luther's view. Otherwise, one may say that for Luther, no sin imperils salvation and even this sort of faith-displacing sin is merely evidence that one never was truly justified in the first place.

In sum, Grisez thinks fidelity to vocation is positively sanctifying. Following Trent's teaching on a threefold justification, Grisez acknowledges the possibility that justification can increase.[102] Sanctification for Grisez, is equivalent to Trent's "increase in justification." In contrast, if it may be said Luther thinks fidelity to one's vocation sanctifying, it is only negatively so. For Luther, there is a clear distinction between

---

102. There is (i) an initial justification which can (ii) increase by good works (or conversely be lost by mortal sin), and (iii) be regained by repentance and sacramental absolution if lost. See Trent, Session VI, (DS 1524, 1535, 1542).

justification and sanctification, so whatever may be said about vocation in relation to sanctification, the works of vocation are clearly not justifying. Beneath this contrast on vocation lie two different understandings of justification.[103]

B. Vocation and Justification

For both Luther and Grisez, justification is by faith, not works, and is a free unmerited gift of God (although this does not mean it takes place without the cooperation of freewill, in Grisez's view).[104] But whereas for Luther, the formal cause of justification is Christ's righteousness which is alien to the believer and extrinsically imputed to him or her, for Grisez, the believer receives a participation in Christ's righteousness that is truly his or her own. For Grisez, the formal cause of justification is charity—God's communion-forming and so deifying love poured out into the heart of the believer by the Holy Spirit.[105] In consequence, on Grisez's view, the

---

103. For a clear and careful overview of the differences between the Lutheran and Catholic positions on justification, see Malloy, *Engrafted into Christ*, as well as his earlier article, "The Nature of Justifying Grace," 93–120.

104. Thus, there is a sense in which Catholics can agree that justification is *sola fide*, though it is not the sense usually intended by Protestants (cf. DS 1532). Commenting on Gal 3:26, Aquinas—whose thought later heavily influenced Trent's teaching on grace—even affirms, "*sola fides homines facit filios Dei adoptivos* (faith alone makes man an adopted son of God)." It is significant in this regard however, that Aquinas was writing prior to the theological controversies of the fifteenth and sixteenth centuries, for it is clear from the wider context of his thought he did not mean by *sola fides* what Luther seems to have. Catholics agree that one's initial justification (or re-justification after a fall into mortal sin) is not on the basis of works, whether morally good deeds or works of the Mosaic Law. However, Catholics understand the faith that justifies to be a gift infused at baptism together with hope and charity. Thus, on the Catholic view, sinners are not justified by an alien righteousness, although they are gratuitously justified by God, not themselves. Moreover, while Catholics deny justification is by works, they do not deny there is a movement of freewill moved by (actual) grace consenting to the infusion of (habitual) grace in the instant of justification. See Trent, Session VI, chapter 5 (DS 1525); on the distinction of *auxilium* from habitual sanctifying grace, see Aquinas, *ST* I-II q. 109 aa. 1–4, 6. Additionally, Trent teaches justification can increase (DS 1535), and justification in this sense is by good works, though it is primarily by grace and only secondarily by good works (since there is a subordination of human to divine causality, though not one that compromises the freedom or reality of human agency). While these substantive differences must be acknowledged, there is more similarity between the two positions, particularly on the level of language, than is sometimes thought.

105. Grisez, *CMP*, 24–D.5.

Christian is actually constituted, and not just accounted, holy. Moreover, holiness cannot coexist with damnable sin on Grisez's view. The implication of this divergence is two different understandings of sanctification, and so of vocation. Luther can admit sanctification as an ongoing process, but only because in this life, righteousness coexists with damnable sin in the believer. This coexistence is possible because the righteousness by which the believer is made holy is extrinsic. As we have seen, works in this situation serve the negative function of crucifying the outer, sinful man. But because one is not really changed, really made holy by a gratuitous, intrinsic participation in Christ's righteousness, there is no room for merit or the idea that a believer's good works actually increase his or her holiness. Christ's own, extrinsic holiness is already perfect and so not subject to increase. Hence, for Luther, while sanctification may be a process, justification cannot actually increase.

Like Luther, Grisez does not think the formal cause of justification can be merited or increase—in the sense of undergoing an intrinsic or quantitative change—through the performance of good works.[106] But despite this initial similarity, the two views substantively differ insofar as they conceive of the formal cause of justification differently. Since for Grisez, the righteousness by which we are made righteous is a distinct, intrinsic participation in the righteousness of Christ, it *is* possible for justification to increase. But again, what it means for this righteousness to increase on Grisez's view is that the subject in whom this righteousness inheres—the believer—gets increasingly shaped up around that righteousness by his or her good works. Thus, on Grisez's view, post-conversion works actually effect one's sanctification and are meritorious, though—crucially—because they are wrought by God in us. Grisez's view allows for human cooperation in justification, whereas Luther's does not. Consequently, for Luther, vocation has a strictly horizontal trajectory, whereas for Grisez, it has both a horizontal and a vertical trajectory.

c. Secularism and the Division of Faith and Works

Besides the aforementioned difference in how the relationship of life or human action to what faith initially accomplishes is conceived, there is also a difference in how the relationship of faith to life and human action

---

106. By "quantitative change" I mean what Aquinas means by *augetur per additionem* (increase by addition) in *ST* II–II q. 24 a. 5 s.c.

is conceived. Whereas Grisez's account of vocation welds faith and action, the Gospel and temporal affairs, and is developed in large part as a response to the phenomenon of secularism, I would charge Luther's exclusion of works from the heavenly realm—the sphere of faith and justification—has for its practical consequence the exclusion of faith from the earthly realm—the sphere of works and vocation. This division of faith and works, as well as the corresponding separation of the heavenly and earthly realms entails, at least in principle, the compartmentalization of faith from life. Wingren, for example, suggests that a believer discharges the duties of his station in life not as a believer, but simply as a secular office-holder.[107] It is unclear from this how a Christian's engagement in temporal affairs should be different from that of a non-believer, or whether there are offices or stations incompatible with faith, for faith makes all things clean.[108] But the idea that faith makes all things clean to the Christian is somewhat ambiguous. Combined with the idea that damnable sin is simultaneously present with the state of righteousness, the idea that all things are clean to the believer comes dangerously close to suggesting one may do as one wills, so long as one counts on the forgiveness Jesus offers.[109]

This is an especially serious charge from the perspective of anyone who concurs with the diagnosis proposed by the fathers of Vatican II that the separation of faith from life deserves to be counted among the more serious errors of our age.[110] Antinomianism—which followed historically from Luther's doctrine of justification, but to which Luther himself was strongly opposed—is one extreme outcome of this separation. But a more subtle and pervasive outcome than antinomianism is secularism—something that has taken centuries to develop in the wake of the Protestant Reformation.[111] One significant entailment of the separation of faith and

---

107. See Wingren, *Luther*, 112.

108. See Luther's *Commentary on the Sermon on the Mount*, trans. C. A. Hay, 58–70.

109. In a certain way, it may be possible to glimpse this bifurcation even in Bonhoeffer's life. He seems to have viewed his cooperation in the plot to assassinate Hitler as sinful, but necessary, and sharply distinguished from his life and role as a Christian. See Siemon-Netto, "A Christian Who Opposed Hitler."

110. *Gaudium et Spes*, 43. In 1937 Germany, Dietrich Bonhoeffer expressed a sentiment similar to that of the council fathers thus: "It is becoming clearer every day that the most urgent problem besetting our church is this: How can we live the Christian life in the modern world?" (*The Cost*, 60).

111. Paradoxically, Luther's separation of faith and works, the earthly and heavenly

works that underlies Luther's theology of vocation is the incapacitation of the Gospel from critiquing and transforming the social order. While on the one hand, Luther's view of the universality of vocation corrects the two-track mentality that emerged over the long medieval period, his idea nevertheless remains too feudalistic insofar as it assumes life-stations are simply given rather than assumed by choice, or if given, can simply be accepted more or less uncritically by believers. Except with this difference: On Luther's doctrine of justification, not only are life-stations inscribed in the given order of things, they belong to a different sphere from the Gospel. How then can the Gospel retain its prophetic edge?

Dietrich Bonhoeffer is one of the Lutheran theologians perhaps most alive to the danger incipient in Luther's separation of faith and works. Bonhoeffer warned of what he called "cheap grace": the idea that one could be saved by grace without discipleship.[112] On Bonhoeffer's diagnosis, the Pauline idea of justification by faith had been abstracted from its scriptural (and especially evangelical) context and crystallized into a doctrine or system.[113] This process distorted Paul's original teaching and invited its practical misappropriation. At the heart of Bonhoeffer's critique was the idea that in moving from Scripture to formalized doctrine, from conviction to theory, the teaching on justification lost its biblical moorings and became corrupted. Bonhoeffer thus implicitly saw that while Luther's understanding of justification *as an idea or formalized doctrine* issued in the bifurcation of faith from life, the foundational problem was that this doctrine of justification was not holistically enlivened by Scripture.

D. Scripture and the Faith/Works Division

The exegetical Achilles heel of Luther's doctrine of justification can itself be assessed along two axes. The first is whether that doctrine is based on a sound interpretation of St. Paul, especially the epistles to the Romans

---

kingdoms was in part, precisely a reaction to the secularization of the Church and other abuses of ecclesiastical life consequent on the failure to distinguish the spiritual from the temporal order. As suggested earlier above, Luther's doctrine of the two kingdoms is not solely responsible for the genesis of western secularism. More radically, the problem is the sort of Christian mediocrity fostered by an exclusivist, two-track idea of holiness.

112. Bonhoeffer, *The Cost*, 47, and more broadly, 45–60.

113. Ibid., 53–56.

and Galatians, wherein Paul discusses justification by faith in relation to works of the law. The second is whether the doctrine squares with the canon as a whole, not just a narrow selection of Pauline texts taken in isolation. While it is impossible within this discussion of vocation to undertake a responsibly exhaustive examination of the biblical warrant for Luther's doctrine of justification (or Grisez's), at least the following points are relevant and may serve to indicate a trajectory of further exploration.

An analysis along the first diagnostic axis cannot but take into account the paradigm shift that has occurred in Pauline exegesis since the publication of E. P. Sanders' seminal study, *Paul and Palestinian Judaism* in 1977 and the earlier works of scholars such as Krister Stendahl that foreshadowed it.[114] At the outset, it must be admitted this so-called New Perspective on St. Paul is not a uniform phenomenon, and its various manifestations have been subject to certain points of criticism both from without and within.[115] Nevertheless, however one might ultimately adjudicate these debates—a project worthy of serious attention in its own right—the substantive thrust of the New Perspective cannot be dismissed.

Those who in various ways have adopted and developed the New Perspective have demonstrated the importance of understanding first-century Judaism for interpreting Paul in his own historical context, rather than through the lens of sixteenth-century confessional polemics. From the New Perspective, Paul's juxtaposition of works of the law with faith in

---

114. Sanders, *Paul and Palestinian Judaism*. See also Krister Stendhal, "The Apostle Paul." The literature on the New Perspective is vast. One important essay is Dunn's "The New Perspective."

115. It is impossible here to exhaustively survey these debates. Dunn, in "The New Perspective," makes an appreciative critique of Sanders, charging his portrayal of Paul is unnecessarily idiosyncratic and out of continuity with Paul's Jewish background. Additionally, Dunn introduces a more precise distinction between the Mosaic Law as such and works of the Law. Hahn is also appreciatively critical, acknowledging the correct thrust of Sanders' position, but alleging that Sanders overplays "the continuity in the covenantal relationship between God and his people and the ready availability of atonement for sin by sacrifice and repentance" (*Kinship by Covenant*, 240). Others more critical to covenantal nomism claim Sanders is not sufficiently sensitive to the variance within Jewish religious practices leading up to Paul's day. See for example the essays in Carson, *Justification and Variegated Nomism*, and especially Carson's concluding essay (505–548). The general reaction to the New Perspective from the standpoint of at least certain streams of Reformed Orthodoxy seems to be negative. While one factor in play is certainly the sheer historical evidence that suggests covenantal nomism as described by Sanders may not be entirely adequate, it is also probable that intuitive but mistaken assumptions about divine causality and human free choice (discussed below) fuel some of the resistance to the New Perspective.

respect to justification cannot be understood as a juxtaposition between the Mosaic law as such or exterior human acts and faith, much less as a juxtaposition between human agency (whether expressed interiorly or exteriorly) and divine.[116] To press for these latter distinctions claims more than the text will bear. According to the New Perspective, first-century Judaism was not a religion of works-righteousness in Luther's sense. Accordingly, Paul was not critiquing Judaism as a form of proto-Pelagianism when he juxtaposed works of the Law with faith in Christ. Paul's overarching concern was rather with the conditions for Gentile inclusion in the new-covenant people of God. Was it necessary for them to abide by the stipulations of the Mosaic law—especially dietary regulations and the requirement of male circumcision—in order to be right with God? Paul taught it was not, but that the time of the fulfillment of Israel's destiny as a vehicle of universal salvation had come—now it is faith in Jesus Christ that is required. Thus, on the New Perspective, Paul's juxtaposition of faith with works of the Mosaic law does not underwrite the classical Protestant doctrine of forensic justification (or by extension, the view of sanctification, sin, merit and human agency it entails). This is not to claim Paul's teaching refutes forensic justification, or that the doctrine may not be held as a defensible theological construct for independent reasons. It is only to say that if the New Perspective is right, forensic justification cannot be advanced as a strict interpretation of Paul. This does however raise serious questions about the theological validity of Luther's juxtaposition of faith and works.

An analysis along the second diagnostic axis must take into account the perspective on good works one finds present outside Paul's teaching on justification in Romans and Galatians, both elsewhere within Paul's corpus and within the NT more broadly. While no NT text teaches one's initial justification is on the basis of works, the plain sense of a host of passages still seems to stand in tension with Luther's doctrine of justification insofar as these indicate good works done after conversion play a causal role in one's salvation.[117] For instance, those who are justified by

116. For the distinction of interior and exterior acts, see for example, Aquinas, *ST* I–II q. 111 a. 2.

117. It is impossible to provide an exhaustive overview of such passages here, but representative collection of passages follows (synoptic parallels are assumed but not listed). On the relation between good works and salvation in the NT, see Stanley, *Did Jesus Teach*. While Stanley's reading of the NT is astute and honest, his theological analysis at points lacks precision. Stanley—an evangelical who in a qualified way defends salvation by works—acknowledges, but tends to downplay the significance of

faith are created for the life of good works that awaits them after their initial justification (Eph 2:10).[118] Indeed, faith is completed by these works and is soteriologically impotent without them (Jas 2:14-26). Because one's salvation is not definitively accomplished in this life, but is in the course of being worked out, believers must stand fast through trial and suffering (Matt 10:22; 24:13; Jas 1:12-15) and are enjoined to make their initial calling and election permanent (2 Pet 1:5-11), for incipient salvation can be lost. They are to persevere in grace by being holy as God is holy, by being doers of the law and so practicing a greater righteousness than the Scribes and Pharisees (Matt 5:20-48; 12:50; 19:17-21; 2 Cor 5:10; Jas 1:19-25; 1 Pet 1:13-25). Believers must show mercy (Matt 18:21-35). Ultimately, one's final judgment will be on the basis of works (Matt 10:40-42; 16:27; 25:34-46; Eph 6:8) and not everyone who says "Lord, Lord" will enter the kingdom (Matt 7:21-27), for doing the will of the Father is an entry requirement. Overall, the message of the NT seems clear that discipleship is not only the privilege (or burden) of the elite few, but is intended for every believer.[119]

In sum, Luther and Grisez's respective ideas of vocation contain two very different perspectives on the relationship of faith and life, works and

---

differences between such figures as Aquinas, the Nominalists, Luther, Calvin, and Arminius on salvation, distinguishing only the Free Grace or Salvation-Discipleship view as a sharp departure from the Augustinian-Thomistic tradition (see 19-70). Stanley also sees his own position as agreeing with that of Luther (321-22). However, Stanley seems to mean by this only that (i) initial justification is not on the basis of works, (ii) saving works done after justification are done only in and through grace, and (iii) that (whatever else they might do) post-conversion works are evidence of one's justification. Yet in the context of the present discussion, these three claims are noncontroversial. A substantive agreement between Stanley and Luther can only be seen by eliding the more radical part of Luther's actual position—not just that pre-conversion works do not cause salvation, but that works do not positively cause salvation at all. Thus, I think there is more distance between Luther's view and Stanley's than Stanley suggests, though in my estimation, Stanley's position finds broader biblical support.

118. Note the contrast in this context between good deeds and works of the law in Gal 2:16, for example. In the present context, Paul is not talking about works of the Mosaic Law as such, but morally good actions, the duties of one's vocation, works of mercy, etc. This does not however mean he intends to exclude here the observance of the moral precepts of the old law, such as the Decalogue.

119. In contrast, there is a certain ironic parallel between the Salvation-Discipleship or Free Grace view summarized by Stanley and the medieval marginalization of lay holiness. Both ignore the intrinsic connection between discipleship and salvation and do not see the call to discipleship as an inherent part of faith.

salvation. At the heart of this divergence lie two different understandings of justification.

However, I would like to suggest there is a deeper basis for the divergence between Luther and Grisez on vocation and justification than their reading of the NT, and it has to do with a philosophical presupposition about the relationship of divine and human agency that they bring to their reading of the NT.

3. Divine Causality and Human Free Choice

Behind Luther's doctrine of justification and vocation lies a commitment to theological compatibilism—the view that human acts, while uncoerced and performed by the human agent, are ultimately determined by God. In Luther, there is an implicit juxtaposition of divine and human agency that issues in a denial of free choice. Man is like a beast ridden either by God or the devil. Having denied free choice, Luther also denies man's free cooperation in justification and he also denies merit, which depends on the idea of free choice. What makes the ideas of free human cooperation in justification and merit objectionable to Luther is the thought that these imply Pelagianism—the view that the human person has the initiative in salvation, or can produce a salutary act autonomously from God, *ex nihilo* as it were.

Grisez shares Luther's opposition to Pelagianism. He also holds—though in a different way from Luther—that human acts are caused by God.[120] In contrast to Luther however, Grisez's affirmation of the divine initiative does not lead him to deny human free choice. In Grisez's view, human persons have the capacity of free choice and God causes human free choices. Because God causes human free choices, human cooperation in attaining salvation does not imply Pelagianism: God sees nothing in us save what he himself has wrought.[121] Crucially for Grisez though, God's working our good deeds in us in no way undercuts our own free agency.[122] On his view, precisely what it is God works in us is our own

---

120. See Boyle et al., *Free Choice*, 97–103. See also Germain Grisez, *God?*, 274–285. For other articulations of a view essentially similar to Grisez's, see Grant, "Can a Libertarian," 22–43; McCann, "Divine Sovereignty," 582–98; Ross, "Creation II."

121. See Aquinas' prayer of longing for heaven in vol 1. of *Sancti Thomae Aquinatis Opuscula Theologica*, 288 (as cited in Finnis, *Aquinas*, 327 n. 142, 333 n. c): "*Te Deum totius consolationis invoco, qui nihil in nobis praeter tua dona cernis . . .*"

122. Cf. Aquinas, *ST* I q. 19 a. 8.

free choosing. Ultimately, what drives such a view of divine and human agency is a profound grasp of the implications of the doctrine of creation: Because God is the total cause of the being, he causes whatever is, "all the way down." God's effect, in other words, is not just what the creature does, understood as the specific determination of the creature's act, but rather the creature's very doing it and doing it freely. On this view, God's will is not a determining antecedent to the human act of free choice. God causes the human act of free choice just as such, so that the act is truly up to the human agent and not therefore determined by any causal or temporal antecedent.

But this bedrock issue—the relation of human to divine agency—is admittedly a difficult matter. I would submit the relation of divine and human causality is in fact one of the most difficult theological matters to think straight about, in line with the mysteries of the Trinity and Incarnation, except that with regard to the latter, early ecumenical councils have provided a significant measure of formal clarification. The same is not so of divine causality and human freedom. As Fergus Kerr has pointed out, understanding the relation of these is "the problem central in all Western theology" and it lies at the heart of "the most intractable division in the history of Western Christianity."[123] The matter's complexity arises not only from the inherent human difficulty of thinking about a transcendent God—something we can do only in terms of creaturely categories, which, if not carefully qualified, are as sure to mislead as to convey truth—but also from the fact that the relationship of divine and human agency has been the focus of tendentious debates within Lutheranism, Catholicism, and Calvinism, not only between them. Effectively, the same core issues were at stake in the Lutheran Synergist Controversy as in the Catholic Controversy *de Auxiliis* and the Calvinist Remonstrant Controversy.[124]

---

123. Kerr, *After Aquinas*, 142, 148.

124. For a comparison of these controversies, see Placher, *The Domestication*, 146–63; cf. 88–107; Tanner, *God and Creation*, 141–52; Gaetano, "Rapprochement." All of these theological controversies also basically map on to the contemporary philosophical debate between libertarians and compatibilists. Contrary to the standpoint I propose in this essay, Placher sees Luther upholding a similar appreciation of divine transcendence as Aquinas in contrast to his more rationalistic followers, Matthias Flacius (1520–75) and Philipp Melanchthon. I agree Flacius and the Philippists get caught on the horns of a dilemma because of a failure to appreciate the transcendence of divine causality, and it may be that Luther has more in common with Aquinas and the earlier tradition than is sometimes thought. However, I think it is a mistake to group Luther's perspective with that of Aquinas, some three centuries earlier, rather than with that of his immediate sixteenth-century followers. The reason is that the

That these debates occurred when they did, on the heels of the Protestant Reformers' teaching on justification, is not an accident of history. Moreover, four centuries on, not a single one of these debates has been definitively settled within its respective confession.

My point here is not to equate the Gnesio-Lutheran position with that of the Dominicans or the Synod of Dort, or to equate Melanchthon's view with that of Molina, Suárez or Arminius. It is merely to show that without conflating those positions, significant parallels can still be seen among the three debates, and that, in a way which is perhaps surprising given the confessional polarization of the period, the various positions on the question of divine causality and human free choice tend to align more closely with one another across confessional lines than within each confession. All of this illustrates the complexity of the matter which I am suggesting explains the principal differences between Luther and Grisez on vocation.

The issue of divine and human causality, therefore, is not a mere abstract, intramural, philosophical dispute, but one that touches at the heart of scriptural exegesis and how we conceive of discipleship. Moreover, the question of the relative theological merits of Luther's and Grisez's respective positions on vocation hinges in no small part on how such debates about divine and human agency are adjudicated.

Conclusion

Grisez's position on divine causality and human free choice seems to me more promising than Luther's because it avoids the presuppositions that give rise to the insoluble grace/freedom controversies of the sixteenth

---

intervention of nominalism between Aquinas and Luther was game-changing and arguably led Luther to uncritically assume a univocal view of causality, despite his opposition to certain elements of nominalism, which he perceived as quasi-Pelagian. It is likely Placher takes the position he does because he assumes the truth of compatibilism and does not distinguish Aquinas' position from it (see 149). This is understandable, as both libertarians and compatibilists have claimed Aquinas for their own. This is probably best explained by the fact that while Aquinas covered the issues of the sixteenth-century grace controversies, he did not do so from a sixteenth-century post-Reformation perspective, and so his work was ambiguous or underdeveloped on certain points neuralgic to the later philosophical and theological debates, even though he implicitly had the resources to circumvent them. For a more plausible interpretation that places Aquinas outside the bounds of the later libertarian/compatibilist debates (including the sixteenth-century grace controversies), see Grant, "Aquinas," 221–35; cf. Goris, *Free Creatures*, 289–304.

century, namely the presuppositions that if God causes a human act of choice, his will is a determining antecedent, whereas if a person's choices are truly up to him or herself, they cannot be caused by God. Additionally however, Grisez's appreciation of divine transcendence allows him to have an understanding of vocation and its place in the process of salvation that does not compromise human agency in order to make space for divine causality. Consequently, Grisez's idea of vocation is able to better account for both the divine initiative in salvation and the unmerited character of initial justification, as well as the biblical idea of reward and judgment on the basis of works and the necessity of discipleship for all believers. In contrast, Luther's idea of vocation presupposes a doctrine of justification that lacks the metaphysical sophistication to account as adequately for the full range of scriptural data. The effective consequence of this, at least on the level of ideas, is the introduction of a divorce between faith and life.

Thus, I would submit an accidental tension arises between justification and discipleship in Luther's thought. Certain elements of Luther's theology of vocation set the ground for a radical renewal of our understanding of the way of Jesus, but the possibilities of this theology of vocation are undercut by the limitations of the doctrine of justification that drives it. I propose that the shortcomings of this doctrine with respect to Scripture stem from the deeper metaphysical assumption that in the final analysis, divine and human agency stand in a zero-sum relationship. Thus, while Luther's core insight that each Christian is the beneficiary of a personal divine calling offers a needed corrective to the reductive, preconciliar, two-track mentality of Christian life that is still pervasive among Catholics, to the extent Grisez's theology of vocation can do justice to Luther's most basic concerns (chiefly the universality of vocation and the divine initiative in salvation) while circumventing the shortcomings of his position (a univocal view of causality and a marginalization of certain NT texts), Grisez's theology of vocation represents a promising way forward for a recovery of Luther's best insight, and thus for contemporary ecumenical reflection on the nature of Christian discipleship.

Bibliography

Anderson, Mary Elizabeth. "Gustaf Wingren's *Luther on Vocation*: A Case Study in Research During the Swedish Luther Renaissance." PhD diss., Luther Seminary, 2004.

Aquinas, St. Thomas. *Summa theologiae*. c. 1265–74.

Ashley, Benedict, OP. "The Scriptural Basis of Grisez's Revision of Moral Theology." In *Natural Law and Moral Inquiry*, edited by Robert P. George, 36–49. Washington, DC: Georgetown University Press, 1998.

Aulén, Gustaf. *Christus Victor*. Translated by A. G. Herbert. London: SPCK, 1970.

Bandas, Rudolph G. *Catholic Action*. Paterson, NJ: St. Anthony Guild Press, 1935.

Bethge, Eberhard. *Dietrich Bonhoeffer: Theologian, Christian, Man for His Times: A Biography*, rev. ed. Edited by Victoria J. Barnett. Minneapolis: Fortress, 1999.

Billing, Einar. *Our Calling*. Translated by Conrad Bergendoff. Philadelphia: Fortress, 1964.

Bonhoeffer, Dietrich. *The Cost of Discipleship*, rev. ed. Translated by R. H. Fuller. New York: Macmillan, 1969.

———. *Ethics*. Translated by Eberhard Bethge. New York: Macmillian, 1965.

Boyle, Joseph M., et al. *Free Choice: A Self-Referential Argument*. Notre Dame, IN: University of Notre Dame Press, 1976.

Braaten, Carl E. and Robert W. Jenson, eds. *Union with Christ: The New Finnish Interpretation of Luther*. Grand Rapids: Eerdmans, 1998.

Carson, D. A., ed., *Justification and Variegated Nomism*. Vol. 1, *The Complexities of Second Temple Judaism*. Grand Rapids: Baker, 2001.

Couenhoven, Jesse. "Law and Gospel, or the Law of the Gospel? Karl Barth's Political Theology Compared with Luther and Calvin." *Journal of Religious Ethics* 30 (2002) 181–205.

Dunn, James D. G. "The New Perspective on Paul." In *The New Perspective on Paul: Collected Essays*, edited by James D.G. Dunn, 99–120. Tübingen: Mohr/Siebeck, 2005.

Erickson, Robert P. *Theologians under Hitler: Gerhard Kittel, Paul Althaus and Emanuel Hirsch*. New Haven: Yale University Press, 1985.

Finnis, John. *Aquinas: Moral, Political and Legal Theory*. Oxford: Oxford University Press, 1998.

———. "Object and Intention in Moral Judgments According to Aquinas." *The Thomist* 55 (1991) 1–27.

Finnis, John, et al. *Nuclear Deterrence, Morality and Realism*. Oxford: Clarendon, 1987.

Gaetano, Matthew. "Rapprochement between Dominican Thomists and Reformed Protestants after the Synod of Dordt." Paper presented at *Reformed/Dominican Dialogue*, a session of the annual Sixteenth Century Studies Conference, Cincinnati, October 2012.

Geisler, Norman L. and Ralph E. MacKenzie. *Roman Catholics and Evangelicals: Agreements and Differences*. Grand Rapids: Baker, 1995.

Goris, Harm J. M. J. *Free Creatures of an Eternal God: Thomas Aquinas on God's Infallible Foreknowledge and Irresistible Will*. Leuven: Peeters, 1996.

Grant, W. Matthews. "Aquinas Among the Libertarians and Compatibilists: Breaking the Logic of Theological Determinism." *Proceedings of the American Catholic Philosophical Association* 75 (2001) 221–35.

———. "Can a Libertarian Hold That Our Free Acts Are Caused by God?" *Faith and Philosophy* 27 (2010) 22–43.

Grisez, Germain. *Clerical and Consecrated Life and Service*. Unfinished draft of Volume 4 of *The Way of the Lord Jesus*. Online: http://www.twotlj.org/G-4-V-4.html.

———. *Christian Moral Principles*. Volume 1 of *The Way of the Lord Jesus*. Quincy, IL: Franciscan Herald Press, 1983 (abbreviated above, *CMP*).

———. *Contraception and the Natural Law*. Milwaukee: Bruce, 1966.

———. *God? A Philosophical Preface to Faith*. South Bend, IN: St. Augustine's Press, 2005. (Note: except for the introduction, which includes a sketch of a new argument for God's existence, this volume is identical to the 1976 piece, *Beyond the New Theism*.).

———. *Living a Christian Life*. Volume 2 of *The Way of the Lord Jesus*. Quincy, IL: Franciscan Herald Press, 1993 (abbreviated above, *LCL*).

———. "Natural Law, God, Religion and Human Fulfillment." *American Journal of Jurisprudence* 46 (2001) 3–36.

———. "Personal Vocation: A Key to Authentic Renewal in the Church," *Homiletic and Pastoral Review* 85/7 (1983) 10–20.

Grisez, Germain, and Joseph M. Boyle, Jr. "Response to our Critics and Our Collaborators." In *Natural Law and Moral Inquiry*, edited by Robert P. George, 213–38. Washington, DC: Georgetown University Press, 1998.

Grisez, Germain, et al. "Practical Principles, Moral Truth and Ultimate Ends." *American Journal of Jurisprudence* 32 (1997) 99–151.

Grisez, Germain, and Russell Shaw. *Personal Vocation: God Calls Everyone by Name*. Huntington, IN: Our Sunday Visitor Publications, 2003.

Hahn, Scott. *Kinship by Covenant: A Canonical Approach to the Fulfillment of God's Saving Promises*. New Haven: Yale University Press, 2009.

Hagen, Kenneth. "A Critique of Wingren on Luther on Vocation." *Lutheran Quarterly* 16 (2002) 249–74.

Han, Jin Hee. "Vocation." In *Encyclopedia of Protestantism* 4:655–58.

Kerr, Fergus. *After Aquinas: Versions of Thomism*. Oxford: Blackwell, 2004.

Lawler, Ronald OFM Cap., et al. *Catholic Sexual Ethics: A Summary, Explanation and Defense*. 2nd ed. Huntington, IN: Our Sunday Visitor Publications, 1998.

Lazareth, William H. *Christians in Society: Luther, the Bible and Social Ethics*. Minneapolis: Fortress, 2001.

Luther, Martin. (Note: Primary texts by Luther cited above are either from the American edition of *Luther's Works* or from secondary sources in which they appear, as indicated in the footnotes. For simplicity, I have only listed here in chronological order the works of Luther cited in either fashion above.).

———. *Bondage of the Will* (1525).

———. *Commentary on the Sermon on the Mount* (1532).

———. *Explanation and Defense of all the Articles* (1521).

———. *Kirchenpostille* (1527).

———. *Large Commentary on Galatians* (1535).

———. *Treatise on Christian Liberty* (1520).

———. *Smalcald Articles* (1537).

Malloy, Christopher J. *Engrafted into Christ: A Critique of the Joint Declaration*. American University Studies. Series VII, Theology and Religion 233. New York: Lang, 2005.

———. "The Nature of Justifying Grace: A Lacuna in the *Joint Declaration*." *The Thomist* 65 (2001) 93–120.

Matava, Robert Joseph. "Divine Causality and Human Free Choice: Domingo Báñez and the Controversy *de Auxiliis*." PhD diss., University of St Andrews, 2010.

May, William E. *An Introduction to Moral Theology*. 2nd ed. Huntington, IN: Our Sunday Visitor Publications, 2003.

McCann, Hugh J. "Divine Sovereignty and Freedom of the Will." *Faith and Philosophy* 12 (1995) 582–98.

Newman, Bl. John Henry Card. *An Essay on the Development of Doctrine*. Notre Dame, IN: University of Notre Dame Press, 1989.

Nygren, Anders. *Agape and Eros*. Translated by Phillip S. Watson. Philadelphia: Westminster, 1953.

Peterson, Luther D. "Synergist Controversy." In *Oxford Encyclopedia of the Reformation* 4:133–35.

Pfurtner, Stephen, OP. *Luther and Aquinas on Salvation*. Translated by Edward Quinn. New York: Sheed & Ward, 1964.

Placher, William C. *The Domestication of Transcendence: How Modern Thinking about God Went Wrong*. Louisville: Westminster John Knox, 1996.

Ross, James F. "Creation II." In *The Existence and Nature of God*, edited by Alfred J. Freddoso, 115–41. University of Notre Dame Studies in the Philosophy of Religion 3. Notre Dame, IN: University of Notre Dame Press, 1983.

Sanders, E. P. *Paul and Palestinian Judaism: A Comparison of Patterns of Religion*. Philadelphia: Fortress, 1977.

Shaw, Russell. *To Hunt, to Shoot, to Entertain: Clericalism and the Catholic Laity*. San Francisco: Ignatius, 1996.

Siemon-Netto, Uwe. "A Christian Who Opposed Hitler." *The Atlantic Times* (2006). Online: http://www.atlantic-times.com/archive_detail.php?recordID=435.

———. *The Fabricated Luther: The Rise and Fall of the Shirer Myth*. St. Louis: Concordia, 1995.

Stanley, Alan P. *Did Jesus Teach Salvation by Works? The Role of Works in Salvation in the Synoptic Gospels*. Evangelical Theological Society Monograph Series 4. Edited by David Baker. Eugene, OR: Pickwick, 2006.

Stendhal, Krister. "The Apostle Paul and the Introspective Consciousness of the West." In *Paul Among the Jews and Gentiles*, edited by Krister Stendhal, 78–96. Philadelphia: Fortress, 1976.

Tanner, Kathryn. *God and Creation in Christian Theology: Tyranny or Empowerment?* 1988. Reprinted, Minneapolis: Fortress, 2004.

Taylor, Charles. *Sources of the Self: The Making of the Modern Identity*. Cambridge: Harvard University Press, 1989.

Weber, Max. *The Protestant Ethic and the Spirit of Capitalism*. Translated by Talcott Parsons Mineola, NY: Dover, 2003.

Wingren, Gustaf. *Luther on Vocation*. Translated by Carl C. Rasmussen. 1999. Eugene, OR: Wipf & Stock, 2004.

6

Luther's Linguistic Innovation

Virgil Thompson

The approaching five hundredth anniversary of Luther's Reformation serves as good an occasion as any to drop again the bombshell, God's justification of the ungodly, by faith, apart from works of the law. When Luther reflected in retrospect about the Reformation, the word did it all, as he and his colleagues drank their Wittenberg beer; the proclamation of God's justification is the word to which he was referring. At its dynamic center the Reformation—whether in the sixteenth century or the twenty-first century—names what happens when the church proclaims this word without qualification. Whatever else the church may be, Luther insisted, above all God has established it as a "mouth-house" for this proclamation. In his Commentary on Romans Karl Barth likened ecclesiastical practices and structures, doctrines and dogmas, "to the charred clinkers in a crater marking the fact that here a great explosion took place."[1] Too often academic theology seems content, like anthropologists on a dig, to focus all its attention on the clinkers of this blast from the past. Luther's Reformation has not fared much better among preachers, regardless of denomination, including the Lutheran denomination. As bombshells go, many ecclesiastics seem inclined to regard justification as something of a

---

1. Quoted in Forde, *Justification by Faith*, 1.

dud. They dismiss it as irrelevant to modern experience. Even preachers who continue to see the relevance of justification, more often than not, qualify it endlessly, to the point of delivering it dead on arrival.

There have been and are however exceptions to the rule. The German scholar, Gerhard Ebeling, writing in the 1960s, launched an interpretative approach that remains promising for the recovery of the dynamic center of Luther's theology for today.[2] Ebeling argued that at heart Luther's breakthrough was a reformation of religious language, a linguistic innovation according to which the Word of God was viewed not primarily in terms of its content but in terms of what it does to the hearer. Following Ebeling's approach, Gerhard Forde, one of the more incisive American interpreters of Luther's theology for today, refers to the bombshell of Luther's Reformation proclamation as the radical gospel. Writing in 1987, on the inaugural eve of the Evangelical Lutheran Church in America, Forde counseled the newly amalgamated church: "Let us be radicals . . . radical preachers and practitioners of the gospel of justification by faith without the deeds of the law. We should pursue it to the radical depths already plumbed by St. Paul, especially in Romans and Galatians, when he saw that justification by faith without the deeds of the law really involves and announces the death of the old being and the calling forth of the new in hope. We stand at a crossroads," Forde concluded. "Either we must become more radical about the gospel, or we would be better off to forget it altogether."[3] This essay, a case study in Luther's theological hermeneutics, takes up Forde's call to tell the story of Jesus as the radical gospel of God's justification of the ungodly.

Sailing against the Current

In its aim the essay moves against the strong stream of modern interpretive convention as it has taken up the Bible. Over the past 250 years, interpretation has sought, in the interest of seeing the biblical text more clearly in historical relief, to bracket theology out of disciplinary bounds. Biblical scholarship may have good reason to be leery of theology. Indeed, the whole idea of the historical-critical approach to the Bible has been to free it from the dogmatic stranglehold of theology. The history of modern interpretation suggests, however, that it has proven more difficult to bar

---

2. Ebeling, *Luther*.
3. Forde, "Radical Lutheranism," 8.

the door to theology than Baruch Spinoza might ever have imagined. While the historical approach to the Bible may serve to free the text from the straightjacket of ecclesial dogma, it may just as well be practiced in a way that protects vested interests and advances unannounced theological agendas. In other words, theological prejudice tends to slip into interpretive discourse in disguise and unacknowledged.

Luther for one would not be surprised. In his view humans are inveterate theologians, forever caught between seeking and fleeing God. In this contention Luther is scarcely alone. The insight runs to the heart of the Christian Scriptures. According to the Psalmist, on the one hand, "As a deer longs for flowing steams, so my soul longs for you, O God" (42:1), but on the other hand, "Where can I go from your spirit? Or where can I flee from your presence?" (139:7). The problem, as Forde observes, is simply the very "godness of God."[4] On the one hand humanity may value the idea of an eternal anchor to hold down cherished hopes and ideals, to offer comfort in troubled times, to sanction and enforce a vision of moral order. But the problem, as in the days when Israel was encamped at Mt. Sinai (Exod 19), is that the prospect of God "breaking out against us" never goes away. Merely barring the door to theology has not succeeded in saving readers from the danger of God breaking out against them. Neither, as a matter of fact, has historical interpretation served to defuse the threat of God against us. Consider just one tiny verse from the biblical story, "Jacob have I loved, but Esau have I hated" (Mal 1:3; Rom 9:13). Can either historical or theological interpretation, for that matter, have anything to say that changes God's resolve, "I will have mercy on whom I have mercy, and I will have compassion on whom I have compassion" (Rom 9:15)?

The threat of God breaking out against the reader of Scripture was not unknown to Luther himself. In fact it was under the pressure of that prospect that Luther engaged the biblical writings. In the course of the encounter, questioning and being questioned, it was driven home to him that neither theology nor interpretation—let alone pious acts of contrition—could deliver humanity from the problem of God. God alone could solve the problem of God. As Luther put it, "to flee from and find refuge in God against God, such is the impossibility that makes theology possible." It also establishes the place and limit of theology in the encounter with the biblical writings. Forde explains: Theology, "whatever else it might be for,

---

4. Forde, *Theology Is for Proclamation*, 15.

has to be for proclamation . . . while not itself to be confused with proclamation, [theology] should be the kind of thinking that advocates, fosters, and drives to proper proclamation of the gospel of Jesus Christ . . ."[5] In other words, theology drives to the proclamation of God's promise in Christ, exposing along the way every false harbor of refuge.

Of course to admit theology to our discourse does not require that interpretation abandon historical and literary approaches to the Bible. Both remain essential to respectful and fruitful engagement with the text as we have received it. They have and will continue to enrich the encounter with the biblical text, and especially the biblical text regarded as the Word that God has sent to redeem a lost and condemned humanity from sin, death, and the power of the devil. Just as Luther and his Wittenberg colleagues advocated and employed the latest humanist methodologies in the study of the Bible so contemporary scholars in the tradition continue to use the critical methodologies of their own age.[6] In other words, neither theology nor history nor interpretive methodologies is the problem. To paraphrase Pogo from the Funny Papers, "We have met the problem and he is us."

Not only does the essay take up Forde's call but does so deeply under his influence. Forde himself is deeply under the influence of Luther whose "Reformation breakthrough" has established the orientation and path of his theology. In my own scholarship, it is not always clear to me just exactly where Luther's influence leaves off and Forde's takes up. In any event the essay seeks to stand within the tradition to which both Forde and Luther belong. Ebeling articulates clearly the stance of the tradition: Many today, like Erasmus in the sixteenth century, may "find Luther's thought too assertive, too much a confession of faith, and his mode of thought, in consequence, too little humanist and too barbaric . . . [however that may be] . . . As we inquire into Luther's thought, we are also ready to encounter Luther as a linguistic innovator. For he has no other concern than to give proper utterance to the word."[7] Not only does the essay argue for the necessity of employing a theological hermeneutic in hearing the biblical story in its own voice, but it argues that apart from the proclaimed promise of God's justification of the ungodly there is nothing at all redemptive about the biblical story. This was Luther's point

5. Ibid., vii.
6. See, for example, Luther, "To the Mayors" (1524).
7. Ebeling, *Luther*, 25–26.

in "A Brief Instruction on What to Look for and Expect in the Gospels" (1521). The Gospels proclaim Christ, alone, the promise of salvation and the freedom to live a down-to-earth existence. Only, be sure, Luther continues, "that you do not make Christ into a Moses.... The chief article and foundation of the gospel is that before you take Christ as an example, you accept and recognize him as a gift, as a present that God has given you and that is your own ... then the other part follows ... giving yourself in service to your neighbor just as you see that Christ has given himself for you."[8] In other words, as Jaroslav Pelikan writes in the Introduction to Luther's Exegetical Writings, "It is not what Christ did that believers must do, but what was done to Christ is what believers must learn to recognize as being done to them as well."[9]

What happened to Jesus according to the biblical story was simply that he was crucified, died, buried, and on the third day was raised from the dead (1 Cor 15:3–4). This is the way God makes new creatures in Christ from the old humanity bound by the desire to not want God to be God, anxious in its own finitude to be god over its own existence, clinging desperately to the false hope, "you will not die" (Gen 3:4). God wounds that he might heal. God crushes in order to raise up. He kills in order to give life. This is the story that the Bible tells. It is the story that is to be enacted toward the hearer in the proclamation of the church. As Jesus answered the grumbling about his choice of companions, "I have come not for the righteous, but for sinners" (Mark 2:17). In what follows we take up Mark's Gospel as a case study in exploring the way in which God's justification of the ungodly, alone, promises a new beginning for humanity in relation to God and creation.

"All of Them Condemned Him"

There is no evidence that Luther took any more interest in the Gospel According to St. Mark than any of his contemporaries. That is to say, for Luther, as for most interpreters from antiquity to the middle of the twentieth century, Mark's Gospel remained in the shadow of Matthew and most especially John in Luther's case. Augustine's view of Mark as the "abbreviated version of Matthew," with few exceptions, dogged the reputation of Mark among interpreters until the 1950s. Nonetheless, Mark's

---

8. Luther, "A Brief Instruction," *LW* 35:119–20.
9. Pelikan, *Companion Volume to Luther's Works*, 62.

story of Jesus provides grounds on which to explore Luther's theological assertion that apart from the promise of Jesus to justify the ungodly, the biblical story offers no redemptive promise at all.

As the evangelist Mark tells the story, it did not take Jesus's contemporaries long to make up their mind that in him something unprecedented was afoot (1:21–28). It took only slightly longer, to a person, for the humanity of the narrative to decide what should be done about it. The verdict of the human court was unanimous: "All of them condemned him as deserving of death" (14:64). There was never a great deal of suspense about it, according to Mark. The handwriting was on the wall from the outset. The reader is barely three chapters into the story before the cross begins to cast its shadow over the fate of Jesus. The Pharisees conspire with the Herodians, "how to destroy him" (3:6). Even his own disciples set out at one point to hunt (*katedioxen*) him down (1:36). It does not appear that Mark has chosen his verb lightly. It could be coincidental, but judging from what transpires in the rest of the story, the verb may be employed in the very same way that it is used in the Septuagint to describe how the king of Egypt and his army pursued the fleeing Israelites (Exod 14:8). Nothing suggests that the disciples were malevolently motivated toward Jesus as this point in the story, or at any point of the story for that matter. To all intents and purposes it appears that the disciples, like the rest of the villagers from Capernaum, were merely seeking Jesus and his benefits. However, as Luther never tired of pointing out, there's trouble ahead when seekers do not obtain the benefits for which they seek. In the end there is little difference between those who seek Jesus for his benefits and those who seek Jesus to destroy him.

Upon finding Jesus, his disciples explained, "everyone is searching for you" (1:37). Jesus for his part appears little impressed by the public attention and the opportunity that the disciples see in it. Not just here but throughout the story Jesus defies every attempt to domesticate him to one parochial interest or another, no matter how salutary to the well-being of the "world-as-it-is." Of course he pays a price for it. When he is found to be of no value to the vested interest of established society, or anti-establishment society for that matter, he is wasted. Forsaken. Denied. Mocked. Executed. That would have been the end of it, were the end of the story written by humanity. But the end of the story has been taken out of human hands. The end of the story, as Mark tells it, is written by God. God refuses to accept the final decision of humanity toward Jesus. Death is not the final word. "He has been raised; he is not here!" (16:6). Jesus no longer lies lifeless in the tomb of the biblical story, the inanimate object of endless theologizing, moralizing, politicizing, and socializing. Donald Juel explains, "If [Mark's] story proves good news for any particular reader, it will not be because interpretive cunning or violence permit readers to lay hold of Jesus and confine him long enough to extract a blessing. 'He is not here,' the young man says . . . [T]hat elusiveness also means that the story does not allow for negative closure either . . . the story undermines confidence in anything but trust in the work of God beyond the confines of the story."[10] Juel's explanation locates the promise of the redemption precisely where Luther locates it, in the prospect of God fulfilling God's promises. As Forde contends, only the preached God, the God who lives in the proclamation of the resurrected Christ, can free humanity bound to the blind ambition to be in control as God. Juel's observation illustrates the way in which Luther's theological hermeneutic arises out of the biblical story and then provides the material perspective from which to read and make sense of the story.

The Problem of God

For Mark, the end of the story is "the beginning of the good news of Jesus, Christ and Son of God" (1:1). Mark, however, does not squeeze out the good news by piously touching up the story with redemptive theories of atonement, as though the whole affair could be rescued by adorning the cross with roses. For Mark, Jesus is God breaking into the world, which is intent upon keeping him out. At his baptism the heavens are torn apart and the Spirit of God tears into Jesus and propels him forward along the path of his mission (Mark 1:11–12). And just as certainly Jesus is God breaking out against the world intent on boxing him up in predictable platitudes. As Mark's Jesus declares, "The time is fulfilled, and the kingdom of God has come near!" (1:15). In Jesus God exercises his divine rights over his creation, the right to have mercy upon whom he will have mercy. In Mark 4 the disciples ask Jesus why he teaches in parables and this is the gist of the answer: I will have mercy on whom I will have mercy. In his words, "To you has been given the secret of the kingdom of God, but for those outside, everything comes in parables; in order that they may indeed look, but not perceive, and may indeed listen, but not understand; so that they may not turn again and be forgiven" (4:11–12). This

---

10. Juel, *The Gospel of Mark*, 191.

does not sit well with a humanity that has become accustomed to having a God in whatever image you care to imagine God, or not to imagine him at all. In this respect it would appear, if my own experience as a teacher of Mark's Gospel is any indication, the humanity that reads the narrative is not much different than the humanity within the narrative world. When attempts to explain away or domesticate what Jesus says here flounder against the hard words on the page, readers tend to become one with the protests of characters within the narrative. When Jesus forgives the sin of a real sinner, the theological authorities grumble among themselves, "Who can forgive sins, but God alone?" (2:7). When Jesus is caught living it up with sinners and tax collectors, the pious protest the propriety to his disciples (2:16). When Jesus, like a bull in a china shop, ventures across the established boundaries between us and them, between disease and health, between who's in and who's out, he meets with the same protest and opposition. "By what authority are you doing these things? Who gave you this authority to do them?" (Mark 11:28). His answer is always the same, "new wine for new wine skins!" "I have come to call not the righteous but sinners" (2:17; see also 2:21ff.). In other words, Jesus has not come merely to keep order in the world according to righteousness as defined by the right or the left, by the north or by the south, by Protestants or Catholics, by male or female. He comes to establish the new order of forgiven sinners freeloading on the grace of their Lord. New wine for new wine skins! Jesus is not to be confined within a theological straightjacket, no matter which ecclesial—or academic—tailor has knit it! The promise, as Paul declared to the Corinthians, is a new creation. "So if anyone is in Christ, there is a new creation: everything old has passed away; see, everything has become new! All this is from God, who reconciled us to himself through Christ, and has given us the ministry of reconciliation . . ." (2 Cor 5:17–18a).

But who could see it? To his contemporaries nothing could have seemed further from reality. His own family, upon hearing of his activities, concludes, "He has gone out of his mind" (Mark 3:21b). They go out to restrain him. The religious authority concludes, "he has Beelzebul, and by the ruler of demons he casts out demons" (3:22). They seek to destroy him. Of course, that's what it must seem. Humanity, blind to its own divine ambition, has no eye to see the God in Christ who comes to be for us.

Much like our world, the world of Mark was not exactly waiting with baited breath for God to make an appearance. That's the thing. Mark reads more like a Flannery O'Connor short story than what most people might expect from the Bible. How is God to get through to a world for which the reality of God has become in the words of Friedrich Nietzsche, "the phantom of grammar, a fossil embedded in the childhood of rational speech"? If that's the question, Jesus is not without an answer: "No one can enter a strong man's house and plunder his property without first tying up the strong man; then indeed the house can be plundered" (Mark 3:27). Again, Juel explains the significance of the saying in a way that is consistent with the tradition that runs from Paul through Luther and Forde: Jesus "intrudes into places where his authority is contested. His advent will be marked by family discord and social disruption. Those in authority will view this as socially (and religiously and politically) risky behavior. From the perspective of those in bondage, this 'plundering' is liberation and salvation."[11] The story of Jesus as the radical gospel is the story of God's breaking and entering into a world bound to not want God to be God. God in the person of Jesus is on the loose to unloose the bonds of a world which is bound up in divine pretension.

The problem of God is not as new as either contemporary detractors or contemporary fretters might imagine. According to Luther the problem of God has been the theme of Christian theology from the outset. Theology according to biblical imagination is about the human who is bound to not want God to be God, and God who is determined to have his creation back by faith in the promise of God for us and not against us, as it must seem from the experience of the naked God in his majesty. The problem of God goes all the way back to the beginning of biblical time. As the tempter put it to the first humans, "It won't kill you; God knows that when you eat of it your eyes will be opened, and you will be like God. And so when they saw that the fruit was a delight to the eyes . . . to be desired to make one wise . . . [they] took and ate" (Gen 3:5–6). As promised, it opened their eyes, but they did not see what they had imagined. They saw only their naked vulnerability. So they hid themselves. Not only did they hide from one another, but also from God, especially from God, "we heard the sound of you in the garden, and we were afraid because we are naked; and we hid ourselves" (Gen 3:9).

---

11. Ibid., 95.

The God Not Preached; The Preached God

But if God is the problem, then God is a problem that only God can answer. This is the thing that finally got through to Luther after questioning and being questioned; "a totally other face of the entire Scripture showed itself to me," he declared. For Luther the "totally other face" that showed itself to him was the face of God in Christ. This then became for him the beginning and ending place of theology—whatever proclaims Christ. Take Christ away from the Scripture and what do you have? Theology for Luther has to do with the thinking that goes on between "hearing the promise of Christ for you" and "proclaiming the promise of Christ for you." In a nutshell that is the bombshell of the Reformation, the "Reformation Breakthrough."

The two faces of God, as the Scripture reveals them, Luther spoke of as God not preached and God preached. This distinction allows theology to reflect and speak honestly about God. Forde explains, "To begin with, assuming we have heard God in the proclamation we can be honest about the fact that outside the proclamation God is something of an onerous burden" that, perhaps understandably, we "will" to be rid of.[12] This is Luther's point when he speaks about the bondage of the human will. Not that he imagines a divine puppeteer pulling the strings of humanity, coercing humanity into behavior against its will. Rather, the bondage about which Luther's theology revolves is the human desire to not want God to be God. Willfully, we will not have it.

Who can say about God as God is in God's self, in his naked majesty? Theology may speculate all it wishes, but who can say? God outside of God's self-revelation in Jesus remains hidden to us. Or more precisely, as Forde contends, God in his naked majesty is "a confusing, nefarious brew of presence and absence, of sheer timeless abstractions. Yet the abstractions do not reveal so much as hide God from us. They tell us more about what God is not than what God is. God is infinite (that is, not finite), immutable (that is, not changeable), not mortal, not suffering, not limited by time or space, not relative to anything. As such, God amounts to a deified minus sign."[13] The very godness of God causes all the difficulty. The bare idea of God—absolute, immortal, immutable, infinite, timeless, passionless, omnipotent, omnipresent, and omniscient—is above us, out of our control. And that is what we will not, cannot tolerate. We do not

12. Forde, *Theology is for Proclamation*, 14.
13. Ibid., 15–16.

know what this God is up to. In fact, God as the bare idea of a higher power is impossible to distinguish from Satan. Who can say? "The 'God-pain,'" as Luther taunted Erasmus, "is like the gout. The more theological doctoring is attempted, the worse it gets."[14]

The problem of God as it turns out is simply the freedom of God to be God. When in the course of Mark's story it becomes apparent that God does not conform to human ideas of God, that God is not content merely to stand around with his feather duster to keep order, rewarding the deserving for their good effort and punishing the wicked for their deadly ways, there is trouble ahead. By the end of Mark's story all humanity in its entirety has burned its bridges to Jesus. Not that they were coerced against their will. Their minds were willfully made up against a God that they could not control, against a God who was of no value to their vested interests. Because Jesus had put himself in the place of God in a way that did nothing to advance their interests, the authorities were "looking for a way to kill him" (14:1). They didn't have to look far. In Judas they find a willing ally. Mark is strangely silent on the question of what motivated Judas. Was it disappointment, greed, fear? Similar to the Markan silence on why Jesus's family sets forth to restrain him—To save him from himself? To save themselves from embarrassment?—Mark shows no interest in such questions. It's all the same. "With a kiss, Judas betrays Jesus into the hands of his enemies." Always with a kiss, Forde observes. Jesus is betrayed into the hands of his enemies always with a kiss. Theology imagines to do God the favor of picturing him according to a more acceptable portrait, but like the disciples, despite their pious assurances to the contrary (14:31), theologians, fearing for their lives, forsake and abandon God as God (14:50). It was no surprise to Jesus. It was no surprise to anyone who knew the long history of God and his people as it was remembered in the Scriptures of Israel. "Let the scriptures be fulfilled," Jesus concedes (14:49). Peter, ashamed to be associated with Jesus, denies any association with him, whatsoever (14:66ff.). Not that you or I could blame him. By that point in the story Jesus, in the forum of world opinion, has been written off as a joke. The authorities from the top down ridicule him, likewise the crowd of humanity that happens by Golgotha (15:16ff.). "Let the Messiah come down from the cross now, so that we may see and believe" (15:31). But he does not come down. That is all too clearly seen. On that basis the centurion concludes

---

14. Quoted in ibid., 21.

the obvious. "Now when the centurion, who stood facing Jesus, saw that in this way he breathed his last, he said, [sarcastically!], "Yeah, right, this man was God's Son" (15:39).

Admittedly, unlike in the earlier description of the soldiers' treatment, where the narrator makes it explicit—"after mocking him . . . they led him out to crucify him" (15:16, 20)—here there is no explicit indication of how the words come off the centurion's lips. Did he speak sincerely or did he speak sarcastically? Readers seem desperate to hear the exclamation of the centurion as a sincere confession, perhaps even a conversion. But isn't it just one more attempt at a cunning resolution to the problem of God? A happy ending, after all, at least one person is redeemed; the rest of us can go about our business undisturbed. But what other conclusion could the centurion have drawn but that the claim was a joke, perhaps a sad joke, but a joke all the same, "Yeah, right, that was God's Son." It is to be noted after all that when Pilate inquires of the centurion, "whether Jesus had been dead already for some time," the centurion reports, "yes, as a matter of fact, Jesus has been dead for some time, quite dead" (see Mark 15:42–47).

No one sees it and no one believes it. Even the women who go to the tomb do not go in expectation that Jesus has kept his word, that he will rise on the third day. They go merely to finish the job of giving Jesus a proper burial. And even when they have the news—"You are looking for Jesus of Nazareth, who was crucified. He has been raised; he is not here . . . go, tell!"—they flee from it in fear and trembling (16:6–8). Whether it is the same fear and trembling of which Kierkegaard wrote cannot be said. But it forms a very dark ending to the story. If the future of humanity in relation to God lies in the hands of humanity, then Mark's story brings down the curtain in silent darkness.

Or could it be that the end of the old humanity, which refuses to have God as God, is the beginning of a new humanity? Is it precisely when humanity comes to the end of the road of its own effort to create an acceptable god that there is promise of seeing Jesus for who he is, "I have come to call not the righteous, but sinners." Could this be what Jesus meant when he said, "the end is still to come" (13:7)? If the conclusion of Mark's story writes the definitive end to the story, not by works, including interpretive works, then doesn't it in the same breath speak the promise of Jesus for faith? Donald Juel, reading from the standpoint of the tradition to which Gerhard Forde and Martin Luther belong, sees the end of Mark in just that way.

> Mark's Gospel—and, we might add, the whole Christian tradition—argues that our lack of enlightenment and bondage arise from attempts to box God in or out of experience. All such attempts come to grief in the resurrection of Jesus. He cannot be confined by the tomb or limited by death. In Jesus' ministry God tears away barriers that afforded protection in the past. God cannot be kept at arm's length. Such a possibility that light dawns even on those who inhabit the realm of darkness is disquieting; it means there is no refuge for the cynical any more than for the naïve . . . If the unresolved ending offers promise, it is surely not because we are encouraged to believe that we can do better than the disciples or the women. We do not 'have' Jesus even at the end of the story, and there is no guarantee that we can wrest a promise from him or lock him safely away by hermeneutical tricks . . . But perhaps that is just where the promise resides.[15]

Yes, the ending of Mark's story is full of unbearable disappointment, but isn't it, just so, full of the promise of Jesus, out of the tomb, no longer safely boxed up in worn-out religious institutions but also not bracketed out as a phantom of grammar. If Luther was and is correct, that salvation is God's work within human speech, then there is reason, as Juel puts it, "to hope that our defenses will finally prove insufficient and that we will not have the last word."[16] We are justified to believe that yet the last word, the last laugh, will go to God's justification of the ungodly. And if so that would be justification to live a "free and merry existence," free as down-to-earth humans. Trusting God to be God, humans would be free to live out their days in enjoyment and care of creation, as God intended in the first place (see Gen 2). As the old priest in Bernanos story had it, "That wouldn't have stopped the labourer ploughing, or the scientist swotting at his logarithms, or even the engineer making his playthings for grown-up people. What we would have got rid of, what we would have torn from the heart of Adam, is that sense of his own loneliness . . . . man would have known he was the son of God; and therein lies your miracle."[17]

---

15. Juel, "Disquieting Silence," 11–12.
16. Ibid., 12.
17. Bernanos, *Diary of a Country Priest*, 19.

Bibliography

Augustine, Saint. *Confessions*. Baltimore: Penguin, 1961.
Barth, Karl. *The Epistle to the Romans*. Translated by Edwin C. Hoskyns. London: Oxford University Press, 1933.
Bernanos, Georges. *The Diary of a Country Priest*. Chicago: Thomas More, 1983.
Ebeling, Gerhard. *Luther: An Introduction to His Thought*. Philadelphia: Fortress, 1970.
Forde, Gerhard. *Justification by Faith—A Matter of Death and Life*. Philadelphia: Fortress, 1982.
———. "Radical Lutheranism." *Lutheran Quarterly* 1 (1987) 5–18.
———. *Theology is for Proclamation*. Minneapolis: Fortress, 1990.
Juel, Donald H. "A Disquieting Silence: The Matter of the Ending." In *The Ending of Mark and the Ends of God*, edited by Beverly Roberts Gaventa and Patrick D. Miller, 1–13. Louisville: Westminster John Knox, 2005.
———. *The Gospel of Mark*. Interpreting Biblical Texts. Nashville: Abingdon, 1999.
Luther, Martin. "A Brief Instruction on What to Look for and Expect in the Gospels." In *Luther's Works,* 35:113–24, edited by Theodore Bachman. Philadelphia and St Louis: Fortress and Concordia, 1970.
———. "Luther to the Mayors and Aldermen of the Cities of Germany in Behalf of Christian Schools." In *Luther on Education,* edited by F. V. N. Painter, 169–209. St Louis: Concordia, 1900.
Pelikan, Jaroslav. *Luther's Works, Companion Volume: Luther the Expositor*. Philadelphia and St Louis: Fortress and Concordia, 1959.

7

Luther, Libertines, and Literature

Jeffrey K. Mann

Martin Luther has left us a problem. There is great appreciation for his theology of salvation through faith alone. However, his radical emphasis on God's grace—which abolishes the despair felt from having to achieve salvation with our own efforts—leaves us with the problem of the potential abuse of this freedom from performing good works. If I can do nothing to facilitate, receive, or maintain my salvation, well, I guess I don't have to do anything. Luther's theology leaves itself wide open for libertinism.

Luther did not simply underestimate this problem; at times he seemed to encourage it outright. In 1535 he wrote, "It is a marvelous thing and unknown to the world to teach Christians to ignore the law and to live before God as though there were no law whatever [sic]. For if you do not ignore the law and thus direct your thoughts to grace as though there were no law but as though there was nothing but grace you cannot be saved."[1]

The essential conundrum, which I have written about as the "antinomian question," is this: How do you respond to the professed Christian who makes little effort to be morally upright? After all, she correctly

---

1. *Luther's Works*, 26.6.

points out that she will be forgiven all her sins of omission and commission if she simply believes. While this type of antinomianism could be expressed in a lifestyle of crass libertinism, more often it involves moral apathy and laziness at a more modest level: Nothing will happen to me if I don't volunteer at Habitat For Humanity. That is to say, this question is not the purview alone of the rare individual who wants to spend his life raping and pillaging, but is a common thought when doing the right thing is not really what I want to do today.

This issue has dogged pastors and theologians from the beginning of the Church. St. Paul needed to respond to those who asked, "Shall we sin, because we are not under the law but under grace?" (Rom 6:15). With Luther and his extreme emphasis on faith alone, and his reticence to speak much of sanctification, casual libertinism became much easier to justify. Why did Luther shout justification and whisper sanctification? The most influential factor was that he believed the Church had failed to deliver the pure gospel. Instead, it beat people down with rules and regulations that left them in despair. The corrective for his time was the message of free grace, not more Law. He condemned works righteousness more strenuously than vice because he believed it to be more dangerous—vice imperils the body, works righteousness endangers the soul.

Luther's *answer* to the antinomian question was clear: Of course good works are important and they should be encouraged! Moreover, where there is genuine faith, there will be genuine acts of love. They are essentially connected. "For as naturally as a tree bears fruit, good works follow upon faith."[2] And, "Just as there is not fire without heat and smoke, so there is no faith without love."[3]

Luther was no antinomian. He did not want to preach the gospel alone and let that happy message transform people's lives.[4] The law is to be preached as well, both before and after conversion. *Lex semper accusat*, the law always accuses. That is, one does not preach the law to the unregenerate alone, but every believer must confront it daily. Luther taught, "The repentance of believers in Christ goes beyond the actual sins and continues through our life until death."[5]

---

2. *Martin Luther Werke*, 103.285.

3. Ibid., 172.275.

4. Luther rejected this position during the two antinomian controversies with Johann Agricola, Andreas Poach, and Anton Otto. Cf. Richter, *Gesetz und Heil*.

5. *Martin Luther Werke*, 391.350.

Nevertheless, Luther certainly erred on the side of the gospel. As a result, there has been a real difficulty in the history of Lutheranism, where pastors and theologians have sought to respond effectively to the antinomian question without compromising Luther's theology. How do you tell people that they have to do good works, at the same time that you tell them they don't have to do good works?

The challenge boils down to this: A good Lutheran pastor will comfort the afflicted and afflict the comfortable. That's a tricky job description if ever there was one. Is it even possible when speaking to a group? Most likely, the reassuring words of the gospel will be gobbled up by the comfortable, while the afflicted will focus on the law of God and all of its demands. As a result of this difficulty, Lutheran church leaders have often followed Luther's example and erred on the side of the gospel, speaking more of grace and forgiveness than moral chastisement. This, of course, makes the lazy libertine life all the easier to slip into.

In 500 years of Lutheran history, there have been two types of replies to the antinomian question. These are logical answers and existential responses. For most of the time that I have worked on this issue, I have focused on logical answers. I am, after all, a hardcore left-hemisphere kind of guy. I like rational, consistent, logical answers to problems. I prefer non-fiction to fiction. I was surprised to hear that *Moby Dick* was a metaphor, and not just a cool story about a whale.

First let us briefly consider a few logical responses: Philipp Melanchthon, Luther's right-hand man, was quite concerned with the abuse of Christian freedom, and worked hard on logical responses to this problem. Among his various efforts, he introduced a third use of the law, which instructs believers in how to live their lives. He also warned them that bad behavior has temporal implications. He wrote in his 1555 *Loci Communes*, "Although obedience is for the glory of God, and not principally for fear of punishment, nevertheless God has revealed terrible punishments respecting it, so that we may know his will and earnestly desire to show obedience."[6] And, of course, good works can bring temporal blessings, as the fourth commandment promises. Melanchthon provides us with a good reply to the antinomian question, but it leaves us open to cost-benefit analyses when considering a little walk on the wild side.

Other logical retorts to the antinomian question answered the would-be libertines, but sometimes compromised Luther's theology in

---

6. Melanchthon, *Loci*, 182.

the process. Philipp Jakob Spener is a good example of this. The father of German Pietism did a great deal for spiritual growth among the people of Germany. He strongly encouraged *collegia pietatis*, or conventicle groups, laying the groundwork for what we know today as bible-study groups. And his preaching of the Law made it clear to everyone what was expected of them. However, his theological innovations created some problems.

In order to put the fear of God into the nominal Lutherans of his day, he taught that there are essentially two kinds of sins: sins of weakness (*Schwachheit-sünde*) and sins of malice (*Boßheit-sünde*).[7] The former are accidental sins, committed without forethought. The latter are intentional and performed without regret. The one is committed by believers and forgiven freely, while the other is the work only of those without true faith. Thus, according to Spener, if you are unapologetically planning your weekends of debauchery, that is a good sign that you do not possess genuine saving faith.

There are a number of problems with this harmatology. First, it stands in stark contrast to Luther's insistence that the redeemed remain complete sinners their whole lives, *simul iustus et peccator*. Additionally, this distinction forces the individual into self-analysis, requiring her to examine her own behavior for a sure sign of God's grace. If her daily conduct includes impious behavior that was not accidental, and did not generate much sorrow, that may very well mean that her faith is insincere and worthless. This stands in stark contrast to Luther's theology which focuses entirely on the work of Christ as the proof of redemption. Luther's theology creates freedom; Spener's enslaves us again, condemning us to lives curved in on ourselves.

The second kind of reply to libertinism is existential. Here we find less explicit theology and more communication with the heart and soul. Rather than offering a logical answer, reply is made through personal connection and inspiration. This seems quite fitting in Christianity, given the example of its founder. Jesus was asked for a definition of who qualifies as a neighbor and responded with a story about a guy getting mugged on the road. He regaled his audience with a tale about fertilizing a fruitless fig tree. He brandished a whip and ran people out of a temple courtyard. The gospels are full of this kind of material. Jesus did not respond to people with legal definitions and theology; he communicated in ways that allowed them to personally appropriate his message.

---

7. *Philipp Jakob Spener Schriften*, II.2, 172ff.

Martin Luther, on the other hand, is not known as a story-teller; his radical message and its delivery in the sixteenth century were usually direct, as they would strike at the marrow of his audience. However, not all his works were theological treatises full of spit and fire. Luther also spoke tenderly to his parishioners. To communicate his ideas to the laity, he often took a different tack. For example, his appreciation for the fables of Aesop is well known.[8] When fulfilling his office of pastor in letters and sermons, he understood the value of everyday examples. Citing Marcus Terentius Varro approvingly, he wrote, "[F]or [examples] help one both to understand more clearly and to remember more easily. Otherwise, if the discourse is heard without an example, no matter how suitable and excellent it may be, it does not move the heart as much, and is also not so clear and easily retained. Histories are, therefore, a very precious thing."[9]

Lutheran theologian and philosopher Søren Kierkegaard adopted the more literary approach in the nineteenth century when trying to communicate the true spirit of Christianity. "My task," he wrote, "has continually been to provide the existential-corrective by poetically presenting the ideals and inciting people about the established order."[10] The father of existentialism held the same concern as Spener, that nominal Christians were abusing the freedom of the gospel. However, his own efforts to combat this mistreatment of Christianity were not theological, per se, but personal, directed to the "single individual." The challenge was to assist people to personally appropriate the truth claims of Christianity. As he famously wrote at the end of *Either/Or*, "[O]nly the truth that builds up is truth for you."[11] That is, we only truly believe—and subsequently act on—that which we have personally appropriated.

According to the Dane, the biggest barrier to spiritual growth is objectification of the truth claims of Christianity. And a primary culprit? Assistant professors. "[T]hose vermin who actually have demolished Christianity, the assistant professors, those noble men who build the tombs of the prophets, objectively recite their teachings, turn the

---

8. Springer, *Luther's Aesop*.
9. *Luther's Work*, 34.275.
10. *Pap* X4 A 15, as in *Søren Kierkegaard's Journals and Papers*, 1.331.
11. *Either/Or*, 2.354.

suffering and death of the glorious ones into a profit."[12] After all, "one does not become pious objectively."[13]

Kierkegaard famously chose indirect communication over direct communication, for most of his life. He wrote of emperors, geese, seducers, and vampire bats, all with the intention of compelling his audience to consider his message for their lives. Through his own parables, and the unique perspectives of his pseudonymity (or polyonymity), he wanted to help his readers internalize the truth claims of Christianity. He wrote, "Christianity is spirit; spirit is inwardness; inwardness is subjectivity; subjectivity is essentially passion, and at its maximum an infinite, personally interested passion for one's eternal happiness."[14] For Kierkegaard, the way to deal with the unsanctified lives of his neighbors was to help them deepen their personal faith. This is achieved, not through objective theology, but personal connection. And as Jesus had demonstrated nearly 2000 years prior, indirect communication achieves this quite well.

But this is not really so easy! How do you present a principle, especially to academics, so that it is not categorized, the author pigeon-holed, and the life-changing message reduced to objective knowledge? Kierkegaard did his best, often telling stories in an effort to force his readers to identify with characters. In one particular example, which makes me think of college professors, he wrote, "Like the child who lets his kite go skyward, he lets his knowledge ascend; he finds it interesting, enormously interesting, to watch it, to follow it with his eyes but—it does not lift him up; he remains in the mud, more and more desperately craving the interesting. Therefore, whoever you are, if this in any way is the case with you; shame on you, shame on you, shame on you!"[15]

What Kierkegaard was doing, without explicitly stating it (to my knowledge), was responding to libertinism with literature.[16] He wrote inspirationally of love, as well as its poor imitators, in the stories of Agnes and the merman, the king who loved the maiden of low status, and creatures of habit. He taught us ethics through the letters of Judge William, the Knight of Infinite Resignation, and accounts of tragic heroes like

12. *The Moment and Late Writings*, 290–91.
13. *Concluding Unscientific Postscript*, 132.
14. Ibid., 33.
15. *The Moment and Late Writings*, 260–61.
16. This is, of course, until the end of his life when the poet "threw away his guitar" and began to speak quite directly to the people of Copenhagen.

Agamemnon. He communicated the ideal of faith through the account of Abraham and Isaac, as well as the Knight of Faith. He could powerfully present the moral ideal without telling people what they ought to do. The reader could be brought to that conclusion for herself.

Reading through Kierkegaard, one is constantly drawn away from intellectual objectification of theology and back into life in the world. Poetry, legend, parables, and countless examples—sometimes fantastic, sometimes mundane—force the reader to appropriate the material to his situation, to his life. Kierkegaard understood that the more objective the material, the less life-changing; the more subjective, the more transformative. In desiring to communicate the Christian message in a way that transformed lives, he recognized that objective theology was not the most useful gift he could give the world. He needed to be a poet, a "Poet of the Word."[17]

What is noteworthy about the power of literature with regard to the Christian message is its ability to speak the appropriate message in the ears of both the comfortable and the afflicted. As you will recall, Lutheran preachers have a problem: A sermon should contain both law and gospel—requirement and forgiveness. The problem is that while those despairing should hearken to the gospel most closely, and the contented to the law, the opposite often results. The conscience-stricken hear only God's moral demands while the smug skip ahead to the cheap grace of forgiveness.

With this in mind, we see the value of literature for such a challenge. Literature draws us in and creates identification with certain characters, often ones with whom we relate most closely. The struggles and personalities which resonate with us are what draw us to individuals in the story. As such, different readers may identify with different characters. When I shared the story of the Good Samaritan with my two young sons, it was plain to me that the three of us were identifying with the three different characters: the father, older and younger sons. In our case, this was particularly appropriate, as our counterparts in the story have similar personalities to the three of us. In cases like this, the applicable lesson for the character may then be appropriated by the reader who needs to hear the same message.

This principle, sometimes referred to as "experience-taking," may help us overcome the preacher's paradox. The lessons learned by literary

---

17. Kuethe, "Kierkegaard," 294–302.

figures translate to those readers with whom there is close identification. According to psychologists Geoff Kaufman and Lisa Libby, having looked at multiple studies on this topic, it is clear that "experience-taking as an immersive, simulative experience . . . [has] the power to change readers' self-concepts, behaviors, and attitudes." Moreover, the evidence is that these changes have a durable effect, being displayed days after the reading event.[18] When paired with a character with whom the reader identifies, positive lessons learned by the character can translate into the life, thought, and actions of the individual. The reader with the afflicted conscience can appropriate the message of grace learned by his literary counterpart. And the smug libertine may likewise learn the lesson of her literary equal.

Of course, a preacher is unable to achieve such a level of identification and experience-taking in the course of a sermon. Kaufman and Libby provide evidence that the more one adopts the identity and mindset of the character, the greater the effect on behavioral changes in the reader.[19] And this takes time—more than fifteen minutes on a Sunday morning. So while a greater appreciation for "story-telling" from the pulpit is a positive lesson for some clergy, it is in the realm of great literature that we may find the greater cure for troubled souls.

In the world of fiction, C. S. Lewis is often cited, and for good reason. Throughout the *Chronicles of Narnia* there is ample opportunity for different readers to identify with different characters. The children of the Pevensie family, with their own distinct personalities, offer such a prospect. The underappreciated Lucy turns out to be an essential element in Aslan's master plan. Edmund must come to grips with his betrayal of his siblings, and also accept his redemption. Numerous minor characters are presented in these books, individuals whose personal failings are presented in remarkable prose for the readers, along with paths toward deliverance.

Literature can have particular potency with regard to libertinism. It is able to inspire virtuous behavior without an ultimatum. This does not happen through moral instruction, but inspiration. While Lutheran theologians were struggling with whether or not they could teach, "Good works are necessary for salvation," the Anabaptists were reading the

---

18. Kaufman and Libby, "Changing Beliefs," 1–19.
19. Ibid.

stories of their heroes of faith in *Martyrs' Mirror*.[20] In the late nineteenth century, orthodox American Lutherans were dissecting the theology of C. F. W. Walther's *The Proper Distinction Between Law and Gospel*. Russian Orthodox readers, on the other hand, were being inspired by the character of Alexei in Dostoevsky's *The Brothers Karamazov*. More recently, countless readers in the twentieth and twenty-first centuries have identified with the nameless human in *The Screwtape Letters*. Known only as "the Patient," his struggle with temptations echoed their own, and led them to overcome these same enticements.

Perhaps as a result of Lutheranism's emphasis on egalitarianism, there has been little celebration of moral heroes. All believers are priests; all human beings remain miserable sinners their entire lives; every Christian is a saint. While the theology may be good, it discourages the elevation of virtuous examples. This is a shame, for the tradition has plenty. Luther was not only a theological genius, he was a man of tremendous courage. He rode into Worms prepared for a brutal end to his life, burned to death at a stake—eventually responding to the emperor with "Here I stand; I can do no other."[21] His colleague Philipp Melanchthon was likewise a man of great bravery and resolution, despite his reputation for being too timid. It was he who went into the streets to directly confront rioting students—who had earned a reputation for violence and even murder—even when it meant that a pike was brandished in his face.[22]

While both courageous, these two men were significantly different from one another in personality. Luther was the "wild boar" who rushed ahead recklessly, often needing to apologize later for his actions. Melanchthon had a tender conscience and was too worried about sinning. He could walk through life as on eggshells. And both had to learn and be corrected by the other. What a wonderful opportunity this friendship has for the gifted writer who could tell their story and inspire generations of readers!

The various written and stage productions of the life of John Newton, who wrote the beloved hymn "Amazing Grace," provide this same opportunity. From slave trader to Christian clergyman, his experience of

---

20. It was in the sixteenth century that the orthodox Lutherans initially condemned this phrase, after the Majorist Controversy (Cf. Bente, *Historical Introductions*). *Martyr's Mirror*, or *The Bloody Theatre* was published in the seventeenth century, at a time when some Lutheran Pietists were reconsidering this controversial statement.

21. Allegedly.

22. Scheible, "Luther and Melanchthon," 326.

forgiveness and tireless work as an abolitionist convey what is best and most essential in Christianity—the reception of this amazing grace and the active life of faith. And yet, his story is unfamiliar to most parishioners.

This entire literary-theological endeavor is exponentially more important for children, for whom a connection between academic theology and their own lives is rather difficult. C. S. Lewis is again a model of the communication of virtue. He wrote, "Since it is so likely that children will meet cruel enemies, let them at least have heard of brave knights and heroic courage."[23] These tales can become what Northrop Frye called "myths to live by" and "metaphors to live in."[24]

Inspiration to virtues of courage, fortitude, generosity, and compassion has been communicated through literature far more effectively than objective treatments of doctrine from the pulpit. And they can do so without compromising Luther's radical emphasis on grace. The ideal is presented, and it functions quite effectively as the law does in Luther's theology: to curb society's excesses, to reflect our own shortcomings, and demonstrate the life of faith.[25]

During the year I spent in an orthodox Lutheran seminary, I recall hearing one of my hyper-orthodox professors disparage the homiletics department as the "department of storytelling." While I have as much appreciation for good doctrine as anyone, I find it sad that he placed so little value on the tremendous tool of subjectivity, of indirect communication. Perhaps more than theology, it is storytelling that has the power to transform lives. And on the basis of my reading of the gospels, I suspect Jesus of Nazareth might feel the same.

Bibliography

Bente, F. *Historical Introductions to the Book of Concord*. St Louis: Concordia Publishing House, 1965.
Engelbrecht, Edward. *Friends of the Law*. St. Louis: Concordia Publishing, 2011.
Frye, Northrop. *The Double Vision*. Toronto: University of Toronto Press, 1991.

---

23. Lewis, *On Stories*, 39.

24. Frye, *The Double Vision*, 18.

25. The statement above suggests a third use of the law in Luther, a controversial position, but one which I happen to hold. Cf. Engelbrecht, *Friends of the Law*.

Kaufman, Geoff F. and Lisa K. Libby. "Changing Beliefs and Behavior through Experience-taking." *Journal of Personality and Social Psychology* 103/1 (2012) 1–19.

Kierkegaard, Søren. *The Moment and Late Writings*. Translated by Howard V. Hong and Edna H. Hong. Kierkegaard's Writings 23. Princeton: Princeton University Press, 1998.

———. *Concluding Unscientific Postscript to Philosophical Fragments*, Vol. 1. Translated by Howard V. Hong and Edna H. Hong. Kierkegaard's Writings 12. Princeton: Princeton University Press, 1992.

———. *Either/Or*. Translated by Howard V. Hong and Edna H. Hong. Kierkegaard's Writings 3–4. Princeton: Princeton University Press, 1987.

———. *Søren Kierkegaard's Journals and Papers*, edited by Howard V. Hong and Edna H. Hong. Bloomington: Indiana University Press, 1967–1978.

Kuethe, John George. "Kierkegaard, Poet of the Word." *Word and World* 3 (1983) 294–302.

Lewis, C. S. *On Stories, and Other Essays on Literature*. Edited by Walter Hooper. New York: Harcourt, 1983.

Luther, Martin. *Luther's Work*. 55 vols. Philadelphia and St. Louis: Fortress and Concordia, 1958–1986.

———. *Dr Martin Luther Werke*. 65 vols. Weimar: Böhlau, 1883–1993.

Melanchthon, Philipp. *Loci Communes Theologici* (1555). Translated by Clyde L. Manschrek. New York: Oxford University Press, 1965.

Richter, Matthias. *Gesetz und Heil: Eine Untersuchung zur Vorgeschichte und zum Verlauf des sogenannten Zweiten Antinomistischen Streits*. Forschungen zur Kirchen- und Dogmengeschichte 67. Göttingen: Vandenhoeck & Ruprecht, 1996.

Scheible, Heinz. "Luther and Melanchthon." *Lutheran Quarterly* 4 (1990) 317–39.

Spener, Philipp Jakob. *Philipp Jakob Spener Schriften*. Edited by Erich Beyreuther. Hildesheim: Olms, 1979.

Springer, Carl P. E. *Luther's Aesop*. Kirksville, MO: Truman State University Press, 2011.

8

Release from Torment

Finding Grace in Arthur Miller's After the Fall, John Osborne's Luther, and C. S. Lewis's Till We Have Faces

Elaine Lux

Drawing upon three diverse works that form a continuum of sorts, from secular, to theological, to experiential transformation, this paper explores the dual role of an uncertainty that can create torment within the soul and can open us to grace, as well. Arthur Miller's drama *After the Fall*, John Osborne's drama *Luther*, and C. S. Lewis's novel *Till We Have Faces* are strongly psychological in orientation, contain elements of Christian imagery, contain characters tormented by uncertainty, and demonstrate movement from torment toward grace; however, the role of uncertainty and the nature of grace differ in nuance and degree in the three works. Quentin, the protagonist in Miller's play *After the Fall*, finds his grace in a secular forgiveness based upon accepting "that we meet unblessed," not in an Eden of innocence but "after, after the Fall, after many, many deaths."[1] Martin Luther, the protagonist in *Luther*, finds his grace in a theological awakening based on biblical verses that set him free from

1. Miller, *After the Fall*, 79.

earning salvation by works but that still leave him a somewhat troubled and troubling figure. Orual, the protagonist in *Till We Have Faces*, finds her grace in meeting her god face to face at long last, through visions. In each case, grace involves the protagonist's receiving a forgiveness that is not earned by self-effort, and this unearned but received grace leads to an easing of the protagonist's inner torment.

As we examine the role of uncertainty in the movement toward grace in *After the Fall*, *Luther*, and *Till We Have Faces*, we will take into account the psychological orientation, the Christian imagery, the torment by uncertainty, and the nature of the grace found in each of these works, viewing each one through the redemptive lens of the story of Cupid and Psyche, the myth Lewis "retells" in *Till We Have* Faces, with special attention to the tasks of Psyche. The myth itself is often interpreted as allegorical of God's redemptive love. As Bulfinch explains, "The Greek name for a *butterfly* is Psyche, and the same word means the *soul*. There is no illustration of the immortality of the soul so striking and beautiful as the butterfly, bursting on brilliant wings" [from its deathlike cocoon]. Psyche, then, is the human soul, which is purified by sufferings and misfortunes" and lifted from death by the love of God.[2] I suggest, here, that the four humanly impossible tasks of Psyche, imposed on her by the goddess Venus, can be seen as maturation steps in an adult's journey to discover and be transformed by God's eternal love. Here are the tasks, as described in *The Golden Ass*, by Lucius Apuleius, whom Lewis refers to as a "'source,' not an 'influence' nor a 'model.'"[3] The first task is to sort a mountainous pile of tiny and sundry seeds into orderly piles of their own kind. Psyche is helped to do this by ants. The second task is to gather golden flax from a fierce flock of golden sheep. She is taught how to do this by a reed. The third task is to go to the highest mountain to gather a bowl of water from the river that feeds lower down into the River Styx. She is aided in this task by Jupiter's eagle. The fourth task is to go to the underworld to gather from Persephone a casket containing the secret of beauty. The condition is that Psyche is not allowed to look into the casket. She is taught how to accomplish this very complex task of going to the underworld by a talking tower. Indeed, each of the seemingly impossible tasks gets accomplished, except for the last detail of the final task. Psyche looks into the casket, which contains not the secret of beauty, but the

2. Bulfinch, *Bulfinch's Mythology*, 79.
3. Lewis, "Note," 313.

sleep of death. She faints dead, but, by the forgiving grace of Cupid, she is restored to life and set free to carry the casket to Venus. Cupid then intercedes with Jupiter for Psyche's life, and Psyche is, in fact, granted permission to be Cupid's bride and is granted immortality, as well.[4]

Task 1: Sorting through the Seeds of One's Life and Motives

Though it has spiritual components, too, the agony of uncertainty has to do in large part with psychological factors, in each of the works under consideration here. In particular, it is in this realm that the first task of sorting is most relevant and most time-consuming.

In Arthur Miller's *After the Fall*, the work's psychological orientation is woven into the very set and staging of the play, as well as into the inner psychological drama the play unfolds. The three-tiered stage represents the protagonist Quentin's mind, and "the action takes place in the mind, thought, and memory of Quentin."[5] The characters who move in and out of action as he thinks of them are, dramatically speaking, in his thoughts.

At the play's opening, and almost until the last moment's resolution, the protagonist's mind is torn by his uncertainty over whether or not he can commit himself to love again, as he has had two previous divorces. He grapples with his own lack of innocence in the failure of his two marriages. Connected to this guilt within Quentin is an external symbol: "a blasted stone tower of a German concentration camp" that "ris[es] above," and "dominat[es]" the set.[6] The tower serves as an ongoing reminder of the human capacity for brutality and betrayal.

Throughout the play, Quentin explores the meaning of his memories, in the context of the McCarthy era and the Holocaust, as he tries to work through the past, so as to be able to love in the present. The play's simulation of spontaneous memory associations is reminiscent of a therapy session. Quentin speaks to an unseen and unidentified Listener, just past the edge of the stage. The Listener may varyingly be construed as God, a friend, a therapist, or even another part of Quentin. In his foreword to the play, Miller interprets the Listener as "Quentin himself turned at

---

4. Apuleius, *The Golden Ass*, 75–113.
5. Miller, *After the Fall*, 5.
6. Ibid.

the edge of the abyss to look at his experience, his nature and his time in order to bring to light, to seize and—innocent no more—to forever guard against his own complicity with Cain, and the world's."[7] Regardless of how the individual audience members consciously interpret the Listener, the staging implicates the audience, too, in that role, for Quentin faces the audience as he addresses the invisible and silent Listener. Thus, the audience becomes a participant in what Stephen Marino calls "Quentin's psychic journey to maturity."[8]

In sorting through his psyche's associations, Quentin discovers that his relational imagery of betrayal was formed in his family of origin. As Marino observes, "in Quentin's seemingly aimless wanderings, the images consistently reinforce a return to a psychic childhood which magnifies his indecision."[9] For example, his mother used Quentin as an ally in her mockery of his father's illiteracy. She also tricked Quentin, by sending him out for a walk with the maid and sneaking away with Quentin's father and brother, to go on vacation. Even more harmful, in terms of the relational imagery of the play, is the betrayal inherent in name-calling and insult. Quentin's mother calls her husband Ike a "moron" and an "idiot."[10] This betrayal imagery is later echoed when Elsie, Quentin's friend's wife, calls her husband Lou "a moral idiot"[11] and when Quentin's first wife Louise says of Quentin, "What an idiot."[12] Quentin finds betrayal within himself when, wrestling with his second wife Maggie for the bottle of pills she is threatening to kill herself with, he finds himself "lung[ing] for Maggie's throat," saying "You won't kill me! You won't kill me!"[13] Clearly, Quentin's psychological torment has to do with his most personal past, but it also has to do with his wider life experience: the betrayal he has seen among fellow Communists during the McCarthy Era and with the horror of the Holocaust.

In John Osborne's *Luther*, too, the psychological sorting out of motives is important to the development of the protagonist's characterization. Martin Luther's sorting through his childhood issues, issues which

---

7. Miller, "A Foreward by the Author," 32.
8. Marino, "Language and Metaphor," 46.
9. Ibid.
10. Miller, *After the Fall*, 23.
11. Ibid., 28.
12. Ibid., 30.
13. Ibid., 77.

linger into his adulthood, serves artistically to emphasize his torment of body by constipation, of emotions by his fearfulness about his father's disapproval, and of soul by the numerous sins he feels driven to confess. The implication of Osborne's play is that Martin's constipation has to do with his being stuck in a psychological stage, perhaps at the anal stage of psychosocial development Erik Erikson identifies as the stage of *Autonomy versus Shame and Doubt*.[14] Osborne makes clear that Luther's relationship with his parents, especially with his father, consumes Martin for a large part of the play. His desire to please his father, despite his rebellion against his father's opinions regarding Martin's choice of a religious vocation and celibacy, forms the emotional underbelly of the play. The dramatic irony of his father Hans's lament, in which he talks about how important his son might have been in society had he not chosen to be a monk, emphasizes both Martin's hunger for his father's approval and Hans's disapproval of his son's personality and choices. Martin's primary emotional task of sorting through his longings and motives has to do with his relationship with his father. Ultimately, Martin moves into a life that his father approves of: a life in which he marries and has children.

In addition to his childhood issues, Martin's confessions in the monastic setting are a form of sorting through, too. In their poetic, internal quality, Martin's tormented confessions contrast to the confessions of his fellow monks. Martin confesses "murmurings in [his] heart" rather than deeds like "omit[ing] to shave." Martin's cries echo but go even beyond *Hamlet*'s longing to be released from his flesh: "If my flesh would leak and dissolve, and I could live as bone, plucked bone and brain, warm hair and a bony heart, if I were all bone, I could brandish myself without terror."[15] Martin's sorting through his internal sins foreshadows his later questioning of what is going on within the Catholic Church and his later unleashing of rhetorical power.

It is true, as Charles Marowitz points out, that the characters of the Osborne's Brecht-influenced play "are involved with the intellectual implications of their behavior rather than with the blood and bone of their situations."[16] However, the use of formal historical tableaux and powerful language effectively highlights the sorting through that leads to shifts in Luther's level of confidence in himself and makes salient the strength of

---

14. Erikson, *Identity and the Life Cycle*, 67–77.
15. Osborne, *Luther*, 22, 21.
16. Marowitz, "The Ascension," 177.

Luther's inner conviction, in that he, a weak and self-declaiming monk, afraid even of his own father, now stands against the high officials of the Catholic Church in politically-charged and life-threatening encounters.

In C. S. Lewis's *Till We Have Faces*, as in *After the Fall*, the structure and content of the work and the sorting-through the seeds of the protagonist's life and motives are one. With the exception of a priest's note at the end of it, the entire first-person novel consists of the written musings of Orual, the Queen of Glome, as she accuses the gods of unfairness to her and, in the process, discovers her own selfish and jealous nature—and ultimately discovers the love of God. Using the myth of Cupid and Psyche, Lewis retells the story through the mind and feelings of one of the jealous sisters. In her writings, Orual deals with the recurrent agony caused by her perception of great injustice dealt to her by the gods, who not only have made her ugly and have taken her younger sister Psyche from her, but then have misrepresented Orual as a jealous sister in the sacred story that has emerged from Psyche's life. In her writing, Orual deals with the psychic torment of her relationship with her father, along with chronicling the tasks she accomplishes in her life as Queen after her father dies. She vents her anger at the way the gods left her with uncertainty about their true nature, blaming them for her wrong action and resultant inner torment for having caused the banishment of Psyche by her lover.

Through the sorting-out process of writing, Orual learns that what she perceived as selfless love for her sister Psyche really had to do with possessiveness and the need to be needed and how she, in some ways, sucked the life out of others who loved and served her faithfully. In Part II, a much briefer section that she writes to clear up the misunderstandings in Part I, Orual confides her reason for writing the second part: "Since I cannot mend the book, I must add to it. To leave it as it was would be to die perjured. I know so much more than I did about the woman who wrote it. What began the change was the very writing itself. [...] The change which the writing wrought in me (and of which I did not write) was only a beginning—only to prepare me for the gods' surgery. They used my own pen to probe my wound."[17]

One of the visions Orual has toward the end of her life shows the task of digging and sorting in a symbolic form. In the vision, her father is again alive and forces her into the Pillar Room, the place where official business was conducted, commanding her to dig with him. They

---

17. Lewis, *Till We Have Faces*, 253–254.

break up "the paved floor" and she is forced to throw herself down the hole they dig, along with him. This time it is a smaller Pillar Room they are in, and it is made of "raw earth." Again, Orual and her father "dig a hole in the center of the room." The labor is very hard. He forces her again to jump down the hole, and this time they are "in yet another Pillar Room; but this [is] of living rock, and water trickle[s] down the walls of it."[18] These labors represent her sorting efforts, her digging with her pen, to face her own inner torments, motivations, and needs. This third Pillar Room, however, foreshadows the grace that comes to her through her subsequent visions, for the solid rock and the trickling water suggest hope and life to come.

Task 2: Gathering Golden Flax—Ceasing to Struggle

Psyche learns from the reed a way to accomplish the second task without head-on confrontation with the dangerous sheep. So, too, Quentin learns from his current love, Holga, to accept the need for patient wisdom in life's uncertainties. The psychological resolution for Quentin's fear about making a commitment in his relationship with Holga is related to his learning to accept imperfection and the need for some degree of separateness in relationships. Previously, when his first wife Louise tells him "I am a separate person," he protests, "When you've finally become a separate person, what the hell is there?"[19] However, after two divorces, he works his way to accepting Holga's image of embracing a life that is imperfect and, in many ways, nonsensical. This acceptance is encapsulated in a dream Holga shares: "I dreamed I had a child, and even in the dream I saw it was my life, and it was an idiot, and I ran away. But it always crept onto my lap again, clutched at my clothes. Until I thought, if I could kiss it, whatever in it was my own, perhaps I could sleep. And I bent to its broken face, and it was horrible . . . But I kissed it. I think one must finally take one's life in one's arms, Quentin."[20]

As he waits for Holga at the airport, Quentin shares his resolution of his issues with the Listener. However, the resolution itself is nuanced by its questions: "Is the knowing all? To know, and even happily, that we meet unblessed; not in some garden of wax fruit and painted trees, that lie

18. Ibid., 274, 275.
19. Miller, *After the Fall*, 29, 30.
20. Ibid., 17–18.

of Eden, but after, after the Fall, after many, many deaths. Is the knowing all?—And the wish to kill is never killed, but with some gift of courage one may look into its face when it appears, and with a stroke of love—as to an idiot in the house—forgive it; again and again . . ." Quentin is not certain this is enough, but he is willing to step forward into life again. As the play ends, "his life [in the form of the on-stage actors] follow[s] him as he climbs toward Holga."[21]

As part of learning to live, Quentin confronts his messianic complex and relinquishes the lie that he can be anyone's savior. Quentin's self-aggrandizing relational images are traceable to his relationship with his mother, who tells him, regarding his birth, "And I saw a star, and it got brighter and brighter, and brighter! And suddenly it fell, like some great man had died, and you were being pulled out of me to take his place, and be a light, a light in the world!"[22] In one scene, after a client named Felice has come by to thank and bless him for his role in encouraging her, and has now left, he spreads his arms out, reaching horizontally across to two light fixtures. He recognizes Felice gave him "the power to change her! And you oughtn't have that power unless you're full of love!"[23] This image of crucifixion coalesces with his telling Maggie, his second wife, about Lazarus, whom God raised "from the dead. But He's God, see . . . and God's power is love without limit. But when a man dares reach for that . . . he is only reaching for the power.—(*Aware*)—Yes!—Whoever goes to save another person with the lie of limitless love is not a lover, he is . . ."[24] Quentin's second task allows him, metaphorically speaking, to gather enough golden wool to live by, and he accepts the truth he perceives that he needs to live in an unblessed world, but one in which trust is still possible.

In Osborne's *Luther*, Martin finds grace much as Psyche comes to the golden wool. He ceases struggling to earn forgiveness. In recognizing that his deeds can never be good enough to earn God's favor, he rests in the scripture that people are saved through grace by faith, and not by works. He finds this insight worth all he goes through as his journey leads him forward. In addition, he rests so fully in the protection of supporters

21. Ibid., 79.
22. Ibid., 46.
23. Ibid., 53.
24. Ibid., 74.

who hide him safely that he is able to continue to write his biblical exegeses even while in hiding.

In C. S. Lewis's *Till We Have Faces*, Orual, too, discovers that she cannot beautify her own soul, no matter how hard she tries. However, through her visions, she comes to see the beauty of God, and she too begins to gather the precious wool of unearned grace. She sees that human efforts to understand the divine fall short. She becomes conscious of the mystery of God, and she lays down her resistance.

Task 3: Getting Water That Flows to the River Styx: Substitution

In the Cupid and Psyche myth, the third task, ascending the steep and treacherous mountain to fill a bowl with the water of death, could not be done by Psyche without substitution: the eagle of the gods had to do this task for her. Directions and hints on how to do it would not be enough.

This third developmental task is not accomplished by Quentin, as he never encounters divine assistance in his coping with the bitter waters of his life. Thus, we move on to Luther. Historically speaking, as reported by biographer Martin Marty, the person Luther suffered from *Anfechtungen*, anguishing trials of grave doubt. Because he found himself sometimes unable to reconcile the contrast between a God of thunder and a warm and inviting God, Luther found himself turning more deeply to God to lift him up. He came to see God's hand even in this "delicious despair": delicious, he said, because "such despair offered sinners opportunities to grow in faith. The assaults [on their faith] robbed them of all certainty, until they found no place to go except to the God of mercy and grace."[25] In Osborne's play, as in the case of Luther's life, such anxiety and uncertainty remain with Luther even later on, as do his bowel troubles. In the play, he becomes a troubled and troubling figure, not simply because of *Anfechtungen*, but because of the major decisions his increasing prominence places him in a position to make. The Luther who tells the nobles to put down the peasants' rebellion at any cost, even at cost of their spilled blood, is an enigmatic figure. He stands for what he perceives as truth: that one cannot serve Christ by violence, and yet he seems to turn against the democratic impulse that has caused him to fight to give the Word of God to the common man. The knight's rubbing Luther's robe

---

25. Marty, *Martin Luther*, 23–24.

with the blood of a dead peasant is a very powerful way to portray some of the controversial parts of Martin's influence.

In Act III, Martin's spiritual advisor Staupitz both acknowledges the enormity of what Luther has done and cautions Martin: "You've taken Christ away from the low mumblings and soft voices and jeweled gowns and the tiaras and put Him back where He belongs. In each man's soul. We owe so much to you. All I beg of you is not to be too violent. In spite of everything, of everything you've said and shown us, there *were* men, *some* men who did live holy lives here once. Don't—don't believe you, only you are right."[26] Yet, despite the lurking danger of the power he achieves, Luther has put his trust in Christ's substitutionary atonement on the cross.

In Lewis's *Till We Have Faces*, the third task is accomplished metaphorically, through what Orual sees in the moving pictures painted on walls of a chamber that her now-deceased tutor the Fox shows her in a vision. Orual begins to grasp the mystery of an ongoing interaction in which "human beings flow in and out of each other, and even merge with the gods."[27] In this way, Orual comes to see that she has been helping Psyche by bearing some of her task-linked burden. When Orual, gazing at the image connected with the third task, marvels that Psyche can seem "almost happy" as she seeks to fill her bowl with the "water of death," Orual's former tutor, explains: "Another bore nearly all the anguish."[28] For Orual, perceiving how her efforts have been instrumental in Psyche's achieving her tasks becomes a marvelous gift of grace. Chad Walsh points out that the ideas in the vision section of the novel show "the obvious influence of Charles Williams, with his doctrine of substitution or coinherence." And, as Walsh says, Christian symbolism abounds here, but subtly: "The reader scarcely notices it at first but a glimmer of Christianity is beginning to infiltrate into the rational world of the Greeks and the intuitive wisdom of the old pagans. This foreshadowing of the supreme revelation that lies perhaps several centuries in the future is done quietly and adroitly. There is simply the growing sense that neither the Fox's rationalism nor the bloody cult of Ungit is adequate to make sense of the insights Orual has so painfully arrived at."[29]

---

26. Osborne, *Luther*, 122.
27. Walsh, *The Literary Legacy*, 171.
28. Lewis, *Till We Have Faces*, 300–301.
29. Walsh, *The Literary Legacy*, 171–72.

Task Four: Descending to the Underworld and the Experience of God's Resurrecting Love

In Osborne's *Luther*, Martin seems to turn to God for comfort; however, perhaps because he is not of a mystical bent, Martin never completes the fourth task of Psyche: that of journeying to the underworld of self and then experiencing a face-to-face meeting with his Savior. Naturally, neither does Quentin reach this stage in *After the Fall*, in which Quentin makes peace with being able to live more wisely as a human in the human world but does not experience any sense of a divinity's presence in his life. Perhaps it is the mytho-fictional nature of *Till We Have Faces* that allows Lewis to bring Orual, through visions, into the completion of the fourth task. She gets a glimpse of herself in glorious transformation; she, like Psyche, is now a bride of the god. Orual's visions before she dies allow her to see her savior face to face and to write about what she has seen. She dies in the midst of writing, in fact. In this way, Lewis's work is the only one of the three in which the protagonist's uncertainty and torment become fully transformed within the cycle of the Cupid and Psyche myth.

It takes Orual until nearly the end of her life to recognize her own psychologically needy and self-seeking behavior and to be done with the anger and torment aroused by her stumbling upon the temple in which the priest tells her the story of Istra (another name for Psyche), the event that triggers her outrage that the sacred story has taken a form that is all wrong—one that attributes jealousy to the sisters of Istra. In her final vision, Orual is reunited with Psyche, who gives Orual the casket of beauty she obtained in the land of the dead. Psyche now tells Orual that the day has at last come "when you and I [. . .] meet in my house and no cloud between us."[30]

Thus, at the close of the novel, we most clearly see the transformational, redemptive myth of Cupid and Psyche blended with the transformational, redemptive aspects of Christianity, though Christ is never mentioned per se in the novel. The god is coming, and Orual understands at last that "the earth and stars and sun, all that was or will be, [exist] for his sake." With the god coming to greet them, Orual "cast[s] down her eyes" to see in the water the reflection of "Two Psyches. [. . .] both beautiful. [. . .] 'You also are Psyche, came a great voice.'" Orual's uncertainty and torment about the true nature of the gods is over, for she has certainty now: "I ended my first book with the words *no answer*. I know

30. Lewis, *Till We Have Faces*, 306.

now, Lord, why you utter no answer. You are yourself the answer. Before your face questions die away."[31]

The uncertainty that can cause torment is not unique to these three works. As Madeleine L'Engle writes, in *Walking on Water: Reflections on Faith and Art*, "We are trapped in un-knowing. Nothing is certain." It is natural, then, for literature to "[deal] with this inability to see around the corner, and the disastrous results when we play at being God. [. . .]"[32]

After the Fall, *Luther*, and *Till We Have Faces* allow us to experience the torment of uncertainty and the movement toward grace in a variety of ways. Although Aristotle's term *mimesis* is most often taken to mean life-like *imitation* or *representation* in art, Keith Oatley points out, citing Stephen Halliwell's research, that "the Greek word, *mimesis* also had a second family of meanings [. . .]. This second set of meanings—of *mimesis-as-dream*—has to do with world-making, with model-building, with imagination, with recognizing what goes on beneath the surface."[33] The beneath-the-surface world into which these well-honed works of literature invite us can help us to move beneath the surface of ordinary faith-life experience, even as dreams invite us to a deepened meaning just beyond our ordinary consciousness.

And if we look at the soul's torment of uncertainty as an impulse to narrative in the way Arthur Frank, in *The Wounded Storyteller*, looks at bodily suffering, we may find ourselves agreeing with Frank's observation that "the self must continue to wrestle and continue to be wounded in order to rediscover the ground it now stands on as sacred. *To be is to wrestle with God.*"[34] To draw on images from *After the Fall*, *Luther*, and *Till We Have Faces*, perhaps, when trials of doubt come to us, we may accept doubt's presence in our faith-lives and even learn to embrace the fruitfulness of times of doubt, as Miller's Holga and, ultimately, Quentin embrace the idiot child of their lives; perhaps we may push ever closer to God's word, studying it, claiming it, standing on it, even as Osborne's Luther does when he feels the buffets of the world and of his own inner doubt; perhaps we may move even deeper into meditation on God's mystery, as Lewis's Orual does, gaining a glimpse of the transforma-

---

31. Ibid., 307–8.
32. L'Engle, *Walking on Water*, 152.
33. Oatley, *Such Stuff as Dreams*, 12–13.
34. Frank, *The Wounded Storyteller*, 182.

tional process we are undergoing and the glory that is before us and, even now, forming in us.

In contemplating the well-known biblical account of Jacob wrestling with the angel, Frank asks an interesting question: "Is Jacob wrestling a blessing out of the angel, or is the angel wrestling the petition for a blessing out of Jacob?"[35] In like manner, we may want to ask: Are we wrestling a blessing out of our torment of uncertainty, or is God, through our trials of doubt, wrestling the petition for blessing out of us?

Bibliography

Apuleius, Lucius. *The Golden Ass*. Translated by P. G. Walsh. New York: Oxford University Press, 1994.

Bulfinch, Thomas. *Bulfinch's Mythology: A Modern Abridgment by Edmund Fuller*. New York: Dell, 1959.

Erikson, Erik H. *Identity and the Life Cycle*. New York: Norton, 1980.

Frank, Arthur. *The Wounded Storyteller*. Chicago: University of Chicago Press, 1997.

L'Engle, Madeleine. *Walking on Water: Reflections on Faith and Art*. New York: North Point Press / Farrar, Straus and Giroux, 1996.

Lewis, C. S. "Note." In *Till We Have Faces*, 311–13. New York: Harvest/Harcourt Brace Jovanovich, 1956.

———. *Till We Have Faces*. New York: Harvest/Harcourt Brace Jovanovich, 1956.

Marino, Stephen A. "Language and Metaphor in Arthur Miller's 'After the Fall.'" *South Atlantic Review* 70/2 (2005) 41–56.

Marowitz, Charles. "The Ascension of John Osborne." *The Tulane Drama Review* 7/2 (1962) 175–79.

Marty, Martin. *Martin Luther: A Life*. New York: Penguin, 2004.

Miller, Arthur. *After the Fall*. New York: Dramatist Play Service, 1964.

———. "'A Foreword by the Author.' *After the Fall*: Complete Text of the New Play." *Saturday Evening Post* 237/4 (1964) 32.

Oatley, Keith. *Such Stuff as Dreams: The Psychology of Fiction*. Hoboken, NJ: Wiley-Blackwell, 2011.

Osborne, John. *Luther*. New York: Signet/New American Library, 1961.

Walsh, Chad. *The Literary Legacy of C. S. Lewis*. New York: Harcourt Brace Jovanovich, 1979.

---

35. Ibid., 181.

9

Luther's Theology of the Cross
Redemptive Suffering and Vivian Bearing's Death in Margaret Edson's play, Wit

Anthony Grasso

For those who may not be familiar with it, Edson's Pulitzer Prize winning play offers a stark look at the treatment and death of Dr. Vivian Bearing, specialist in the metaphysical poetry of John Donne. Vivian, alone and in her early fifties, is diagnosed with terminal, metastatic ovarian cancer. Faced with the difficulties of her pain and the probability of her untimely death, she agrees to participate in a research project testing a new and powerful treatment for her cancer, run by Dr. Kelekian, prominent in the field, and his research assistant, Dr. Jason Posner, who also happens to be one of Vivian's former students from a class on Seventeenth-Century Poetry. In addition to an uncompromising treatment of death, *Wit*, as its title suggests, looks carefully at Donne's and Vivian's fascination with language, as well as the ironic humor contained in verbal conceit, as a means of coping with and transforming the experience of human suffering. While not overtly religious, one can see much in the play that is theological because of its content and Edson's allusions to Donne and to the existence of a life beyond.

In one of the most jarring moments of the play, Jason attempts to revive Vivian at the end, in spite of the DNR (Do Not Resuscitate) order that she had arranged to have in place through Susie, her intensive care nurse. The conflict of this moment is heightened because the audience is aware that Vivian has consented to be a part of a long-term study on the experimental cancer drug she has been receiving. One has to imagine the scene and that overwhelming sense of panic which Jason feels as he witnesses Vivian in her demise. He leaps across the bed onto her to call in the code from the phone on her nightstand. Vivian is laid out, seeming comatose, still hooked to the morphine drip with wires emanating from her skeletal frame. The doctor's body is splayed across hers, arms outstretched reaching for the phone. Her vertical body crossed horizontally by the doctor's is an image which creates the shape of a cross. Whatever religious imagery we see fleetingly is immediately undone by nurse Susie's screaming at him *not* to call in a code, because there's a DNR which he knew about, and that Vivian did not want to be revived: "Hasn't she been through enough?" She screams, until Jason, normally unaffected by the emotion of dealing with the terminally ill, becomes unhinged and breaks down into tears, screaming "I MADE A MISTAKE," and repeating, "Oh, God . . . Oh, God" (84–85).[1]

I would suggest that Edson, from her experience of living at a convent with Catholic sisters for a time, was familiar enough with Christian topoi to know what the cross means and to be aware of its implications. More importantly, the idea of taking up or bearing one's cross, in the obvious reference to Vivian's surname, is an authorial choice, no doubt based upon the reference in scripture: "Jesus said to his disciples, 'Whoever wishes to come after me must deny himself, take up his cross, and follow me. For whoever wishes to save his life will lose it, but whoever loses his life for my sake will find it. What profit would there be for one to gain the whole world and forfeit his life?"[2]

Edson seems fully aware of the power of the cross in Donne and certainly in Vivian's life as well, even though she might not label it as such. The cross has been called by Luther and other theologians "a judgment,"[3]

---

1. Page references to Margaret Edson's, *Wit* appear in the main text.

2. Matt 16:24–26 (New American Bible).

3. Several of Luther's sermons and treatises refer to death as a "judgment." For example, Paul Althaus, cites from Luther's Lectures on Psalm 90 and other topics, delivered between 1534 and 1535, that he saw human death ". . . not as the result of a natural process created by God. Rather death is 'laid upon him and executed through

and as both the gospel text and the play suggest, it requires a conscious and free choice to enter into. And it serves as a fitting symbol in this play to think of both the form and theological content of the cross as involving a number of judgments, or moments of decision, in the lives of both Vivian and Jason, whose paths intersect on two significant occasions. The play's final scenes offer the cross, or its suffering and vulnerability, as the main differentiation between the experience of theological salvation which Vivian receives, in Luther's sense of the cross as judgment, and the missed opportunity that this spiritual moment of Vivian's passing ends up being for Jason.

Within Luther's theology the cross was the foundation from which his understanding of Christianity emerges, as was captured in the *Heidelberg Disputation* in the phrase, "The cross alone is our theology" ("Crux sola est nostra theologia").[4] Alister McGrath, a respected commentator on Luther's theology, has identified his understanding of the "theology of the cross" as: (1) a revelation, which (2) must be regarded as "indirect and concealed" because the God revealed in the passion and cross of Christ is not immediately recognizable as God. Only those who have faith understand the true meaning of the cross. He quotes Luther as saying that the theologian of the cross recognizes the "crucified and hidden God ('Deus crucifixus et absconditus'), who is not merely present in human suffering but actively works through it."[5]

As the play implies, and Vivian's experience bears out, every human life comes to many points which call for decision. Vivian's choice of profession and her manner of functioning as an educator were choices she made to emulate those who were her mentors, at least insofar as she understood them at the time. Those choices came with consequences for the kind of teacher she became. At the midpoint of her life and career she has come to another major crossroad, the question of how to respond to the diagnosis of ovarian cancer. Vivian's central academic study of Donne's theological poems provides a direct experiential link; however, she views her work on the Holy Sonnets—replete as they are with issues of mortality, faith, and afterlife—as mainly involved with cracking the verbal code of Donne's "intellectual conceits." In so doing she had hoped

---

God's wrath,'" referring to the judgment of humanity after the Fall from Eden (*Theology*, 403). Our relationship to death has to be understood within the relationship between God and man, according to Luther.

4. *Martin Luther Werke*, 5.176.32–3.
5. McGrath, *Luther's Theology*, 149–50, 175.

to impress her mentor, E. M. Ashford, professor of seventeenth-century literature. Having called Vivian in to discuss the problem of her reliance on the wrong edition of Donne's poems, Ashford comments:

> Do you think the punctuation of the last line of this sonnet is merely an insignificant detail? The sonnet begins with the valiant struggle with death, calling on all forces of intellect and drama to vanquish the enemy but it is ultimately about overcoming the seemingly insuperable barriers separating life, death, eternal life ... In the edition you chose this profoundly simple meaning is sacrificed to hysterical punctuation. And Death—*capital D*—shall be no more *semi-colon*. Death—*capital D*—thou shalt die—*exclamation point*! Gardner's edition of the holy sonnets returns to the Westmoreland manuscript source of 1610—not for sentimental reasons, I assure you, but because Helen Gardner is a *scholar*. It reads: And death shall be no more, *comma*, Death, thou shalt die ... Nothing but a breath—a comma—separates life from life everlasting. It is very simple really. With the original punctuation restored, death is no longer something to act out on the stage, with exclamation points. It's a comma, a pause. This way, the *uncompromising* way, one learns something from the poem, wouldn't you say? Life, death. Soul, God. Past, present. Not insuperable barriers, not semicolons, just a comma.
>
> *V*: Life, death ... I see (Standing). It's a metaphysical conceit. It's wit! I'll go back to the library and rewrite the paper—
>
> *E. M.*: (Standing emphatically) It is *not wit*, Miss Bearing. It is truth (*walking around the desk to her*). The paper's not the point.
>
> *Vivian*: It isn't?
>
> *E. M.*: (*Tenderly*) Vivian. You're a bright young woman. Use your intelligence. Don't go back to the library. Go out. Enjoy yourself with your friends. Hmm?
>
> *V*: (*As she gradually returns to the hospital*) I, ah, went outside. The sun was very bright. I, ah, walked around, past the ... There were students on the lawn, talking about nothing, laughing. The insuperable barrier between one thing and another is ... just a comma? Simple human truth, uncompromising scholarly standards? They're *connected*. I just couldn't ... I went back to the library. Anyway. All right. Significant contributions to knowledge. Eight cycles of chemotherapy. Give me the full dose, the full dose every time (14–16).

It has taken Vivian half a lifetime to realize that she had missed Ashford's point on both counts. She wasn't able to make the connection between Donne's experience and insight as metaphysical truth, rather than simply being a clever conceit about what separates the finite from the eternal. More than a mental game of wit or something to fear, death could be seen as a natural pause before the next phase of life which Christianity posits. Ashford hints that Vivian needs to learn to understand the "truth" of Donne's insights in human, as well as in intellectual, terms. Good scholarship is required but in order to comprehend life and its intricacies in a deeper way, we can't live it solely "from the neck up." Unless we engage in the emotional enterprise of rubbing shoulders, working with and laughing alongside others, how to love or to be loved, everything else is meaningless.

By opting for the library to achieve her dream of academic success, Vivian had missed the opportunity to fulfill her human potential. Ironically, she'd not been able to deal with the theological point that Donne had dwelt upon and which Prof. Ashford had called a "truth," that the cessation of life is but a "comma," a partial caesura. Perhaps owing to her father's sudden death when she was young, she dared not risk another emotional attachment or to think too deeply about death. And although she published widely on Donne, becoming a recognized scholar of his sonnets, Vivian reveals little excitement about her achievement, saying: "My book, entitled *Made Cunningly*, remains an immense success, in paper as well as in cloth. In it, I devote one chapter to a thorough examination of each sonnet, discussing every word in extensive detail . . . I summarize previous critical commentary on the text and offer my own analysis. It is exhaustive" (19). Vivian's description of her life's work is remarkably devoid of emotion, suggesting that she knows something is missing. In fact, it appears to be as exhausting a venture as it was "exhaustive," and not such a labor of love as one might expect. Matter of fact in tone, her description parallels the interchanges she has with hospital staff, doctors, and technicians, about to commence her chemotherapy treatments; they ask both intimate and vital questions in the same tone one might use when asking whether a person wished to take her coffee with cream.

Her sense of emptiness becomes all the more poignant when she encounters Dr. Posner, a "clinical fellow" in the medical oncology branch working with Dr. Kelekian, her oncologist and the major researcher. We discover from Kelekian's diagnosis that Vivian suffers from stage four ovarian cancer, which he terms "insidious" in the medical sense, but which she immediately translates into the darker undertones that the word conveys. Jason, as antiseptic as his mentor, must create his own medical history of the new patient. Before he begins, he reminds Vivian, who clearly doesn't recall him, that he:

> . . . was an undergraduate at the U. I took your course in 17th Century Poetry.
>
> *V*: You did?
>
> *J*: Yes, I thought it was excellent.
>
> *V*: Thank you. Were you an English major?
>
> *J*: No, Biochemistry. But you can't get into medical school unless you're well-rounded. And I made a bet with myself that I could get an A in the three hardest courses on campus.
>
> *Susie*: How'd ya do, Jace?
>
> *J*: Success.
>
> *V*: Really? (*Doubtful*).
>
> *J*: A minus. It was a very tough course (21–22).

We not only see Vivian's assessment that none of her students could achieve an "A" grade in her course, but we also learn that Jason is the medical version of his former teacher: a cerebral, socially awkward overachiever. The course was for him a challenge in order to better prepare for the rigors of medical school. It seems that nothing of Donne's powerful comment on doubt, faith, or his struggles with death, had much impact on Jason either.

During the interview, the same tone of emotional distance prevails as the facts of Vivian's life are summed up in a minimalist catalog:

> *J*: How old are you?
>
> *V*: Fifty.
>
> *J*: Are you married?
>
> *V*: No.
>
> *J*: Are your parents living?
>
> *V*: No.
>
> *J*: How and when did they die?

> V: My father, suddenly, when I was 20, of a heart attack. My mother, slowly, when I was forty-one and forty-two, of cancer. Breast cancer.
>
> J: Cancer?
>
> V: Breast cancer.
>
> J: I see, any siblings?
>
> V: No.
>
> J: Well, that about does it for your life history.
>
> V: Yes, that's all there is to my life history (23–24).

This passage is almost as hard to digest as the original diagnosis. Vivian admits to having no family, no love interest, nor anybody in her life; she clings only to her reputation as a "tough" professor. And now Vivian is faced, not only with terminal cancer, but with a former student who must administer her pelvic exam which, as Vivian describes it, "was thoroughly degrading—and I use that term deliberately—but I could not have imagined the depths of humiliation that . . ." (31). Here she interrupts her speech to vomit again. The sarcastic descriptions used about her treatment sum it up: "discomfort" in exams; the "agony" of proctosigmoidoscopy; the "embarrassment" of wearing two hospital gowns all day long; and "watching myself go bald" is, she says, "highly educational. I am learning to suffer" (31). Within this ironically delivered line lies the key to the play's theology.

While Vivian is initially appalled by everything she endures during her treatment and hospitalization, eventually she comes to understand that she must embrace her suffering, in order to experience emotions she had avoided for much of her life. Jason, her accidental student, who had inadvertently found in Vivian a professional mentor, reveals the same tendency toward intellectual pride. He is as consumed with research and the notoriety he hopes it will attain for him as Vivian had been in her quest to "conquer" Donne's wit and his poetic conceits. Edson would have us see that, if they are to develop into full humanity and be "saved," which is to understand what is needed to pass from this life to the next, any suffering they will endure is both essential and ultimately life-giving.

In one crucial flashback Vivian faces the audience recalling how she dealt with her students:

V: in this sonnet what is the principal poetic device? I'll give you a hint. It has nothing to do with football. What propels this sonnet?

S1: I—um . . .

V: (*speaking to audience*) did I say (*tenderly*) "You are 19 years old. You are so young you don't know a sonnet from a steak sandwich." (*Pause*). By no means.

(*Sharply to student*) you can come to class prepared, or you can excuse yourself from this class, this department and this University. Do not think for a moment that I will tolerate anything in between. (*To the audience defensively*) I was teaching him a lesson.

(*She walks away from the students, then turns and addresses the class*)

So we have another instance of John Donne's agile wit at work; not so much *resolving* the issues of life and God, but *reveling* in their complexity.

S2: But why?

V: Why what?

S2: Why does Donne make everything so complicated? (*The other students laugh in agreement*). No really, *why*?

V: What do you think?

S2: I think it's like he's hiding, I think he's really confused. I don't know maybe he's scared, so he hides behind all this complicated stuff, hides behind this *wit* . . . Well, if he's trying to figure out God, and the meaning of life, and big stuff like that, why does he keep running away, you know? (59–61).

There is obvious student insight here which Vivian opts not to pursue because the comment strikes too close for comfort. Donne's speaker was not alone in running from God and life; Vivian had spent her life doing so. Her emphasis on Donne's verbal acuity hardly accounted for the depth of struggle in which the speaker of those poems had engaged. However, it did fit her recollection of her father's love of language, recalled in the flashback from her fifth birthday, when he taught her the meaning of the word, "soporific" (41–43), an event which influenced and symbolized her vocational choice.

There were moments when Donne's speaker had embraced the truth of God's love and his conquest in the cross and resurrection even of death itself, paraphrasing Paul in his own Holy Sonnet X. Yet Vivian focuses solely on the complexity of his language and can only respond to such claims from students harshly because they challenge her feelings. She retreats to the realm of the intellect to forestall dealing with her own pain and with questions of a religious or spiritual nature. Donne's "wit" becomes her cover and his language the cloak which neither does full justice to the poetry, nor allows her to account for the depth of feeling that guided the speaker, and likely the poet, on his spiritual journey. In another flashback Vivian recalls a student who is seeking a paper extension. She responds sarcastically:

> V: Don't tell me. Your grandmother died.
>
> S: You knew.
>
> V: It was a guess.
>
> S: I have to go home.
>
> V: Do what you will but the paper is due when it is due.
>
> V: (*to audience*) I don't know. I feel so much—what is the word? I look back, I see those scenes, and I . . ." (63).

Vivian's chemo-befuddled brain can't see quite through to identifying her shame and guilt over such treatment of her students, yet we sense the strong emotion in her inability to find the words to admit it. Because of her suffering, Vivian has now been brought to the point of losing words and of experiencing the raw emotion of her humanity. She finally emerges from behind language to dwell in the vulnerability from which she had, for most of her life, sought to protect herself. Ironically, her father's death, at a deep psychological level, may have driven her toward Donne's poems on the subject. The retreat into Donne's intellect soothed her own, enabling her to avoid the turmoil she must have felt at being left abandoned by his untimely passing.

Once the exterior defenses of her pride and intellect had been cracked, Vivian began to see how much she depended upon and really needed the simple, caring Nurse Susie. At one point near to the end, when Vivian feels the sting of her isolation, she intentionally pinches her line to bring in the nurse.

V: I was awake.

S: You were? What's the trouble, sweetheart?

V: (*to the audience, aroused*) Do not think for a minute that anyone calls me "sweetheart." But then I allowed it. (*To Susie*) Oh, I don't know.

S: You can't sleep?

V: No, I just kept thinking.

S: If you do that too much, you can get kind of confused.

V: I know. I can't figure things out. I'm in a *quandary*, having these *doubts*.

S: What you're doing is very hard.

V: Hard things are what I like best.

S: It's not the same. It's like out of control, isn't it?

V: (*Crying, in spite of herself*) I'm scared.

S: (*Stroking her*) Oh honey, of course you are. It's alright. I know. It hurts. I know. It's alright. Do you want a tissue? It's alright (silence). Vivian, would you like a popsicle?

V: (*Pulling herself together*). The epithelial cells in my G.I. tract have been killed by the chemo. The cold popsicle feels good; it's something I can digest, and it helps keep you hydrated. (*To audience*) For your information. (*Susie returns with an orange two-stick popsicle. Vivian unwraps it and breaks it in half.*)

V: Here.

S: Sure?

V: Yes.

S: Thanks. (*Susie sits on the commode by the bed. Silence*). When I was a kid we used to get these from a truck. The man would come around and ring his bell and we'd all run over. Then we'd sit on the curb and eat our popsicles. Pretty profound, huh?

V: It sounds nice (64–66).

What, in Vivian's normal realm of articulation, would seem incredibly banal, being called "sweetheart" and splitting a popsicle, ends up being the first kind gesture Vivian has engaged in since she entered the stage. The human act of sharing, even something so mundane as a frozen treat, takes on theological significance at this crucial juncture of the play. The moment is Eucharistic because it involves the act of giving, raising a simple item into something meaningful. Not bread and wine, but something equally elemental and life-giving, flavored water, is elevated to profound significance. A poignant moment of comfort and appreciation in this dying woman's experience leads to the realization of what living is really about, and it has nothing to do with verbal gymnastics or mental acuity.

Susie, the least educated person on the scene, is the only one who shows Vivian any compassion. She is also the only one who brings up the question of setting up the DNR ("Do Not Resuscitate") order to avoid a "full code," something her doctors should have explained. Susie provides Vivian the opportunity to discuss what she suspected, that she was not going to get any better, reviewing in plain English the end-of-life options over which she can exercise some control, so that she can pass naturally when the time comes.

> *V:* That certainly was a maudlin display. Popsicles? "Sweetheart?" I can't believe my life has become so, *corny* . . . Now is not the time for verbal swordplay, for unlikely flights of imagination and wildly shifting perspectives, for metaphysical conceit, for wit. And nothing would be worse than a detailed scholarly analysis. Erudition. Interpretation. Complication. (*Slowly*) now is the time for simplicity. Now is the time for, dare I say it, kindness. (*Searchingly*) I thought being extremely smart would take care of it. But I see that I have been found out. Ooohhh . . . I'm scared. Oh, God. I want . . . I want . . . No, I want to hide I just want to curl up in a little ball (69–70).

In a rare moment of lucidity, Vivian admits that she had made a home inside her mind, as it were, to avoid the pain and fear that have shadowed her through life. Even in the face of this revelation, she struggles with the old habit of using words to shield her emotions. And that thought shames her back into herself, expressed in her desire to hide from God, afraid that he will be angry.

Earlier, Vivian had flashed back to teaching Holy Sonnet IX, which dwells upon sin and forgiveness. She has an interesting take on the speaker's crisis. The poem reads:

> If poysonous mineralls, and if that tree
> Whose fruit threw death on else immortal us,
> If lecherous goats, if serpents envious

> Cannot be damn'd; Alas, why should I bee?
> Why should intent or reason, borne in mee,
> Make sinnes, else equall, in mee, more heinous?
> And mercy being easie, 'and glorious
> To God, in his sterne wrath, why threatens hee?
> But who am I, that dare dispute with thee?
> Oh God, Oh! If thine onely worthy blood,
> And my teares, make a heavenly Lethean flood,
> And drowne in it my sinnes blacke memorie.
> That thou remember them, some claime as debt,
> I think it mercy, if thou wilt forget (49).

She comments to the class that the speaker has ". . . a brilliant mind and he plays the part convincingly but in the end he finds God's *forgiveness* hard to believe, so he crawls under a rock to *hide*" (49). Further on she expounds that:

> When the speaker considers his own sins, and the inevitability of God's *judgment*, he can conceive of but one resolution, to disappear . . . Doctrine assures us that no sinner is denied *forgiveness*, not even one whose sins are overweening *intellect* or overwrought *dramatics*. The speaker does not need to hide from God's *judgment*, only to accept God's forgiveness. It is very simple, suspiciously simple (50).

Vivian's projection, attributing to the speaker her own guilt and sense of sinfulness, results in a map of mis-reading of the poem, something she'd done throughout her career. Donne's speaker frets about sin, creating the rationalized "plea" for why he should not to be condemned; however, he comes round in the poem's resolution to suggest that he ought not to "dispute with" God (l.9).

His remorse is implied as well in the closing couplet: "That thou remember them, some claim as debt, / I think it mercy, if thou wilt forget (ll.13–14). This sentiment reveals no desire "to hide," as Vivian had interpreted the impulse, but emanates from a sound theology of the cross expressed so well in the earlier part of the sonnet: "If thine onely worthy blood, / And my teares, make a heavenly Lethean flood / And drowne in it my sinnes black memorie" (ll.11–12), which evokes what the salvific act involves. The speaker doesn't wish to be forgotten or hidden, but counts on God's mercy, and the assurance of salvation, to "forget" his sins.

Although she struggles with a desire to hide from the judgment to come, eventually the small dose of kindness shared between the two women wins over her impulse. While Susie begins her morphine drip (73), Vivian flashes back to the time with her father when she learned that the word "soporific" means "to make you sleepy" (42), teaching it to Suzie who of course has never heard the term before. The two share a good laugh together in spite of Vivian's severe pain, at first seemingly at Susie's expense, but mainly over how silly the word sounds.[6] In these last, fleeting moments Vivian is able to let her guard down completely. She has abandoned the falsity of the intellect and returns to the childhood status of playground joy, sharing popsicles and laughing at funny sounding, archaic words. She is again the five-year-old, only this time able to act appropriately.

As she is dying, the play comes full circle with the visit of Prof. Ashford, who not coincidentally is in town for her great-grandson's fifth birthday. Once she sees her condition, she immediately crawls into bed next to her, enfolds Vivian in her arms, and reads from *The Runaway Bunny*, a storybook she had bought for her great-grandchild, after Vivian declines to let her recite anything by John Donne. Thinking aloud about the story of the bunny who wishes simply to get lost, she says "Look at that. A little allegory of the soul. No matter where it hides, God will find it. See, Vivian" (79–80). When she is asleep, Ashford, the first person who seemed to care what happened to Vivian, "*leans over and kisses her*," as the stage direction states and utters: "It's time to go. And flights of angels sing thee to thy rest. (*She leaves*)" (80).[7]

---

6. Madeline Keveaney suggests that "In addition to seeing in this scene, the way in which language fuels humor, we also see it tied to the theme of the power of naming . . . this scene forecasts . . . the way language can be used to provide emotional comfort and connection" (Keveaney, "Death," 43). She argues that the simplicity of language shared with Susie and Prof. Ashford provides a physical and psychological connection for Vivian, seemingly the only one in her life that offers comfort.

7. Jaqueline Vanhoutte deduces that "in Edson's allegorical schema, cancer is God's method for finding the runaway souls of overweening intellectuals" ("Cancer," 404), but that makes the disease into a literal punishment, rather than the means to reflection on one's life, to which Edson alludes. Later she suggests that the reference to Shakespeare's *Hamlet*, which could also refer to the "In Paradisum" from which those lines about angels are drawn, suggests that Edson favors Shakespeare as "engaging emotions" and ". . . show[ing] the way to a more spiritual illumination." While that comment may be true to an extent, it makes a facile comparison between one reference in Shakespeare to the more complex theology contained in Donne's poems quoted throughout the play, which doesn't adequately account for the various emotions revealed in the Holy Sonnets.

John Sykes, in his article on the play's faith, comments that, "The message for Vivian is twofold. First, this simple tale [*The Runaway Bunny*] is an antidote to the anxiety-producing complexity of Donne and the competitive, interpretive hubris to which Vivian and her medical counterparts have fallen prey... The hopefulness of the book springs not from human kindness, but from trust in God's overriding mercy."[8] This point about redemption as the play's theme has been in part corroborated by Edson's own comments: "Grace... is the opportunity to experience God in spite of yourself, which is what Dr. Bearing ultimately achieves."[9] While she has spent life in a paradox, isolating herself to study language while paradoxically using it as a barrier against others, Vivian realizes that her life and scholarship have both missed the mark. Her simple conversations with Susie have helped her to see the authentic function of language and to accept Susie's ministering to her as friendship; a sacred relationship and bond is forged. Some critics of the play argue that the character of Vivian does not evince a developed sense of Christian redemption, because she dies without ever mentioning God or faith, per se.

However, in his analysis of Luther's theology of preaching, Dennis Ngien sees "... a correspondence between God hiding in his humanity to reveal himself and God hiding in human language to communicate with us... in the day to day language of human beings." Quoting one of Luther's sermons, he concludes that "God does everything through the ministry of human beings."[10] Thus, the relationship with her nurse and the ultimate sharing of mundane things—a popsicle, a smile, and giddy laughter—so easily taken for granted, assume significance because they occur during Vivian's experience of the cross, amid her excruciating battle with cancer.

An intelligent woman, Vivian had entered into last-stage experimental treatments with the obvious knowledge, expressed or not, that there would be no cure. It may have been initially an "intellectual" decision like all the others in her life, but she may also have consented because she had felt the need to repent, to experience some of the suffering which she had often inflicted on others. Ultimately, Vivian achieves relief from all of her life's pain, and makes up for whatever hurts she had

---

8. Sykes, "*Wit*, Pride," 169.

9. Quoted in Eads, "Unwitting Redemption," 241. The comment is taken from the published text of an interview of the playwright by Adrienne Martini for *American Theatre*.

10. Ngien, "Theology of Preaching," 34.

caused. Her ability to care for and need another person is evident when she asks whether Susie would "still be taking care of" her (69), no small thing in an otherwise alienated life. As well, her rediscovery of childlike joy in the midst of physical and emotional torment is a concrete sign of God's redemptive love at work. Edson consciously eschews theological language in the play in favor of symbol. After all, such a decision is in keeping with the play's theme that language, as Tennyson had said in *In Memoriam*, only "half reveals and half conceals the grief within," as well as the God who remains partially "behind the veil" (Canto V). It is also endemic in liturgical drama, which this play approximates, to allow the symbols of faith, bread and wine, cup and plate, to stand for themselves; they require no translation once engaged in the dramatic moment of re-enacting God's sacrifice.

Theologian Karl Trueman suggests, commenting on Luther's "Heidelberg Disputation Against Scholastic Theology" from September, 1517—precursor to the famous *Ninety-Five Theses* posted in October of that year—that, "He deserves to be called a theologian, however, who comprehends the visible and manifest things of God seen through suffering and the cross."[11] God's power is hidden in the form of weakness which ironically turns all theological and even human language on its head. When discussing Christian ethics and experience as the lived aspect of faith according to Luther, Trueman further comments that ". . . The cross is seen as it really is. God is revealed in the hiddenness of the external form. And faith is understood to be a gift of God, *not a power inherent in the human mind itself*."[12] Edson has managed to capture the essence of Luther's theological concepts in a simple and evocative way, which would clearly be in keeping with her purposes to reveal grace at work in Vivian, as well as her desire not to "force" religious language into the play. Interestingly, that decision ends up revealing Luther's own idea that God's grace works through the everyday language and gestures of human beings.

Nothing in the human mind or its capacity either fully understands or really deserves the gift of faith, which is precisely that: a mystery and a gift freely given by God. It is what Vivian comes to understand as she experiences the limitation of language, left as she is without words to

---

11. Trueman, "Luther's Theology." He argues that Luther sees God's wisdom and power as being "demonstrated in the foolishness of the Cross."

12. Ibid., my emphasis.

express remorse, to confess her guilt, or even to ask God for pardon.[13] All she has to offer at the end is a half-popsicle, but the gesture is itself a symbol of deeper realities, as her memory of reciting of Holy Sonnet IX is her way of seeking God's mercy. Edson correctly intuits what is expressed in Luther's belief that God and his goodness are always revealed in the cross and through human expression. Such intense suffering, willingly undertaken and nobly endured, must lead to compassion and real love. One is reminded also of the Anglo-Saxon poem, "The Dream of the Rood," obliquely referenced in the "Tree" of salvation in Sonnet IX (l. 1) , in which the wood of the cross, itself a tree, gladly bears the pain of the savior's death and its own complicity in that act, because of what it yields for humanity.

While some critics argue that the play doesn't provide a developed theology of the cross, one commentator does regard Vivian's suffering as redemptive.[14] Chad Wriglesworth interprets Vivian as enacting the role of a "suffering servant" who, like the reference to Christ in Isaiah, "suggests a deliberate and volitional carrying of metaphysical weight."[15] Although not expressed, Vivian is complicit in accepting her own suffering as redemption for her earlier inability to embrace her humanity. I would extend this insight even further. As Jason and everyone else struggle over "calling the code" which Susie finally succeeds in getting canceled during those last, frantic moments of the play, Edson has allowed Vivian to pass. The symbolic ending in which Vivian drops every item of hospital

---

13. Valerie Raoul, et al., speaking of how language performs in the play, suggests beyond medical terminology or literary conceit, that ". . . the overall message of the play seems to defend the simplicity of kindness and respect for the other as person over the verbal pyrotechnics of sophistic poetry or medical jargon. Thanks to Susie, there will be no code; Vivian will be allowed to die, rather than to continue as a painful experiment. The state of *coma* functions as Donne's *comma*, indicating a painless passage from life to death" ("Margaret Edson's Play," 294). I would also add a *silent* one, in that the sign, or symbol, eliminates any need for obfuscating language.

14. Chad Wriglesworth comments that "The theological depth of *Wit*'s ending leaves many critics baffled. As Martha Greene Eads states, although some critics recognize that the play is about redemption, 'the nature of that redemption . . . is difficult for many of them to describe.' (241) . . . We have lost the language to express depth, and Edson's play, like much of art, confronts these issues 'more profoundly than most directly religious expressions of our time.'" Wriglesworth calls *Wit* an example of "theological humanism" requiring an "interpretive praxis" for reading, and acknowledges that ". . . below the surface of things she [Vivian] is mysterious—even sacred—a more complicated character than anyone in the production or the audience might begin to imagine" ("Theological Humanism," 219, 213).

15. Ibid., 217.

garb—the nails and wood of her cross (bracelets, cap, awful gowns, wires, and tubes)—as she reaches "toward a little light," is an understated, yet effective, way of expressing her "kenosis," the emptying of physical form at the moment of transformation. She moves from a lifetime of being an "intellectual posturer," an empty human being, to becoming a fully redeemed human soul, which reflects Donne's poetic representation of God's triumph over Death in Holy Sonnet X. After all, she has endured being ". . . bent, blown and broken" anew, to paraphrase slightly his Holy Sonnet XIV.[16]

Such a view also illustrates Luther's idea that in the "hiddenness of this form," both in Vivian's body and in that of the cross, is God's ultimate gift, the reality that the sufferings of life act not so much as termination but become the means of transformation, owing to Christ's having died once and for all. We, as the witnessing audience, have intimately re-lived those sufferings through Vivian's flashbacks, and discover in their trajectory as part of God's plan that they are not devoid of meaning, but have led to this moment of redemption.

Paul Althaus, well-known commentator on Luther's theology, quotes from his key sermons on death and offers some exegesis of Luther's idea:

> 'Death, then, which previously was a punishment of sin, is now a remedy for sin. Thus, it is now blessed.' Death, freed of the wrath of God in this way, is now asleep. 'Death is become my slumber' is the way in which Luther puts it in his hymnal paraphrase of Simeon's song [Luke 2:29–32]. Or to illustrate with another picture which Luther used in his *Treatise on Preparing to Die* (*Sermon von der Bereitung zum Streben*) (1519), death is only 'the narrow gate and the small way to life,' corresponding to the narrow exit through which a child is born into this world from the body of his mother. Thus, when a man dies, he passes through the narrows and straits of anxieties to be born into the world to come. 'Thus a dying man must courageously enter into anxiety with the knowledge that there will be great space and much joy afterwards.' The voice of the law says, 'In the midst of life, we are in death.' The voice of the gospel says, 'In the midst of death, we are in life.'[17]

---

16. Although Martha Eads does question how overtly Christian a play this is, she also suggests that, "Whether or not she realizes it, Edson has depicted in her play the same desire that Donne expresses in Holy Sonnet XIV: 'Batter . . . make me new' (11. 1–4)" ("Unwitting Redemption," 253).

17. Althaus, *The Theology*, 408.

These descriptions, compiled from Luther's preaching, corroborate Vivian's experience as she dwelt with her fears in the face of death. Luther's reference to St. Paul on Death's "lack" of a victory over us, on which Donne had based his reflections in Holy Sonnet X, also parallels the action of the play. Vivian had overlooked the role of faith in Donne's poetry as she pursued the intellectual paradoxes of his words; however, in her embrace of the dying process she came to experience the joy beyond the anxiety, as Luther had aptly phrased it, on the way to redemption.

At play's end Vivian remains an enigmatic character: a deep thinker and a troubled soul; in short, somewhat of a mystery like all human beings, but one whose suffering and recognition of past failings have "saved" her in the theological sense. With uncanny *simplicity*, to use her own and Vivian's word, Edson reveals in this play more than a humanist understanding of suffering. She offers a visual and vividly portrayed theology of the cross as redemptive, similar to that expressed by St. Paul and Luther, and contained in the Reformation thought of Donne's metaphysical sonnets. Vivian "Bear[s]" her Cross amidst pain and reluctance, until the moment of her final "letting go," the acceptance of death, and joyful transformation into "a little light," in spite of how much she'd have liked simply to run away.[18] The fact is that she did not; she took, as she said early on in the play, "the full dose" every time. In the end, she literally became Donne's "comma," curled up on her bed of pain, temporarily shaped into that pause, of which Edson has Prof. Ashford speak so eloquently, moving, in Vivian's own words, *steadfast*[ly] and *resolute*[ly] (53) beyond death into light.

Bibliography

Althaus, Paul. *The Theology of Martin Luther.* Translated by Robert C. Schultz. Philadelphia: Fortress, 1966.

---

18. Paul Althaus, discussing Luther's view of Christ faced with the human dilemma of death, explains it this way: "Certainly he feels as the damned feel. He trembles before God and *would like to flee from him*; but at the same time, he is able to love him. This is how Luther expresses it in his *Sermon von der Bereitung Zum Sterben*, 'Treatise on Preparing to Die.' Christ is the heavenly image of one who, although forsaken by God as damned, has yet to overcome hell through his omnipotent love; and he bears witness that he is the dearest Son and offers the same status to us as our own if we believe" (Ibid., 206–7).

Eads, Martha Greene. "Unwitting Redemption in Margaret Edson's *Wit.*" *Christianity & Literature* 51 (2002) 241–54.

Edson, Margaret. *Wit.* New York: Faber & Faber, 1999.

Keveaney, Madeline M. "Death Be Not Proud: An Analysis of Margaret Edson's *Wit.*" *Women and Language* 27 (2004) 40–44.

Luther, Martin, *Dr Martin Luther Werke*. 65 vols. Weimar: Böhlau, 1883–1993.

McGrath, Alister. *Luther's Theology of the Cross*. Oxford: Blackwell, 1985.

Ngien, Dennis. "Theology of Preaching in Martin Luther." *Themelios* 28/2 (2003) 28–48.

Raoul, Valerie, et al. "Margaret Edson's Play, *Wit*: Death at the End or the End of Death?" In *Unfitting Stories: Narrative Approaches to Disease, Disability, and Trauma*, edited by Valerie Raoul et al., 285–96. Waterloo, ON: Wilfred Laurier University Press, 2007.

Sykes, Jr. John D. "*Wit*, Pride and the Resurrection: Margaret Edson's Play and John Donne's Poetry." *Renascence* 55 (2003) 163–74.

Trueman, Carl R. "Luther's Theology of the Cross." Online: http://www.opc.org/new_horizons/NH05/10b.html.

Vanhoutte, Jacqueline. "Cancer and the Common Woman in Margaret Edson's *Wit.*" *Comparative Drama* 36 (2002–03) 390–410.

Wriglesworth, Chad. "Theological Humanism as Living Praxis: Reading Surfaces and Depth in Margaret Edson's *Wit.*" *Literature and Theology* 22 (2008) 210–22.

10

Never Such Innocence Again
The Persistence of Hope in Cormac McCarthy's The Road

STEPHEN SICARI

"Never such innocence again." So writes Philip Larkin in "MCMXIV," a poem about how World War I impacted western culture so ferociously that "innocence" is shattered beyond any salvaging. Paul Fussell uses this poem in his classic study of the effects of the Great War on modern culture, and the phrase "Never such innocence again" functions as a lament for a way of being permanently lost by the horrors of that war.[1] What's odd is that Larkin writes this poem in the mid-1960s, and therefore in the midst of another age of innocence being battered by yet another war. It's as if the lesson had not been learned, as if the poet had to instruct us, once and for all, to be done with innocence.

Perhaps the lesson needs repeating, over and over, because innocence can never wholly be effaced. Perhaps innocence is as Wallace Stevens, that most philosophical of poets, sees it, an *a priori* concept of

---

1. Quoted in Fussell, *The Great War*, 19. Fussell uses the phrase, "Never Such Innocence Again," as a section title in his first chapter. This section begins with this sentence: "Irony is the attendant of hope, and the fuel of hope is innocence" (18).

the human mind. This is from the seventh section of "The Auroras of Autumn," written in 1947, and so after Auschwitz and Hiroshima and in response to the new atomic age:

> There may always be a time of innocence.
> There is never a place. Or if there is no time,
> If it is not a thing of time, nor of place,
>
> Existing in the idea of it, alone,
> In the sense against calamity, it is not
> Less real. For the oldest and coldest philosopher,
>
> There is or may be a time of innocence
> As pure principle. [. . .]
>
> It is like a thing of ether that exists
> Almost as predicate. But it exists,
> It exists, it is visible, it is, it is.[2]

"Never such innocence again"? Despite recent horrors and the prospect of global annihilation, Stevens insists—"it exists, it exists, it is visible, it is, it is"—that the idea of innocence is outside time and space, ideal and permanent and absolute.[3] Stevens provides a way to appreciate the surprising persistence of innocence and hope in Cormac McCarthy's *The Road*.

William Blake established the poetic model for understanding the ideal nature of innocence in his *Songs of Innocence and Experience*, and he did so largely by presenting images of children under severe economic oppression. "The Chimney Sweeper" poem in *Innocence* may well be the classic expression of Blake's vision of innocence. It is clear that the children in the poem are being abused, and the corresponding "Chimney Sweeper" poem in *Songs of Experience* has a child express his own awakening consciousness of his oppression at the hands of his parents, the Church, and the State. In the *Innocence* version of the poem, one of the children has a consoling dream:

---

2. Stevens, *Collected Poetry*, 360–61.

3. In Stevens' conviction that innocence is not a thing of time and place yet exists, in a way that is not less real, in its idea, I am reminded of Rudolf Otto's understanding of the holy as an a priori category of the human mind. Stevens associates innocence with holiness in lines that end this section of *The Auroras of Autumn*, when he bids us "lie down like children in this holiness" (ibid., 361).

> And by came an Angel who had a bright key
> And he open'd the coffins & set them all free;
> Then down a green plain leaping, laughing, they run,
> And was in a river, and shine in the Sun.
>
> Then naked and white, all their bags left behind,
> They rise upon clouds and sport in the wind;
> And the Angel told Tom, if he'd be a good boy,
> He'd have God for his father & never want joy.[4]

This dream of heavenly joy is certainly an instance of childlike innocence, and the Angel's parting words express a hope that can console the child in the midst of his oppression. The poem ends with little Tom able to accept his lot in life with innocent hope:

> And so Tom awoke; and we rose in the dark,
> And got with our bags & our brushes to work.
> Tho' the morning was cold, Tom was happy & warm;
> So if all do their duty they need not fear harm.[5]

Clearly the ambivalence is intended and rich. It's as if Blake was reading Marx and delivers an image of religion as the opium of the people, and the off-rhymes of the last stanza indicate that this "innocent" ending jars mightily with our sense of justice. The "experienced" reader may ignore the consolation offered by the dream and focus on the continued abuse and oppression, and Blake surely intends for us to remain outraged at such a situation. Those who need to "do their duty" to escape harm include the members of Church and State who sanction such abuse. But to reject the consolation and hope as false is just as one-sided as ignoring the injustice of the system. We are being asked to feel the depth and richness of the innocent hope even as we deplore the unjust circumstance; we should "turn and become like children" who can maintain innocence even under the most horrible conditions.

The last poem in *Songs of Innocence* called "Night" refreshes one of the most conventional images of consolation and hope in Jewish-Christian scriptures. It presents angels as they watch over the innocent animal world as it goes to sleep, and they are especially worried about the lambs, that most traditional emblem of innocence. They want to keep them safe from tigers and wolves, but they make no guarantees and even

---

4. Blake, *Songs of Innocence*, 43.
5. Ibid.

appear impotent to prevent attacks. But they assure the lambs that, in the long run and ultimately, all will be well, in the heavenly fold. Here's the last stanza (and so the last words of *Songs of Innocence*), as sung by a lion who would have been their enemy on earth:

> And now beside thee, bleating lamb,
> I can lie down and sleep;
> Or think on him who bore thy name,
> Graze after thee and weep.
> For, wash'd in life's river,
> My bright mane for ever
> Shall shine like the gold
> As I guard o'er the fold.[6]

The lion shall lie down with the lamb: that's the ultimate Christian image of innocence that Blake works to renew. There is no denying the violence and horrors of life, but as we are wash'd in life's river, we are restored to an innocence that was certainly in doubt but never wholly lost.

In *The Road* Cormac McCarthy presents a world as horrible as any I have ever encountered in literature, and at first glance, it may seem ludicrous to claim that *The Road* offers any grounds for consolation or hope.[7] It takes place in a brutal post-apocalyptic landscape populated by creatures no longer recognizably human. It's a bleak and dying world inhabited by monsters. But the two characters we follow—the man and the boy, as they are called, father and son—remain human in this posthuman world. Some truly gruesome scenes are scattered through the novel that create a monstrous setting. One scene suffices. The two come to a grand house, and whenever they come to such a place the father investigates, to see if there is anything they can use—food especially, but clothing, blankets, fuel, tools, anything that helps them survive. "Mostly he worried about their shoes. That and food. Always food" (17). In this pursuit, he goes down a cellar and discovers "naked people, male and female, all trying to hide, shielding their faces with their hands" (110). They are prisoners kept alive for torture and as food. The man and the boy hear hideous shrieks from the house that night. It takes the boy a few days before he can even talk about it, asking his father if those people were going to be eaten. Yes, he answers.

---

6. Ibid., 55.

7. All quotations from *The Road* come from the First Vintage International Edition, 2006. The page numbers are provided in the main text.

In this world the man and the boy struggle not only to stay alive but to remain human, and they use a phrase to describe the higher purpose that they hope ensures their well-being. "We're going to be okay, aren't we Papa? / Yes. We are. / And nothing bad is going to happen to us. / That's right. / Because we're carrying the fire. / Yes. Because we're carrying the fire" (83). The boy is not asking questions but making statements that the father verifies; they have had this conversation before, and it motivates their journey. This phrase may be viewed skeptically as something the father invented to comfort the boy. He may be desperate to believe it himself. But the oft-repeated phrase provides the basis of a more hope-filled plot. Even in this most monstrous world, we see the hopeful persistence of holiness and light.

From the novel's first words we know that the father sees something special in the boy. "In the dream from which he'd wakened he had wandered in a cave where the child led him by the hand. Their light playing over the wet flowstone walls. Like pilgrims in a fable swallowed up and lost among the inward parts of some gigantic beast" (3). A page later, "He knew only that the child was his warrant. He said: If he is not the word of God God never spoke" (5). "Warrant" is precise and unexpected. It means a sanction, an authorization, a justification. The boy justifies the man's life, justifies perhaps human life on the planet. He tells the boy directly, "My job is to take care of you. I was appointed to do that by God. I will kill anyone who touches you. Do you understand?" (77).

"If he is not the word of God God never spoke." Not a ringing assertion of faith, but it brings God into the picture, even if only as a remote possibility. The father wavers back and forth, but for the most part he uses language and images that retrieve an almost forgotten tradition of the divine presence in the world. But the man is no naïve idealist who could be in this world? The only time he directly addresses God is early in the novel: "Then he just knelt in the ashes. He raised his face to the paling day. Are you there? He whispered. Will I see you at the last? Have you a neck by which to throttle you? Have you a heart? Damn you eternally have you a soul? Oh God, he whispered. O God" (11–12). That's a post-apocalyptic prayer. The Book of Job is explicitly evoked when the man utters the words of Job's wife, "Curse God and die." What she actually said, "Are you still holding to your innocence? Curse God and die." An innocent man suffering and maintaining his innocence before a God who allows that suffering: that's how Job figures in *The Road*.

An old man appears late in the novel who wants the universe shorn of all traces of the divine: "There is no God and we are his prophets." Upon hearing that when he saw the boy he thought he had died, the father asks, "What if I said he's a god?" The old man's reply: "I'm past all that now. Have been for years. Where men can't live gods fare no better. You'll see. It's better to be alone. So I hope that's not true what you said because to be on the road with the last god would be a terrible thing so I hope it's not true. Things will be a lot better when everybody's gone" (172). The father needs clarification, and the old man obliges: "When we're all gone then there'll be nobody here but death and his days will be numbered too. He'll be out in the road there with nothing to do and nobody to do it to. He'll say: Where did everybody go? And that's how it will be. What's wrong with that?" (173). Having witnessed horror, the old man wants no enchantment, no mystery, no trace of the transcendent. Pure nothingness.

Perhaps this is the appropriate place to allude to the work of Charles Taylor, especially his monumental *A Secular Age*. Taylor's argument, in the smallest of nutshells, is that since the Enlightenment there has been a steady emptying out from the world of magic and mystery, the gradual elimination of the divine from the world in the name of science and progress. While some may welcome and wish to encourage the disenchantment of the world described by people such as Max Weber (the term is often credited to him), as freeing us from the stranglehold of superstition and intolerance; thinkers like Taylor lament the accompanying flattening out of experience. In *A Secular Age* Taylor painstakingly documents a shift from what he calls a porous world, in which the divide between human being and the divine was permeable and allowed interpenetration, to a buffered world, in which we are increasingly closed off from magic and enchantment. The disenchantment of the world leads, in Taylor's view, to a loss of richness in lived experience not compensated by the progress made possible by science and technology.[8]

Taylor's ideas are also the implicit subject of a series of essays collected by George Levine under the title *The Joy of Secularism*.[9] The debate

---

8. Taylor, *A Secular Age*. There is no one place in *A Secular Age* where these ideas are stated as baldly as this, but the introduction and conclusion are places where Taylor presents his overview.

9. Levine, *The Joy of Secularism*. This book assembles eleven essays that address the loss of enchantment from various perspectives, including essays by biologists and psychiatrists, anthropologists and political scientists. Only Taylor laments the loss.

between someone like Taylor, who wants to enact what he calls the reenchantment of the world, and the secular humanists Levine champions, who hail the world's disenchantment, provides a powerful context in which to read a text like *The Road*, which presents the bleakest of worlds and the barest possibility of reenchantment. Taylor's essay in Levine's book is titled "Disenchantment-Reenchantment," and in it he lays out his case for the desire to reenchant the world, to find a way to return to a way of being that feels the divine in the world, a sense of mystery and higher purpose, without which we lose value and maybe even wonder.[10] The secularists whom Levine lines up against Taylor insist, strongly and uniformly, that we should welcome the disenchantment of the world, as it frees us from the superstitions and hostilities that religious views of the world have fostered, and that we are free to create our own (superior) values based on an exclusively human world. The title of Bruce Robbins' essay says it all: "Enchantment? No, Thank You!"[11] Secularists like Robbins feel strongly that they can live a life of value and wonder without the divine, in a disenchanted world, while Taylor fears a loss of value attends the loss of the divine. The plot of McCarthy's novel provides a powerful argument in favor of enchantment, for without a sense of the divine we will not remain human, but instead become vicious monsters.

Raimon Panikkar also provides a theological context for my argument. Like Taylor, he sketches a view of history in which scientific progress, which has given us many good things and cannot be reversed even if we would so wish, has estranged us from nature and has drained the world, and ourselves, of our divine aspects. Whereas primitive people felt the earth as a living organism imbued with divinity, we see it as something to exploit and master, and this loss of innocence is much to be regretted. But Panikkar does not call for a "recovery of lost innocence. Innocence is innocent precisely because once spoiled, it cannot be recovered. We cannot return to the earthly paradise, much as we might long to. The desire itself is the greatest threat." Instead, what he calls for "is a conquest, the difficult and painful conquest of a new innocence."[12] We have come

---

10. Ibid., 57–73.

11. Ibid., 74–94.

12. Panikkar, *The Cosmotheandric Experience*, 50. Panikkar sketches three phases in human history, ending with what he calls a "Catholic" moment in which we may be able to respond to the scientific humanism of the Enlightenment with a renewed sense of the intimate relation of the world, the divine, and the human, the "cosmotheandric" trinity. The Enlightenment severs the divine from the world and from the human, and

so far along the path of progress that we are in the process of destroying the earth, and a return to an original innocence seems impossible indeed. But a "difficult and painful conquest of a new innocence" may be precisely what we are watching in *The Road*.

The world McCarthy presents lies in utter ruins as the bitter fruit of scientific progress; yet the father never yields in his hope that something divine has survived in the world, and survived especially in the boy. Perhaps it's nostalgia for a world fading into oblivion, but he cannot help but use language from religious ritual—much of it seems quite Catholic. When it starts snowing, the boy "looked at the sky. A single gray flake sifting down. He caught it in his hand and watched it expire there like the last host of christendom" (16). It's a gratuitous simile, one that brings "Christendom" into the text even if it's only to note its fading. Describing the first years after the nuclear event: "Creedless shells of men tottering down the causeways like migrants in a feverland" (28). Isn't "creedless" an odd description of the "shells of men"? Watching the boy stoking flames: "God's own firedrake. The sparks rushed upward and died in the starless dark. Not all dying words are true and this blessing is no less real for being shorn of its ground" (31). Some ritual of blessing still has validity, despite having lost its ground.

After the father shoots a man who held the boy against him with a knife: "This is my child, he said. I wash a dead man's brains out of his hair. This is my job. [. . .] All of this like some ancient anointing. So be it. Evoke the forms. When you've got nothing else construct ceremonies out of the air and breathe upon them" (74). A wild simile, comparing washing a dead man's brains out of a boy's hair to an anointing, but there it is, as if he cannot help laying on a layer of sacerdotal language upon the actions surrounding the boy. As he strokes the boy's hair: "Golden chalice, good to house a god" (75). That's pretty Catholic language. In a world desperately in need of reenchantment, the man and the boy are its agents.

It's clear that the phrase—"carrying the fire"—is meant to suggest that the two, and especially the boy, are the bearers of some special quality of sacred significance. The notion that humans contain a spark of the divine, is a long one limited to no single religious tradition. In a bleak world of cruel violence, these two keep moving on, motivated by the

---

without the divine we came to see the earth as something to dominate and master; hence, our exploitation of the earth that is now endangering our ability to remain on the planet. Without using the language of disenchantment-reenchantment, Panikkar's work can be read as a theological version of Taylor's thesis.

conviction that they are perhaps the last with this spark, with this fire. Without them, without it, the world will be thoroughly disenchanted, completely bereft of the divine. They bear an awesome responsibility.

And the boy feels this burden. One of his chief concerns is that he and his father not eat anyone, because that would be a sign that they are no longer "the good guys." A typical exchange: "We wouldn't ever eat anybody, would we? / No. Of course not. / Even if we were starving? / We're starving now. / You said we weren't. / I said we weren't dying. I didn't say we weren't starving. / But we wouldn't. / No. We wouldn't. / No matter what. / No. No matter what. / Because we're the good guys. / Yes. / And we're carrying the fire. / And we're carrying the fire. Yes. / Okay" (128–29). These two ideas are linked, being the good guys and carrying the fire, and the boy is totally committed to this ideal, even more than his father. The boy wants to help the few people they meet on the road, even if at their expense and at their risk. Late in the novel, the father catches up with a thief who was taking all their belongings. Because the boy is so adamant, they go back to help even this man. Their exchange: "What do you want to do? / Just help him, Papa. Just help him. / The man looked up the road. / He was just hungry, Papa. He's going to die. / The man squatted and looked at him. I'm scared, he said. Do you understand? I'm scared. / The boy didn't answer. He just sat there with his head bowed, sobbing. / You're not the one who has to worry about everything. / The boy said something but he couldn't understand him. What? He said. / [The boy] looked up at him, his wet and grimy face. Yes I am, he said. I am the one" (259). That's how the boy sees himself, as the one who has to worry, as the one maintaining a morality of good and bad, as the one who keeps compassion and love operating in an otherwise desolate universe. Carrying the fire indeed.

So who is this boy? As the story draws to its close and the father is in his final hours, we are told clearly what the father sees in the boy: "He'd stop and lean on the cart and the boy would go on and stop and look back and he would raise his weeping eyes and see him standing there in the road looking back at him from some unimaginable future, glowing in that waste like a tabernacle" (273). The father cannot imagine the future but sees the boy there, like the receptacle on the altar that contains the transubstantiated bread of the Eucharist. As he watches the boy kneel before him with a cup of water: "There was light all about him." "He lay watching the boy at the fire. He wanted to be able to see. Look around you, he said. There is no prophet in the earth's long chronicle who's not honored here today. Whatever form you spoke of you were right" (277).

The boy as a prophet carrying the fire into an unimaginable future: that's how the father sees him. The last scene between the two is heart-rending: "You're going to be okay, Papa. You have to. / No I'm not. Keep the gun with you at all times. You need to find the good guys but you cant take any chances. No chances. Do you hear? / I want to be with you. / You cant. / Please. / You cant. You have to carry the fire. / I don't know how to. / Yes you do. / Is it real? The fire? / Yes it is. / Where is it? I don't know where it is. / Yes you do. It's inside you. It was always there. I can see it. / ... You said you wouldn't ever leave me. / I know. I'm sorry. You have my whole heart. You always did. You're the best guy. You always were. If I'm not here you can still talk to me. [. . .] Just don't give up. Okay? / Okay" (278–79). And he doesn't.

The father had them heading southwards and toward the ocean. It's not as if there is reason to believe there will be anything worthwhile down south or seaside; when they get to the ocean they find a ship with supplies that provision them for a bit but otherwise, nothing. It's just a hunch. At one point, when the father was clearly dying, the boy says, "I don't know what we're doing. The man started to answer. But he didn't. After a while he said: There are people. There are people and we'll find them. You'll see" (244). There are still *people* somewhere out there, not only the monsters they have been encountering. And when the father dies, the boy does find some people. That's the kind of coincidence that seems like fate. Or like providence.

The boy asks the man who finds him, "Are you one of the good guys?" The man says he is. A few moments later, the boy asks, "Are you carrying the fire? / Am I what? / Carrying the fire. / You're kind of weirded out, aren't you? / No. / Just a little. / Yeah. / That's okay. / So are you? / What, carrying the fire? / Yes. / Yeah. We are. / Do you have any kids? / We do. / Do you have a little boy? / We have a little boy and we have a little girl. / How old is he? / He's about your age. Maybe a little older. / And you didn't eat them?" (284–85). A woman in the group "would talk to him sometimes about God" (286). Early in the novel, the father had thought, "On this road there are no godspoke men. They are gone and I am left and they have taken with them the world" (32). The father fulfilled his God-appointed task and managed to bring the boy to godspoke people. The world has not been taken away.

The very last words of *The Road* present an image of renewal: "Once there were brook trout in the streams in the mountains. You could see them standing in the amber current where the white edges of their fins wimpled softly in the flow. They smelled of moss in your hand. Polished and muscular and torsional. On their backs were vermiculate patterns that were maps of the world in its becoming. Maps and mazes. Of a thing that could not be put back. Not be made right again. In the deep glens where they lived all things were older than man and they hummed of mystery" (286–87). I first misread the beginning, "Once there were brook trout," as recalling a past where such healthy creatures once lived. I saw it as retrospective and nostalgic. But that's wrong. "Once there were brook trout" is in the present of the group's onward journey. These godspoke people, including and especially the boy, find a place of health on the earth where the mystery that is life continues. We are invited to speculate that the boy, who has been carrying the fire, has been appointed to re-enchant the world, and this ending signals the hope that human beings, lighted by this fire, can restore the earth to its innocence again; or, to follow Panikkar, have captured a new innocence. While the world may not be made right again, and of a thing that could not be put back, there will be a future with life and health. The universe hums with mystery still.

Bibliography

Blake, William. *Songs of Experience*. New York: Dover, 1971.
———. *Songs of Innocence*. New York: Dover, 1971.
Fussell, Paul. *The Great War and Modern Memory*. New York: Oxford University Press, 2000.
Levine, George, ed. *The Joy of Secularism: 11 Essays for How We Live Now*. Princeton: Princeton University Press, 2011.
McCarthy, Cormac. *The Road*. New York: Vintage International, 2006.
Otto, Rudolf. *The Idea of the Holy*. Translated by John W Harvey. New York: Oxford University Press, 1973.
Panikkar, Raimon. *The Cosmotheandric Experience: Emerging Religious Consciousness*. Maryknoll, NY: Orbis, 1993.
Stevens, Wallace. *Collected Poetry and Prose*. New York: Library of America, 1997.
Taylor, Charles. *A Secular Age*. Cambridge, MA: Belnap, 2007.

11

Allusions to Wittenberg, the Four Last Things, and the Character of Hamlet, Prince of Denmark

Brigid Brady

Shakespeare has created a rich if subtle context for the character of Hamlet, Prince of Denmark. Foil characters Fortinbras and Laertes share a similar filial duty of retribution for evils suffered by their parents. How each young man addresses this responsibility contrasts with the other and with Hamlet's approach. Study at Wittenberg offers additional context for Hamlet's analysis of the injury done his father and consequently of his planned revenge. Earlier in *Hamlet's* century, Henry VIII's *Assertio Septum Sacramentum* opposed Luther, seconded by Thomas More; the Elizabethan audience, especially the courtiers and well-read citizens among them, would recognize the significance of the Wittenberg allusions in the play.

Shakespeare's *Hamlet* involves three young men, confronting the violent death of a father in ways that are unique to each. Fortinbras seeks to regain the land lost through his royal father's challenge to the King of Denmark. Forestalled by the reigning king from military action against Denmark, Fortinbras marks time pursuing other military targets, and winds up with the throne of Denmark as the reward for his patience. Laertes storms back from Paris seeking vengeance for the death of Polonius. He looks for retribution in the form of the life of the killer for the life of his father, all very contained in this world. Hamlet's schema of retribution alone goes beyond this life to the judgment, which he fears may have awaited his father as the result of his "sudden and unprovided death." He sees himself as not having fully avenged his father if his killer is not brought to a similar fate.

All of these young men are introduced either in person or by reference in the second scene of the play. Ambassadors are dispatched to the King of Norway to forestall an attack by Fortinbras. Laertes is given permission to return to school in Paris. Claudius addresses Hamlet's similar petition:

> For your intent
> In going back to school in Wittenberg
> It is most retrograde to our desire ... (1.2.112–14)[1]

Hamlet finds his return to study at Wittenberg thwarted by the will of his uncle Claudius, the newly crowned king and his newly acquired stepfather.

While the temporal setting of the play is unclear, the history of the University of Wittenberg is not. Founded in 1502, Wittenberg attracted the young Martin Luther in 1508. Luther rose quickly to the position of Doctor in Bible, retaining that position for life. During this period, an active campaign of preaching indulgences, related to raising funds for the restoration of St. Peter's Basilica, was underway. Luther, who vehemently opposed the practice of indulgences, prepared a statement of ninety-five theses for disputation, and according to legend, nailed them to the door of the church in Wittenberg on the 31st of October, 1517. The debate never actually happened, but the theses were widely circulated. Responses to the ninety-five theses and other writings by Luther, among them the *Babylonian Captivity of the Church*, came from Henry VIII of England and from his Lord Chancellor, Thomas More. Henry VIII personally presented his *Assertio Septem Sacramentorium* to Pope Leo X, who bestowed on him the title "Defender of the Faith."

Horatio, already at Elsinore in the first scene of the play, is Hamlet's fellow student at Wittenberg, and a close personal friend. A warm

---

1. References to Shakespeare's *Hamlet* (Norton Critical Edition, 2010) appear in the main text.

reunion occurs toward the end of the second scene. It would hardly seem possible that Shakespeare was not drawing upon the Wittenberg allusion and the controversy surrounding Luther to help in shaping the characters of these two young men and some aspects of the conflict in the play. While Luther's name is not mentioned, his presence is on Shakespeare's mind as is evident from the fourth-act pun on the Diet of Worms, when Hamlet reveals the whereabouts of Polonius' body saying:

> Not where he eats, but where he is eaten: a certain
> convocation of politic worms are e'en at him. (4.3.19–20)

Central to the controversy surrounding Luther is the very lucrative practice of indulgences which Luther opposed in the *Ninety-five Theses*, as well as the doctrine of Purgatory, which he dismisses in the *Smalcald Articles* as an "illusion of the devil."[2] *Hamlet* seems not to be following Luther's thought but the thought of those who opposed him, including Henry VIII, in *Assertio Septum Sacramentorum* and Thomas More in *Responsio ad Lutherum*.[3]

Henry VIII and Thomas More disputed Luther's challenges to traditional Catholic doctrine in the first quarter of the sixteenth century. By the time *Hamlet* was being written at the end of the century, much had changed. The Church of England, headed by the Henry's younger daughter Elizabeth, claimed a fundamentally Catholic theology while repudiating allegiance to Rome. Ironically, Denmark became a Lutheran kingdom at virtually the same time that Henry VIII engineered the separation of England from the Roman Catholic Church, establishing the Church of England with himself as its Supreme Head. That action led to an irreconcilable rift with More whom Henry then ordered beheaded, his head exhibited for the month following on London Bridge. These were tumultuous events leaving a context for allusions to Wittenberg in the minds of Englishmen who remembered Henry and the conflict with his friend that ended so disastrously for More.

It is the purpose of this paper to explore the significance of the Lutheran controversy concerning indulgences and even more its connection to the doctrine of purgatory and allusions to these in the play, for the character of Hamlet and the retributive justice he comes to seek against Claudius.

---

2. Luther, *Basic Theological Writings*, 506.
3. Henry VIII, *Assertio*, 196.

The drama is set in motion by an apparition closely resembling Prince Hamlet's recently deceased father. The first sightings of this figure precede the first scene of the play, as the guards on the night shift report to Horatio. The scholarly Horatio is skeptical of their report until the apparition returns. The former king, whom this ghostly figure resembles, is known to be dead. Horatio attests to that fact as well as to resemblance of this apparition to the dead king. As the audience also observes the figure, they are drawn into the subsequent discussion about the nature and meaning of what has been observed. Interrogating the speechless figure, Horatio runs through the popular explanations for ghosts walking. Clearly he has set aside his skepticism, but not all of his caution. Perhaps the ghost needs something done; can Horatio do this while staying in grace himself? Does the ghost know something that can allow Denmark to avoid pending disaster? Is there ill-gotten wealth for which restitution must be given before the ghost may rest in peace?

A cock crows and the figure departs in haste. The sorting of evidence continues. Horatio observes the manner of its departure; "It started like a guilty thing / upon a fearful summons" (1.1.148–49). The three men agree that the summons has something to do with the crowing of the cock. Horatio offers "something he has heard," suggesting that this may be "an extravagant and erring spirit" called back to its "confines" (1.1.146–48). The men appear to be moving toward the hypothesis that the figure may be the soul of a distressed deceased person confined during the day to a place like purgatory and walking at night. Morning dawns with little progress toward a definitive answer. They agree to refer the matter to Hamlet, whom, it would appear, the matter more nearly concerns. Horatio has not dismissed the distressed ghost idea. Neither has he dismissed the purgatory question as might an ardent disciple of Luther who calls purgatory and its accompanying practices "illusions of the devil."

What do this investigation and its provisional solution reveal about the character of Horatio? It seems he is cautious but willing to expand his options to include explanations that his previous study might indicate are impossible. He takes risks such as attempting to engage the apparition in conversation. He possesses a store of folk wisdom to draw upon when confronted by experiences that do not conform to his formal education.

On the following night, Hamlet joins the others on the ramparts. The apparition returns. Sighting the figure, Hamlet exclaims:

> Angels and ministers of grace defend us!
> Be thou a spirit of health or goblin damned,
> Bring with thee airs from heaven or blasts from hell,
> Be thy intents wicked or charitable,
> Thou com'st in such a questionable shape
> That I will speak to thee. (1.4.39–44)

Hamlet offers just two possibilities for his interpretation of what he sees: The apparition is from heaven or from hell. Perhaps this initial response arises from his Wittenberg education; purgatory is not an option. He goes on to identify the figure with his father, confirming Horatio's judgment in the first scene. He poses the question that all his companions and the audience share: "Why?" The figure, mute till now, answers Hamlet's question about whence he comes:

> I am thy father's spirit
> Doomed for a certain term to walk the night
> And for the day confined to fast in fires,
> Till the foul crimes done in my days of nature
> Are burnt and purged away. (1.5.9–13)

The answer the apparition gives is the one Hamlet had not considered. The "certain term" eliminates the only other option "fasting in fires" suggests. The spirit is not confined to hell because its "sentence" has a term. Obvious though it may be, this response does not resolve all questions and ambiguities. If the elder Hamlet had been judged worthy of avoiding the eternal punishment of hell, what is he doing here urging his son to: "Revenge his foul and most unnatural murder!" (1.5.25).

The ghost offers a traditional view of purgatory as a place of temporary punishment for evil done while in life. However, Catholic/Anglican tradition does not support the idea of purgatorial ghosts walking at night (Celtic tradition related to the festival of Samhain may). Wholly incompatible with traditional Christian theology is a blessed ghost inciting his son to avenge his murder. This behavior validates Hamlet's suspicion that the ghost may be demonic, intending to entice him to his own damnation. Once it can be seen that the demon "speaks true," which Claudius's behavior at the play seems to confirm, Hamlet sets aside this caution.

The ghost of Hamlet's father describes his murder in detail and then points to the most grievous element of it:

> Cut off even in the blossoms of my sin
> Unhousseled, disappointed, unaneled
> No reckoning made, but sent to my account
> With all my imperfections on my head. (1.5.76–77)

The deprivations of which the ghost complains include the last rites of the Church, the sacraments that Luther questions in *The Babylonian Captivity of the Church*—the document which Henry VIII refuted in the *Assertio Septum Sacramentum,* and which forms one basis for More's *Responsio ad Lutherum*: Eucharist ("unhouseled"), Extreme Unction ("unaneled"), and Penance ("no reckoning made"). These are of course the complaints of the ghost and do not originate with Hamlet, but they are the basis on which Hamlet discovers an obligation to take revenge and the criteria for determining an appropriate revenge.

In the second act, Hamlet expresses some uncertainty about the nature of the ghost:

> The spirit that I have seen
> May be a devil and the devil hath power
> T'assume a pleasing shape yea, and perhaps
> And out of my weakness and my melancholy
> As he is very potent with such spirits,
> Abuses me to damn me. (2.2.555–60)

This uncertainty becomes the motivation for the "Mousetrap." The king's reaction to the play may help reassure the audience that Hamlet is not overly gullible in regard to the ghost, but the play also contributes to Hamlet's undoing, in that it provides him with the certainty he feels he needs in order to act. Hamlet has engaged Horatio to second the observation of Claudius at the play. The play having sent the king rushing from the room in distress, Hamlet is certain of Claudius's guilt and the ghost's honesty. He is ecstatic. He checks with Horatio for confirmation of his judgment, saying "Oh, good Horatio, I'll take the ghost's word for a thousand pounds. Did'st perceive?" (3.2.262–63). Horatio responds that he did indeed perceive, but exactly what he perceived remains unspoken. In his excitement, Hamlet goes on to other things.

On his way to Gertrude's closet, he passes Claudius at prayer and contemplates taking his revenge at this moment, but determines that killing Claudius under these circumstances will not balance the injustice Claudius has done to his father.

> Now might I do it pat, now a's a praying,
> And now I'll do't—and so a' goes to heaven,
> And so am I revenged. That would be scanned.
> A villain kills my father, and for that,
> I, his sole son, do send that same villain up to heaven.
> Why, this is hire and salary, not revenge. (3.3.73–39)

On that reasoning, Hamlet returns his sword to its scabbard, determining to kill Claudius "when he is about some act / that hath no relish of salvation in it" (3.3.91–92). At this crucial moment, Hamlet must decide and act (or not) alone. The possible outcomes he considers for Claudius include heaven and, by implication, hell. Purgatory is not an option here, as it would not have been for Luther.

Neither Aquinas (speaking for Catholic tradition) nor Luther seems anywhere to endorse an obligation of revenge for sons of murdered parents. Hamlet's turning-point determination to send Claudius's soul to hell is incompatible with any reading of the Gospel. However, it may be argued that when Hamlet ultimately stabs Claudius with Laertes poisoned sword and forces the remains of the poisoned chalice on him, he acts as the legitimate royal authority in Denmark, executing justice for the publicly evident crimes, attested to by Laertes dying words, including the attempt on his own life and what might be called the felony murder of Gertrude who dies as a result of Claudius's attempt on Hamlet's life. The prince seems to act in the royal role when he speaks for Fortinbras's succession to the Danish throne.

The final episode which directly addresses matters related to the Lutheran controversy about destinies confronting the Christian at death happens in the final scene as Hamlet lies dying and before Fortinbras arrives. He has achieved the perfect vengeance that retributive justice would demand of him, having killed Claudius with the very wine Claudius had prepared to kill him, and which in fact was the cause of Gertrude's death. The King's guilt is evident to all present. Hamlet has exacted justice for his victims, from the senior Hamlet to Gertrude to Hamlet himself. He makes his final requests of Horatio: explain things to Fortinbras, including Hamlet's dying voice for his succession to the throne of Denmark, and provide a fair description of all that has transpired. As Hamlet breathes his last, Horatio offers a parting prayer: "Good night, sweet prince. / And choirs of angels sing thee to thy rest." The words are a simpler version of an antiphon from the traditional Catholic funeral liturgy, traditionally called the "*In Paradisum.*"

This traditional prayer fits in well with the play's apparent reliance on the possibility of purgatory. If purgatory exists, the ghost is conceivably what it claims to be, the spirit of the dead king. However tortuous and dreadful purgatory may be, the dead king has been judged a certain candidate for redemption and therefore the audience is free to assume that even the awful revenge Hamlet contemplates in the third act may somehow be morally necessary. However, if purgatory is, as Luther teaches, an illusion, then interpretation that the visitor is from hell is entirely possible and his visits to Hamlet may be intended to lure him to his damnation. Hamlet has acknowledged the possibility of such a trap. The "*In Paradisum*" allusion leaves the impression that, in Horatio's mind at least, Hamlet has incurred no guilt in carrying out his mission of justice against the now obviously guilty Claudius.

Horatio is less emotionally impetuous than his friend, methodical and logical in his investigation of the ghost's appearance. He initially doubts the ghost story he hears from the guards, and relies more heavily on observation than on teachings he would have heard at Wittenberg. Hamlet, more closely involved in all that transpires, is also more passionate in dealing with it. He holds to the Wittenberg view of life beyond death until the words of the ghost (who apparently has returned from "the undiscovered coountry") attest to the existence of a place of temporary purgation. Even then, he looks for further confirmation of the accusation he hears from the ghost and the quest for vengeance laid upon him.

The ambiguities about the ghost's nature have been made possible by the competing theological positions that confronted Christians during the time of the Reformation. Questioning the practice of indulgences had been familiar to English audiences at least since the fourteenth-century works of William Langland and Geoffrey Chaucer. The satiric tone of these earlier works makes the questioning less threatening. *Hamlet's* inclusion of an uncertain purgatory and the possibility of "erring and extravagant spirits" intensifies the atmosphere of terror in facing an afterlife of competing absolute teachings that claim eternal consequences.

Bibliography

Henry VIII. *Assertio Septum Sacramentorum*. Edited by Louis O'Donovan. New York: Benziger, 1908. Online: https://archive.org/stream/cu31924029398223#page/n5/mode/2up.

Luther, Martin. *Martin Luther's Basic Theological Writings*. Edited by Timothy F. Lull. Minneapolis: Fortress, 1989.

More, Thomas. *The Yale Edition of the Complete Works of Sir Thomas More*. New Haven: Yale University Press, 1990.

Shakespeare, William. *Hamlet*. Norton Critical Edition. Edited by Robert S. Miola. New York: Norton, 2010.

www.ingramcontent.com/pod-product-compliance
Lightning Source LLC
Chambersburg PA
CBHW062047220426
43662CB00010B/1684